There Was a Woman

La Llorona from Folklore to Popular Culture

DOMINO RENEE PEREZ

UNIVERSITY OF TEXAS PRESS, AUSTIN

The publication of this book was
made possible in part by a University
Cooperative Society Subvention Grant
awarded by the University of Texas at
Austin.

Requests for permission to reproduce
material from this work should be sent to:
> Permissions
> University of Texas Press
> P.O. Box 7819
> Austin, TX 78713-7819
> utpress.utexas.edu/index.php/rp-form

♾ The paper used in this book meets the
minimum requirements of ANSI/NISO
Z39.48-1992 (R1997) (Permanence of
Paper).

Library of Congress Cataloging-in-
Publication Data
Perez, Domino Renee, 1967–
  There was a woman : La Llorona from
folklore to popular culture / by Domino
Renee Perez. — 1st ed.
     p.   cm.
  Includes bibliographical references and
index.

— ISBN 978-0-292-71812-8 (pbk. : alk.
paper)
  1. Llorona (Legendary character)
2. Legends—Mexico.   3. Popular
culture—Mexico.   4. Mexican
Americans—Folklore.   5. Mexico—
Folklore.   6. United States—Folklore.
I. Title.
GR115.P47   2008
398.20972—dc22
2008006870

For my mother Maria Elsa Ortiz Perez, my husband James H. Cox, my son Ewan James Alejandro Cox, and all the storytellers in my family who have shared with me the stories "we see in our eyes."

And for Joan M., who was the first to believe.

CONTENTS

AT THE AGE of seven in Yorktown, Texas, I heard my first La Llorona stories from my tíos and primos. Concealed behind an ancient pecan tree, I listened one evening as they exchanged late into the night terrifying stories about a woman in white who tried to seduce them to their deaths with her pitiful cries. In turn, each related a personal encounter or passed along a story he had heard from a compadre whose sobrino, or some such removed person of good authority, had had a run-in with the crying lady. One tío said the ghost woman could hover above water. Another encountered her along a deserted road and described her wearing a tattered white dress. My favorite cousin offered details about how she turned into a flock of birds before his very eyes. His version was enough to send me running away from their stories that night without ever looking back. After that evening, despite living in Texas and being part of an enormous family of storytellers, I did not hear about her again from the men in my family or from anyone else for more than twenty years. La Llorona's absence from and reappearance in my life corresponds to my own journey away from and eventually back to my cultural community.

La Llorona is an important part of Mexican storytelling traditions on both sides of the US/Mexican border. Also known as the Weeping or Wailing Woman, she is a ghost said to haunt the river banks and lake shores. Some know La Llorona as a murderous mother who killed her children in an act of revenge or grief, and they believe she is condemned to wander the earth in search of the children she sacrificed or, as others see it, relinquished willingly. For people of Mexican ancestry, La Llorona traditionally serves as a cultural allegory, instructing people how to live and act within established social mores.[1] At times, however, she is simply a spooky bedtime story. Her tales are told to children to induce good behavior. When I was growing up, though, no one ever used La Llorona or her story to make me behave. My parents, neighbors, and relatives used El Cucuy, La Llorona's male counterpart, for that job. The sum of my own childhood knowledge about La Llorona was that she was a scary woman who had done something bad, wandered crying in the night, and posed a threat to the men in my family.

While working on my Ph.D., I was reintroduced to La Llorona in Rudolfo Anaya's *Bless Me, Ultima* (1972). Anaya's Llorona was much like the one in my own family, for she, too, from the perspective of the young male protagonist, Antonio, threatens the men in his family, his brothers in particular. In Antonio's nightmares, she is a demon that *"seeks the blood of boys and men to drink"* as she wanders along the riverbanks crying (23). Anaya attaches neither infanticide nor betrayal to the legend in his novel.[2] Meeting her again, but this time more directly, impacted my life in two very important ways: first, I began to think about La Llorona in a broader context for the first time, one outside of my family and the oral tradition; second, it marked the beginning of a ten-year devotion to studying and amassing artifacts that represent her.

My adult encounter with La Llorona was one from which I could not, and still cannot, walk or even run away. I began to think about the parts of her legend that had been hidden or kept from me, such as her identity and the murder of her children. I wondered about La Llorona's origins. I wanted to know how long she has been a part of Mexican culture. I was troubled by the fact that men were the exclusive source of my limited knowledge about this woman, and I was struck by the fact that I had not encountered a single La Llorona story by a woman. This absence not only led me to question the existence of such a story but also contributed to my initial speculation that women's relationships with La Llorona had to be different than those of men. I needed to know what had been written about her and if it revealed how La Llorona or her story had at all changed. I initiated a search for anything I could find on La Llorona, turning first to academic sources, which led me to Mexican as well as Euroamerican folklorists, cultural anthropologists, and other scholars cataloguing and tracing the origins and variations of La Llorona stories.

All of these studies fueled my interest, and I was glad finally to read La Llorona stories collected from Mexicans and Chicanas. I was surprised, though, to find accounts from people not of Mexican ancestry included in some of these studies, because, growing up, I had never seen or heard her represented outside of my family or cultural community.[3] Still, I had yet to hear a Llorona story directly from, or read one penned by, a woman. As my research progressed, I began to share my findings with my mother. Over a period of weeks, she patiently listened to me regurgitate all that I was learning, until one day she politely inquired, "Why don't you ask me about La Llorona?" I was taken aback by her question. I had no answer at the time, yet I now understand that in my mind I had separated my personal life from my academic one, taking care that the two did not meet except under the most benign circumstances, such as graduations and other official gatherings. The gesture was more a method of protection than evidence of shame. I did not want my family unfairly scrutinized by outsiders, but I should have had more faith in them and known that shielding can be perceived as shame. The two worlds I had worked to keep apart were now coming together. Fittingly, my mother was the first woman to tell me a Llorona story.

She explained to me that the story of La Llorona has been passed down by the women in my family for more than four generations: my great-great-grandmother Porfíria, great-grandmother Inés, grandmother Eugenia, and mother, Maria. My mother told me that when the wind would moan softly in the fields of my great-grandparents' farm, the tiny woman who raised her, whom I would know as "the little grandma," would suddenly grow quiet and take a deep breath, holding it long enough to catch the attention of my mother and her siblings.[4] Then she would exhale, saying, "Oye. La Llorona." The children would immediately set aside whatever they were doing and run into the kitchen, begging to hear the story about the woman who, according to the women in my family, including my mother, died of loneliness:

Fue una mujer, who married a man con tres niños chiquillos [*sic*]. Now the man loved his children very much, pero esta vieja fue muy celosa. She was vien [*sic*] jealous of those kids because he showered them with love every day. She told him how she felt but nothing changed. One day, she had had enough and told him, "Oyes, hombre. Un día vas a perder lo que quieres más en este mundo." Well, one day he was working late or cual cosa, but he was late getting home. So she took those kids down to the río and drowned them thinking that with them out of the way, she would be able to get more of his attention. Después cuando el señor regresó a la casa and found those kids gone, he knew immediately what had happened. The loca had killed them. He was heartbroken. Pues, he left her and she died of loneliness. Y cuando ella murió y fue al cielo, God told her, "You cannot enter the kingdom until you find the lost souls of the children." Because she didn't know where they were, she wanders the earth to this day looking for them. (Maria Perez)

She concluded by adding, "That's our family's version, but you know now, there are others." I sat in a stunned silence not knowing what to say. I was proud of my mom, embarrassed for not asking her sooner, and excited all at once. My mother, who must have sensed my conflicting emotions, effortlessly closed the uncomfortable gap between us when she asked nonchalantly, "That reminds me, did I tell you about little grandma and grandpa's house?" I was grateful for the finesse she used to avoid pointing out my ignorance.

Our conversation soon ended, and we did not discuss La Llorona again until a couple of weeks later. In the interim, I thought about the superficial differences between the versions circulated in my family: the women had one agreed upon story, while the men had many versions, and the women did not position La Llorona as a threat outside of her own family. For the women, the focus was on telling La Llorona's story rather than encountering her directly. I finally called my mom back to review the story and ask if we could talk a little bit about La Llorona. After asking her permission to tape our exchange, to which she reluctantly agreed, the rest of our conversation unfolded naturally. The following is a transcript of our conversation. Rather than summarize the exchange, I include it in its entirety in order to privilege my mother's voice as a storyteller and document her specific reactions to being asked to interrogate critically a story told in her family primarily for entertainment.

DRP: I want to ask you about the Llorona story the little grandma told you. How was the story told? Was it a ghost story? Was it used as a warning?

MP: No, it was mostly for entertainment. Me, your tío Freddy and tía Pola liked hearing it, and the little grandma liked telling it.

DRP: Did the little grandma ever change the story in later tellings to emphasize different points?

MP: No, not really. But there *are* different versions, like the one where the man is running around on the woman or where he sees her children as being in the way.

DRP: Going back to the first version you heard, what does the story mean?

MP: Overall or to me?

DRP: In general.

MP: Jealousy overtook the woman's love for the man. She became obsessed and could only think about what was interfering. She probably thought that if she could remove the obstacles, the children, she would get more affection.

DRP: And to you, specifically?

MP: I've never given it much thought. We would ask Amá Inés to tell us stories, scary stories, any kind of stories. And then when we heard any noise, it became the Llorona. That's it really.

DRP: What do you think the story says about women?

MP: (Long pause) I think it says a woman will go to any means to remove the obstacles in the way of what she loves. In the story, so much jealousy overcame her, she couldn't see what was right. Because she is wandering forever, she has time to realize what she did was wrong.

DRP: And about men?

MP: That they're all cabrones. (Laughter)

DRP: Can I quote you?

MP: I don't know. Is it okay to say that? (Laughter)

DRP: Well, if that's what you think . . .

MP: You know that's a good question. They don't ever really talk about the man. The focus is on the man because he was good and loved his kids. And then it switches to the woman because she's the one who committed the sin. In the story, when he gets home, he doesn't go looking for the children. He doesn't try to help her. He just leaves. I mean, there once had to be some love there for him to marry her, right?

DRP: You would think. Maybe he married her for other reasons.

MP: I don't know.

DRP: Does the story have a moral or is it just entertainment?

MP: Well, it does have a moral. But the people who told the story when I was growing up didn't stress one because it was just a story to tell. Something to pass the time. Because it was a . . . what's the word? Not a myth but you know . . .

DRP: A folktale?

MP: Yes, a folktale. Because it was a folktale, I don't think that anyone ever thought, "What is the moral?" I say it has a moral, but I'm confused where the moral is. Are we done?

The richness of our exchange helped me to see that I had ignored an obvious authority, and it became a valuable lesson I have not forgotten. More than anything I read, the interview/conversation with my mother became a vital critical lens through which to view La Llorona stories and artifacts. It taught me to set aside everything when listening to a storyteller, not to ignore, take for granted, or obscure vital and valuable sources in my own cultural community, and that everyone has the capacity to be a critical cultural reader.

The last point was made clear when my mother read the story to mean, in part, that men can be cabrones, even though the idea is not stated directly in my family narrative. The exchange also showed me that the story told by the women in my family revealed familial gender politics when placed in dialogue with the men's stories. I saw these same gender politics reflected in the Mexican American community where I spent the early part of my life. I realized that before moving forward with my research, I had to revisit that night when I was seven. For much of my life, the incident remained a sacred childhood memory, one frozen in time and not to be looked at critically. It called to mind family, wholeness, and innocence. I worried that these sentiments would be stripped away if I were to scrutinize the episode thoroughly. As it turns out, I was right. Nevertheless, it was exactly what needed to be done. I had to determine how my own family was using La Llorona before venturing into the lives and productions of others.

My understanding of the event itself, the composition of the group, gender politics, and cultural knowledge all helped me to see clearly the following: (1) As a little girl, I was somewhere I was not supposed to be—outside with the men at night; (2) My willful disregard for familial and cultural mores was an act of defiance; (3) Eavesdropping—also an act of defiance, or rather resistance—during the transmission and exchange of stories by the men in my family provided a glimpse into a male-dominated space where my uncles and cousins had the authority to determine what was "real" and to define characteristics of or traits in women that they perceived as threatening, which they then wrote across La Llorona; (4) Within the storytelling circle, no one's authority was questioned; (5) Of the stories I heard that night, none included infanticide, adultery, or betrayal.

Needless to say, I did not retain my romantic ideas about what was taking place that night in that circle of men, but critical reflection did teach me, or rather reinforce, a valuable lesson about power and authority. Their storytelling circle was more than simply an arbitrary setting; it was a safe place for them to create, however problematically, a world of words, where they faced the dangers and challenges of life, embodied by a woman, and survived. They helped me to understand that the lore represented a powerful, dynamic, culturally specific way to address the larger issues (the effects of racism, poverty, classism, and gender role expectations) at work in their lives.

The exchange with my mother has also served as a guiding principle for my work. For this project, as well as all of my scholarly endeavors, I turned first to

the voices and the wisdom of my family and community members before venturing into the mainstream cultural and critical arena. Without their knowledge,
my tíos (Raul, José, Nicolás, and Lalo) and older primos (Pete, Johnny, Little Joe,
Hector, Harry, Richard, Larry, and Ralph) became my first sources of information for this book. I include them here as a way to honor them and so readers
might see that my family and other less visible storytellers like them are the
people who attend to the continuation of the lore.

Gloria Anzaldúa, José Limón, Cordelia Candelaria, and Tey Diana Rebolledo
were my initial critical guides on this journey with La Llorona.[5] They showed me
the different ways to privilege a Chican@ worldview in my work, especially when
engaging and discussing dominative ideologies.[6] More importantly, they were
the first Chicana and Chicano scholarly voices I heard in the larger discussions
about La Llorona, and they both challenged and inspired me to find my own
voice and approach. Family and community are sources to which I will always
return, for from them I first learned that "There was a woman."

ACKNOWLEDGMENTS

I WOULD FIRST like to thank my mother for her strength, sacrifice, and love. Without her care and support, the completion of this project would not have been possible.

I am also grateful for the insight and generosity of my husband, who committed himself to my vision and its realization. When I doubted, he never did.

To my brother Michael and his family, Cindy, Aaron, and Matthew; my tío Freddy Ortiz, tía Ofelia, and tío Raul Ortiz; and Papi Gerardo Alanis, thank you for your love and stories.

The project in its original form was shaped by the guidance of my dissertation director, Maureen Honey, at the University of Nebraska–Lincoln. I wish to extend my thanks to Ralph Grajeda, Barbara DiBernard, Venetria Patton, Mark Busby, Paul Cohen, and Wheeler Winston Dixon for their insights and ongoing support.

In the early stages of my work, Jane Hafen, Daniel Heath Justice, Jacqueline Vanhoutte, Alex Pettit, and DeNara Hill called my attention to—and in some cases located or made copies of—key Llorona artifacts included in this or other publications. I appreciate their professional support as well as their friendship throughout this process.

The insights and thoughtful recommendations of Norma Cantú, a mentor since my time as a graduate student, Alicia Gaspar de Alba, and Ralph E. Rodriguez have strengthened the work overall, and to them I am deeply indebted.

My University of Texas colleagues in the Center for Mexican American Studies and Department of English, particularly Gloria Gonzalez-Lopez, Ann Cvetkovich, Lisa Moore, and Don Graham have encouraged my project by reading drafts of my work or passing along Llorona artifacts. Michael Winship and Sue Heinzelman offered their classes as forums to present my work in its various stages. I am also indebted to Douglas Bruster, Frank Whigham, Wayne Lesser, and Elizabeth Richmond-Garza for allowing me to draw on their expertise.

I wish to thank T. Jackie Cuevas for assisting me initially in the arduous task of cataloging the at times overwhelming number of artifacts; Crystal Kurzen, my assistant for the majority of the project, for her positive spirit and meeting each daily calamity with her trademark calm; Lacey Donohue for her candor, critical insights, and extra set of eyes during crunch time; Amara Graf and Jennifer Styperk for their exemplary cheering skills; David Morgan Jones for his devotion and keeping me on task; and Dr. Michael Turner for safeguarding my spiritual and physical well-being.

The generous support of the University of Texas at Austin—through a U.S.-Mexico Relations/Borderlands Research Award, Dean's Fellowship, Proposal Award, Ransom Fellowship, and a University Co-operative Society Subvention Grant—was crucial to my project, allowing me both the financial resources and leave to complete my work. I especially want to thank James Garrison, former English Department chair, and José Limón, director of the Center for Mexican American Studies, for their guidance and encouragement.

I wish to extend a personal thanks to the artists whose works are featured in this study, especially Ray Martín Abeyta, Diana Bryer, Xavier Garza, Rob Jefferson, Lizz Lopez, David Salas, and Stephanie Saint Sanchez, who checked in regularly on me and the project. I am indebted to several authors: Cherríe Moraga for sharing the page proofs of the version of *The Hungry Woman: A Mexican Medea* that appears in *Out in the Fringe;* Rudolfo Anaya for providing me a copy of his unpublished play, "The Season of La Llorona"; Jorge Huerta for retrieving his play *La Llorona*, which was set to be archived, in order to make a copy for me; and Don Daglow for his generosity and enthusiasm.

An earlier version of my analysis of the film *Mulholland Drive* appeared in "Lost in the Cinematic Landscape: Chicanas as Lloronas in Contemporary Film," included in *Velvet Barrios: Popular Culture and Chicana/o Sexualities,* edited by Alicia Gaspar de Alba (New York: Palgrave Macmillan, 2003). I thank Palgrave Macmillan for allowing me to reprint a revised version of that analysis.

My mother's story about La Llorona first appeared in "Caminando con La Llorona: Traditional and Contemporary Narratives" as a part of *Chicana Traditions: Continuity and Change,* edited by Norma E. Cantú and Olga Nájera-Ramírez (Urbana: University of Illinois Press, 2002). I am grateful to the University of Illinois Press for allowing me to include my mother's story and other brief sections from the essay.

An earlier version of my analysis of *So Far From God* appears in *Proteus: A Journal of Ideas* 16 (1) (Spring 1999), and the definitions I offer of *myth* and *legend* first appeared in *The Oxford Encyclopedia of Latinos and Latinas in the United States,* edited by Suzanne Oboler and Deena J. Gonzalez (Cambridge: Oxford University Press, 1995). My thanks to *Proteus* and Oxford University Press for allowing me to reprint portions of these articles.

Finally, my sincerest thanks to all of the wonderful people who have shared their work with me and with whom I have corresponded as a result of this project.

There Was a Woman

Haunting Our Cultural Imagination

*How is it that there is so many lloronas? [. . .] in my family we believe its a
mexican legend and that La Llorona is one woman who drowned her kids
in a river and she wanders by the river in some place in Mexico.*

— MAYRA DEANDA

NO WORDS STRIKE more fear in the hearts of students and faculty than "on-
campus parking." It is a frustrating and at times futile endeavor. What should be
a simple act can be dangerous and costly. All who attempt it are potential victims,
stalked by unseen forces waiting to tow, ticket, or affix the bright orange "boot of
shame" onto a front tire. On this day, I am one such likely prey. The temperature
is 104°. My infant son is strapped in his car seat in back, and I need to get both
of us in and out of the library before he awakens. I have been driving for twenty
minutes around a parking lot so small that I feel as though I am maneuvering
through a go-kart course. I lost one space to a cabrón who upon entering the lot
immediately drove the wrong way down a one-way row to get to an open space
before me. The other available space went to a colleague, whom I did not recognize, although the exasperation she wore was certainly familiar. My son begins to
stir, and I want to shout, "I NEED ONE BOOK! TEN MINUTES, THAT'S ALL
I NEED. JUST TEN MINUTES!"

    In desperation, I contemplate the double-park, flashing-light maneuver but
know that I will emerge from the library to find my vehicle gone, or worse, made
immovable by a steel clamp. As if on cue, my son awakens screaming, hot, wet,
and hungry. I know I have lost my window of opportunity. The completion of

my task has been made infinitely more difficult, yet I resolve not to leave without Rudolfo Anaya's epic poem *The Adventures of Juan Chicaspatas* (1985). Rounding an impossibly tight corner, I see a blue Chevy Astro van exiting halfway down the row. I pull up to wait patiently for the space to become available, and that is when I see it. Affixed on the back bumper is a sticker that reads: "Honk if you've seen La Llorona."[1] In spite of my circumstances, or perhaps because of them, I cannot help but laugh. I know she is testing me. As the van pulls away, I honk. The sound startles my son, who suspends his tears. A large brown hand appears from the driver's side window of the van, waving in recognition of the shared cultural knowledge that has momentarily united two strangers in a parking lot. Over the years, La Llorona has revealed to me her many sides, and on this day, she is reminding me that she is not without a sense of humor.

La Llorona (the Weeping Woman) is one of the most famous figures in Mexican and, for the specific purposes of this study, Chican@ oral and literary traditions. According to a popular traditional version of the legend, La Llorona is a woman abandoned by the man she loved and left alone to raise their children. Grief or desire for revenge compels La Llorona to murder her children and throw their bodies into a river. Despair ultimately contributes to La Llorona's death, and in the afterlife, she is condemned to wander for all of eternity until the bodies of her children are recovered.[2] The legend of La Llorona is as old as it is dynamic. From a pre-conquest portent, which consisted of a woman howling in the night months before Cortés' arrival, to the Houston mother from Mexico accused of murdering her children, who stated in an interview, "Yo soy La Llorona," the Weeping Woman has permeated the consciousness of her folk community.[3] To those who participate in the transmission of the lore, either through storytelling or as interlocutors, La Llorona is alternately, and sometimes simultaneously, a person, legend, ghost, goddess, metaphor, story, and/or symbol. In an attempt to account for all of these views, I speak about her as a legend, spirit, symbol, and living entity.

Thirty-five years ago, La Llorona remained largely a part of oral stories, but the figure has wandered out of this genre onto pages, canvases, celluloid, and even into cyberspace where, in a substantial change in the narrative's structure, we must instead look for her. Complicating this movement is the fact that La Llorona is used now around the world to sell or promote everything from coffee and women's underwear to films and academic conferences.[4] An Internet search will yield more than five hundred non-redundant entries, excluding images, from sites generated in such locales as Singapore and Australia.[5] Record albums by Lhasa de Sela (Mexican, Jewish American) and Chavela Vargas (Argentinean); a park in Las Cruces, New Mexico; a punk band in a graphic novel series by the

Hernandez brothers; and an art gallery in Chicago are named after her.[6] Children's books by Rudolfo Anaya and Gloria Anzaldúa, sketches and paintings by artists such as Santa Barraza, Isaura de la Rosa, Elizabeth "Lizz" Lopez, and Stevon Lucero, and Kathleen Anderson Culebro's play feature La Llorona or her legend as a subject.[7] She appears in poems and short stories. Her tragedy is used to promote tourism in New Mexico and sell T-shirts on the Internet. La Llorona has made appearances on the short-lived ABC television series *Cracker* (1997–1998), the PBS family drama *American Family* (2002–2004), and in a commercial for the California Milk Processor Board (CMPB), in which she is crying not for her children, but for milk.[8] Her film career in the United States is one most aspiring actors would envy; she has gone from bit player in a David Lynch movie to a feature film star.[9] La Llorona has not yet reached the commercial status of the Virgen of Guadalupe—we have not seen La Llorona night-lights, dashboard figurines, or rear-window decals—but I suspect she soon will.

The sheer number and variety of these productions can be overwhelming, and some may conclude that the Llorona they know is unrecognizable, or decide that La Llorona's function in these works is indeterminate and, therefore, irrelevant. For many people who hear and pass on the story, La Llorona was condemned to suffer, not to become a celebrity. Others may worry that she is losing her ability to illustrate or convey the specific moral, social, or political concerns of Mexicans and Mexican Americans who continue to disseminate the lore. One thing, however, is clear: as La Llorona's stories have evolved, storytellers and artists continue to adapt her story to new contexts.

Contemporary Mexican American and Chican@ cultural producers who represent La Llorona reconfigure the power relations between La Llorona and her lover, conflate La Llorona with powerful Aztec goddesses, subvert traditional narratives to allow the Weeping Woman to transcend her tragedy, and draw La Llorona into futuristic landscapes. She is sketched in so many ways that deciphering her social and cultural function in relationship to traditional versions of the lore in which she only weeps and wanders can be difficult. For people like Mayra, quoted in the epigraph, who grew up believing there was only one version of the story, a short film featuring La Llorona as a chain-smoking, snack food obsessed, stand-up comic might appear strange indeed.[10]

This book participates in the theoretical practice of privileging Chican@ storytelling traditions as sources of critical inquiry. It also offers a critical catalog and analysis of the many ways La Llorona has been put to use in and outside of Chican@ culture, as well as methods for creating a dialogue, inclusive of a vast number of disparate "texts" featuring Llorona, that can account for the stand-up comic Llorona along with more traditional depictions. More than two hundred artifacts featuring La Llorona—works authored by artists, filmmakers, poets, and dramatists, to name a few—were considered for this analysis, a significant number of which appear or are noted in this work. Although each has been cataloged and categorized, I do not include an individual analysis of every item. Due to the number of representations and the scope of this study, I exclude representations of La Llorona generated in Mexico, Central America, South America, and the Caribbean, and limit my focus in the first four chapters to Chican@ cultural productions. A consideration of the rise and dissemination of La Llorona folklore in these countries or locales would require a political, historical, and cultural contextualization particular to the nation or region, which is beyond the scope of this project. The three primary objectives of this interdisciplinary study are: (1) to provide a critical cataloging of artifacts generated by Chican@s that are illustrative of the wide range of La Llorona representations across genres; (2) to offer reading strategies devised to empower audiences and aid them in deciphering these images; and (3) to consider the ways in which La Llorona folklore promotes intercultural dialogue.

In the formulation of these reading strategies, I draw heavily from my training in film studies and am indebted to Jacqueline Bobo's work in *Black Women as Cultural Readers* (1995) and Víctor Fuentes' analysis "Chicano Cinema" (1992). Because so many of the works included in this study are visual in nature, include a visual component, or were displayed to wide, diverse audiences, the visual nature of film and the interdisciplinary approaches the medium inspires make film studies a productive theoretical basis for the conceptualization and reading of cultural texts across genres. Bobo goes beyond textual analysis to examine how black women readers of film and fiction contextualize narratives in their own cultural frameworks. In her view, "Members of a social audience—people who are actually watching a film or television program—will utilize interpretive strategies that are based upon their past viewing experiences as well as upon their personal histories, whether social, racial, sexual, or economic" (87). Similarly, Chicano theorist Fuentes states that in "the plurality of relationships that are established within and around an artistic text, the perspective of the reader (in cinema that of the viewers) is of utmost importance. Each reader brings to the reading her or his own cultural baggage, expectations, and personal and socio-historical circumstances" (210). This "cultural baggage," including folklore, positions the reader/viewer to engage these images from a distinct cultural location. It is from within a Chican@ cultural framework, in particular one informed by the legend of La Llorona, that I read the works included in this study. These cultural readings reveal how La Llorona has evolved from pre- and post-conquest oral narratives to contemporary films. They also reflect the changing cultural, economic, political, and social concerns and positions of Chican@s and contribute to a critical understanding of the impact of non-Chican@s' use of La Llorona, a consideration I make, specifically, in Chapter 5.

The first chapter is a historical overview of La Llorona's movement from a pre-conquest portent to contemporary Mexican American and Chican@ cultural productions, starting with the testimonio about a wailing woman included in Book Twelve of the Florentine Codex and moving to La Llorona's wandering through cyberspace.[11] The artifacts discussed in this chapter represent exclusively traditional and contemporary versions of the lore, categories I define in detail and which serve as the foundation for all of the strategies offered in the subsequent chapters. These productions, such as Rosemary Catacalos' poem "A Vision of La Llorona" (1984), Silvia Gonzalez S.' play *La Llorona Llora* (1996), and José L. Cruz's film *Haunted from Within [Spirit Hunter: La Llorona]* (2004) reflect on social and cultural issues involving Chicano nationalism, rigidly defined gender roles, poverty, and heterosexuality.[12] Mexican Americans and Chican@s who transmit traditional and contemporary versions of the legend emphasize basic elements found in Llorona stories, like wandering or weeping, and make visible or allude to her various permutations. At times, some also assume an audience familiar with the oral tradition.[13] The emphasis in this chapter is on those productions that seek to replicate or render the lore in ways that do not trouble La Llorona's traditional position as a threat, which is not to say that all reflect a single set of concerns. The conventional and traditional renderings of the tale included in this chapter help cultural readers to prefigure the more radical revisions to La Llorona and her story discussed in the subsequent three chapters.

Chapter 2 is a discussion of artifacts that represent *revisions* of the lore. One way in which this category differs from traditional or contemporary renderings is that it places greater demands on cultural readers. Reading for revisions is dependent on the audience's ability to be fairly conversant in the legend and to have awareness of its different versions in order to see the ways in which La Llorona and her story are being changed; for instance, her crying for milk instead of her children as in the CMPB's "La Llorona, Got Milk?" television commercial. Cultural producers revise the legend by changing its primary features, reconfiguring or renaming the source of La Llorona's oppression, recasting the roles of the major players in the tale, or reworking the somber tone to illicit sympathy and even laughter from audiences. Chican@s who revise La Llorona lore frequently interrogate the misogyny, classism, or colonialism at the center of some versions without discarding familiar themes entirely. Pieces like Victoria Moreno's poem "La Llorona, Crying Lady of the Creekbeds, 483 Years Old, and Aging" (1977) and Monica Palacios' short story "La Llorona Loca: The Other

Side" (1991) have decidedly political overtones in that they highlight sources of oppression embedded in traditional narratives or point to contemporary oppressive forces, though they are not specifically counter-narratives that dismantle or overtly challenge them. When authors like Anaya, in *Rio Grande Fall* (1996), and Angel Vigil, in the short story "La Llorona's Final Cry" (1994), attempt to offer "new" truths about the lore aimed at challenging our conventional understanding of the tale, the power of the lore is such that these revelations, as represented in these texts, have no effect on the community's perception of La Llorona.

In Chapter 3 I focus on *resistance* narratives in which La Llorona acts against and on sources of oppression or empowers women to do the same. Often these women are written into Llorona narratives or cast as Llorona figures. Such is the case with Cleófilas in Sandra Cisneros' short story "Woman Hollering Creek" (1991) and the washerwoman in Helena María Viramontes' short story "The Cariboo Cafe" (1985). Not all, though, are receptive to her presence or see her as a means of liberation. Therefore, resistance, as conceived of and conveyed in these works, sometimes means resisting La Llorona outright and turning away a potential ally and figure of liberation. The category of resistance is comprised of artifacts that include La Llorona as a direct example or metaphysical manifestation of economic, gender, political, or sexual oppression, for example. In some artifacts, La Llorona is used as a vehicle for resisting specific subjugating forces that cause her disenfranchisement not only as a woman but as a Native woman, as in Pat Mora's poem "Llantos de La Llorona: Warnings from the Wailer" (*Agua Santa*, 1995) and Cherríe L. Moraga's play *The Hungry Woman: A Mexican Medea* (2001).

Chapter 4 features a catalog of artifacts that demand the most of audiences familiar with the lore. In addition to distinguishing among traditional, revised, or resistance narratives, readers are looking for the ways that Chican@s are returning—literally, turning to—lost or forgotten elements of La Llorona's life. These elements can include, but are not limited to, La Llorona's name before she assumed the mantle of weeping and wailing; moments of her life not attached to the tragedy; or antecedents in the Mesoamerican pantheon.[14] Through these strategies, Chican@s return La Llorona to a past or a historical moment not often featured in the lore. In this chapter, I argue that recuperations, like the ones we see in Cordelia Candelaria's poem "La Llorona at Sixteen" (1993) and Xavier Garza's mixed media artwork *La Llorona* (2001), can show that the girl/woman people would come to know as La Llorona was not always a figure of sorrow or that her suffering began well in advance of the murder that would mark her. Recuperations of La Llorona also identify antecedents that were a part of a Mesoamerican worldview but that were set aside, erased, or written over as a result of "conquest," the same ones brought to the fore in works like Juana Alicia's mural *La Llorona's Sacred Waters* (2004). The recovery of these buried historical and Native antecedents can serve to empower characters, as in the case of the matriarch in Ana Castillo's novel *So Far From God* (1993).

Throughout the book, I have selected the artifacts most representative of each category, which means that some productions were necessarily excluded.[15] My study, while extensive, is not meant to be exhaustive. Many artifacts can be read as belonging to more than one category (for example, a resistance narrative has probably been revised), so they are arranged by their primary features. This model allows me to show the complexity and scope of portrayals of La Llorona as a person, spirit, and/or story, for clearly in the work of Chican@s, she is all of these and much more, including metaphor and muse.

I am not the first person to conceive of cultural productions featuring La Llorona or the figure herself in terms of revision, resistance, or recuperation. The critical categories offered in each chapter were created in conversations with and in response to primarily Chican@ scholarship on La Llorona, in particular the work of Anzaldúa, Candelaria, Limón, and Rebolledo. Anzaldúa recovers some of La Llorona's antecedents found in the pantheon of the Mexicas and asserts that wailing is an act of resistance, sometimes the only one available to Indigenous women. Candelaria questions the possibility of a re/visioning and/or re/reading of La Llorona by radical artists, and Limón argues that La Llorona has the potential to become a Chicana feminist figure of resistance and urges further contemplation of her as such. Rebolledo reconceptualizes La Llorona to consider the ways in which she represents not only women but also Chican@ culture as a whole. This study, however, is the first book-length interdisciplinary study of representations of La Llorona across genres.

My theoretical and critical perspectives are informed by sources across disciplines. Whenever possible in the first four chapters, I privilege the work of Chican@ and Latin@ studies' scholars in fields ranging from folklore and literature to art and film. In the area of folklore studies, I turn to the early, regional work done in New Mexico by Aurelio M. Espinosa in 1910 and in Texas by Soledad Pérez in 1951.[16] Antonia Castañeda Shular, Tomás Ybarra-Frausto, and Joseph Sommers effectively bridge folklore and Chican@ literature in their anthology *Literatura Chicana* (1972) to show how one medium for storytelling can inform or take shape in another. I also rely on the oft-cited seminal historical studies of La Llorona done by early folklorists such as Thomas A. Janvier, Betty Leddy, Bacil F. Kirtley, Robert A. Barakat, and Michael Kearney. The use of these works is problematic because in some instances the native informants are represented as superstitious, quaint, or exotic. The later work of Bess Lomax Hawes, Shirley

Arora, Pamela Jones, Mark Glazer, and Ed Walraven reflects a more enlightened, culturally sensitive view of informants and their respective communities.

More broadly, in the areas of border, cultural, literary, and gender and sexuality studies, many of the creative writers—like Anaya, Anzaldúa, Candelaria, Alicia Gaspar de Alba, Jorge A. Huerta, Moraga, and Naomi Quiñonez—whose work appears among the artifacts included in this collection, also contribute theoretical perspectives on La Llorona. Other critical investigations that either focus exclusively or in part on La Llorona include, but are not limited to, Rosemarie Coste's creative/critical quest to recover or locate the source of a woman's voice in the legend; Clarissa Pinkola Estés' La Llorona entry in her best-selling book *Women Who Run With the Wolves* (1992), a Jungian approach to women's mythology; Arturo Ramírez's replication of the legend, giving particular attention to the issues of gender and nationalism, to determine its "fundamental elements" and their meaning (21); Maria L. Figueredo's analysis of La Llorona's cultural history as a means of determining the legendary figure's continual ability to resonate for her cultural community; and Alicia Schmidt Camacho's feminist study of "feminicidio" in Juárez, Mexico, and the use of La Llorona stories as a subversive means of transmitting cultural and gendered information among the women of the maquiladoras.[17] The combined work of these critics reveals that La Llorona has moved beyond the boundaries of her singular tragic fate, while maintaining prominence in Mexican, Mexican American, and Chican@ culture.

In the area of literary studies, Ana María Carbonell sees La Llorona, when attached to her indigenous precursors, as a resistant figure that teaches women how to holler instead of wail in the works of Sandra Cisneros and Helena María Viramontes. Juan Bruce-Novoa discusses La Llorona as a barrio resident whose story creates, in part, the backdrop for the poetry of raúlrsalinas and Ricardo Sánchez. Rebolledo presents La Llorona as one of many female archetypes, along with la bruja or Coatlicue, for instance, found in Chicana literature. José David Saldívar considers Viramontes' use and revision of the legend in a transnational context to "produce cultural simultaneity in the Américas (uniting Central American and North American borderlands history) [. . .]" (105). Sonia Saldívar-Hull provides explicit discussions of what she sees as revisions of and resistance to conventional constructions of La Llorona's narrative and "other misogynist plots" that forestall Chicana subjectivity, as also found in the work of Cisneros and Viramontes (123).

In the first four chapters, I bring together the many different conversations taking place about La Llorona, not simply the Chican@ scholarly ones that focus on literature. The readings and representations of La Llorona included in this study reflect the ideological diversity of thought about this complex figure, while providing us with strategies to determine our relationship(s) to her and the role we want her to play, if any, in our lives.

The last two chapters are devoted to intercultural dialogues, ones in which La Llorona serves as a kind of cultural ambassador who can bring diverse communities into conversation about the cultural, economic, political, and social issues that inform the lore. Chapter 5 offers the reading strategies presented in the first four chapters as methods for Chican@ cultural readers to engage in conversations about how non-Chican@s or Mexican@s participate in disseminating the lore. La Llorona's story is an ideal vehicle for creating intercultural dialogue because she does not recognize any border, and similar figures appear across cultures.[18] As performance theorist and artist Guillermo Gómez-Peña asserts, "In order to dialogue, we must learn each other's language, history, art, literature, and political ideas. We must travel south and east, with frequency and humility, not as cultural tourists but as civilian ambassadors" (48). Respectful readings of La Llorona or ones that privilege a Chican@ worldview can challenge existing forms of power in the colonial context of America and serve as a starting point for respectful intercultural conversation. Some readers may be surprised to find a commercial product such as coffee from the Coffee Shop of Horrors and a novelette that appeared in *The Magazine of Fantasy and Science Fiction* included in a discussion about art by Diana Bryer and Dan K. Enger or a David Lynch film. But regardless of the medium or genre, all of the above artifacts serve as sites for the dissemination of information about La Llorona by non-Chican@s, who not only transmit the lore, but also, in many cases, transform it using the same strategies as Chican@s.

Rather than avoiding questions about appropriation or engaging in, according to Stanley Fish, the "moral algebra" of figuring out who did what to whom (4), I am locating my discussion of non-Chican@ cultural productions about La Llorona in Mexican American, Chican@, and Latin@ studies contexts, a strategy that presents its own kinds of difficulties. As Gómez-Peña reminds us:

> The social and ethnic fabric of the United States is filled with interstitial wounds, invisible to those who didn't experience the historical events that generated them, or who are victimized by historical amnesia. Those who cannot see these wounds feel frustrated by the hardships of intercultural dialogue. Intercultural dialogue unleashes the demons of history. (47)

We must confront these demons, those that were unleashed upon us and those of our making, if we are to chart La Llorona's future and our own.

It is my belief that by shifting the discussion to this new site, we can offset the privilege of Anglo dominative culture and equalize the power on both sides of the conversation. This move is crucial for intercultural dialogue to be effective, for as Gómez-Peña observes, "Dialogue is a two-way, ongoing communication between peoples and communities that enjoy *equal* negotiating powers" (48; emphasis mine). I am aware that "dialogue," like "multicultural education," is often a substitute for real substantive work on sociopolitical problems. The intercultural dialogue that I am calling for, therefore, involves both sides speaking and *listening* from equal positions. Portions of this chapter are in conversation with the works of noted cultural theorists: Jean Baudrillard, Coco Fusco, Gómez-Peña, and Trinh T. Minh-ha. Many of their views inform my own analysis of La Llorona's representation in the cultural mainstream. By bringing all of these perspectives, approaches, and works by authors and artists of diverse cultural backgrounds together in one place, I see my work as promoting, through its singular focus on the figure of La Llorona, intercultural dialogue about the contemporary artistic and political struggles inherent in the act of storytelling and attached to the cultural groups who transmit the legend.

Chapter 6 is a study of artifacts featuring La Llorona generated by artists, educators, and storytellers of various ethnicities primarily for younger audiences to determine what we are telling future generations about La Llorona. The stories we pass on to our children and those we choose to pass over will determine her status as heroine or villain. Through the pairing of traditional and revised narratives, writers and artists are teaching children to become sophisticated cultural readers from an early age. Authors like Anaya in *Maya's Children: The Story of La Llorona* (1997) and *My Land Sings: Stories from the Rio Grande* (1999), and Anzaldúa in *Prietita and the Ghost Woman/Prietita y la Llorona* (1995); theatre troupes such as Magical Rain, ChUSMA, and Great Leap; and productions such as Express Children's Theatre's performance of *The Ghost of La Llorona* (1995), written by Rodney Rincón, ensure La Llorona's survival in the cultural imaginations of children and teens as well.

I conclude the work by considering the larger theoretical and practical possibilities of reading representations of Chican@s as Llorona figures even when La Llorona does not appear or is not mentioned by name in a work. I also illustrate how reading non-Chican@ texts through the lens of the lore can open new paths for critical consideration of canonical texts, such as *Moby Dick* (1851), by privileging, for example, socially or racially marginalized characters in those productions or foregrounding the historical and cultural mechanisms in place that contribute to their marginalization.

The cultural readings offered in this study are not the only methods for interpreting or deciphering artifacts featuring La Llorona lore. Because *lore* refers generally to particular kinds of learning acquired or transmitted through sources generated by a cultural community, an examination of these representations through the lens of La Llorona lore will provide readers with a way to make meaning, but will not reveal an ultimate meaning.

In addition to the setting of parameters for this discussion, certain terms used in this study warrant clarification. *La Llorona* and *Weeping Woman* refer exclusively to the woman attached to the legend. The latter is used primarily to avoid repetition rather than announce her Anglicization or assimilation into the dominant cultural mainstream. I use *Llorona* without the article to refer to a woman who is drawn similarly to the woman in the tale and in cases where the inclusion of the article ("La") would be grammatically incorrect, such as in the case of "the La Llorona legend," which would translate to "the The Weeping Woman legend." The term *llorona* used colloquially means "crybaby" but can also refer to a woman outside of the legend who weeps most often about love, as in the mournful and melancholic Oaxacan folksong that does not include infanticide as a part of the story of lost or unrequited affection.[19]

While La Llorona is unquestionably a US/Mexico transnational figure that represents broad Mexican@ and Chican@ folkloric and storytelling traditions, at times I identify the legend as predominately Chican@. As Jean Franco notes, Chicana feminists especially centralize, actively reconsider, and reconfigure in distinct ways prominent Mexican icons such as La Llorona in their expressions of cultural, gendered, sexual, and political identities in the United States, a point I consider at length in other chapters.[20] My identification of La Llorona as predominately Chican@, therefore, is not a proprietary move, but rather a reflection of Chican@ization, a process by which her story is made to reflect distinct cultural and US national concerns of Chican@s. Like the borderland scholars Américo Paredes, Limón, and Saldívar-Hull before me, to name a few, I also use the term *Greater Mexican* to speak of the legend. The designation directly challenges oppositional notions about national identity (Mexican or American). Although the term allows for a reconceptualization, as well as a redrawing, of a cultural and geographic homeland, some scholars, such as Alicia Gaspar de Alba, oppose the term because it "de-privileges the Chicano/a reality that it's attempting to describe and depoliticizes" the border (pers. comm. 2006). Therefore, I use it primarily when speaking of a US/Mexico shared cultural or storytelling history.

In studies across disciplines, scholars refer to La Llorona and her story as myth and/or legend.[21] *Myth* is regularly assigned to sacred stories that explicate and reflect a cultural-specific worldview, though the term is often informally synonymous, especially in a Western worldview, with a story that is not "true."

Traditionally transmitted orally, myths are long-established stories that often serve as the foundations for religious, cultural, and social beliefs. Myths also serve as a means of elucidating abstract or complex ideas about the world, such as creation and cosmography, through narrative. Whereas myths are fairly static in nature, legends are more dynamic, in part because they are often a mixture of accepted fact and fiction. However, they retain a measure of rigidity due in part to their historical basis. Legends are stories usually told in the present about historical figures, places, or events. The relationship between myth and legend is complex because at times myth can give rise to legends or vice versa. Like myth, legend is often transformed, and this can occur on multiple levels to accommodate political, geographic, and linguistic shifts. In previously published work, I have used *myth* and *legend* interchangeably. But now, due to my belief that La Llorona, as we have come to know her, originates in the disembodied voice heard before Cortés' arrival, I will refer to La Llorona's story as legend.[22] I will use *myth* when referring to those stories that point directly to an Indigenous antecedent from the pantheon of Native beliefs.

I use *parent* or *native* culture interchangeably. The people who gave rise to the legend — Indians and mestizos — comprise each term as I conceive of it.[23] I prefer this terminology to *mother culture,* which places emphasis on the woman, in La Llorona's case the Native woman, usually in reference to passivity or violence, though arguably La Llorona can be viewed as a cultural parent. *Cultural community,* on the other hand, is a much more inclusive term that accounts for the people who cultivated the legend and those who participate in its transmission and dissemination, while being respectful of the cultural communities reflected in the tale.

Perhaps the most important concept in need of clarification involves the identity or identities of "cultural readers." While everyone is a cultural reader, members of the dominant culture have the privilege of assuming that their readings are universal, definitive, and somehow cultural without ever having to identify, or consider critically, the lifeways or worldviews that might comprise their "culture." The cultural readers for this study are Mexican@s, Mexican Americans, and Chican@s or their allies, diverse individuals reflecting a vast heterogeneity of thought, educational experiences, sexual alliance, and social or economic positions, for instance. Cultural readers are those who privilege the histories and worldviews generated from the mestizaje that characterizes the cultural territories in which they reside. It is possible, therefore, for non-Chican@s, for instance, to use these reading strategies. Still, as Llorona blogger Desiree Kennedy warns, outsiders might not "understand if [they] weren't raised on the stories" ("More Deaths in Iraq"). Non-natives who engage Chican@ cultural readings willingly commit to and privilege views not their own. Cross-cultural readers metaphorically remove the fence separating themselves and the cultures and/or artifacts under consideration. They must also willingly relinquish their positions as "authorities" to consider first, but not exclusively, readings, strategies, and theories generated by Mexican@s and Chican@s.[24] My vision for this project was to locate in one place a critical mass of La Llorona artifacts to begin wider discussions about La Llorona that may not always rely exclusively on the voices from the Chican@ community, but which I hope will always include them.

As Mexican@s and Chican@s become the numerical majority in cities across the United States, we will need to determine, individually, which cultural values, beliefs, and productions we wish to carry with us across borders and into the cultural mainstream. La Llorona's future is but one consideration. The dynamism of the legend allows for the simultaneous existence of conventional narratives and cultural productions that reflect the changing concerns of Mexican Americans and Chican@s. Both forms ensure the continuation of the lore for a new generation of cultural readers who will define their own relationships to it. This book will play a crucial role, framing our discussion of both La Llorona and, more broadly, the traditions that we consider a distinct part of Chican@ storytelling. Some people may decide that she is too important a figure to leave behind. Others may ultimately determine that La Llorona and her legend are relics that should be buried with the past. In what can be described only as an ironic twist of fate, La Llorona's future has always been in the hands of her cultural and metaphoric children. By continually retelling and reshaping her story to account for new or changing sites of struggle, Chican@s, thus far, have proven that La Llorona is an avatar of social and cultural conflict. Her continued presence in our oral history for almost five hundred years suggests that she and her legend can accommodate dramatic historical and cultural shifts, including the demographic one that is happening now. La Llorona could indeed serve as a powerful symbol for Chican@s as we move into this new era, a reminder of our past and of the obligations that come with power. In determining her fate, we will decide our own.

La Llorona has much to teach us about the world. Instead of finding her that hot summer afternoon in the library, she, in a way, found me in the parking lot. The experience reminded me that while we cannot always control a situation, we can control, in part, our reactions to it. My hasty plans of dashing in and out of the library were abandoned in favor of spending time playing outside of the library with my son and watching from the shade of trees the pulsing fountain in the courtyard shooting water sky-high. The symbolic significance of our proximity, as mother and child, to water and the pulsing spray did not escape me. Eventually, after much laughter and clapping, we retrieved the book. Seeing a representation of La Llorona on the bumper sticker in the parking lot that day helped to create a lasting moment that had nothing to do with suffering, sorrow, or murder, though water and wailing were certainly present. Over the years, I have, indeed, "seen" La Llorona reflected in the cultural imaginations of her people, and what she has shown me is that, regardless of how we feel about her or view her actions, she has the power to bring people together.

ONE

A Five-Hundred-Year History

Traditional La Llorona Tales

JORGE A. HUERTA'S play *La Llorona* (1978) opens with the guitar strains of the traditional Mexican folksong of the same name. Against this backdrop, the actors, who form a semicircle facing the audience, together shout, "¡La Llorona!" The first line is an announcement, affirmation, and invocation of the legendary figure. The actors remain onstage throughout the production and represent visually the diversity of the cultural community that has attended to La Llorona's story for more than five hundred years. This diversity is also represented in the first four scenes of the sixteen-scene, one-act play, in which the audience learns the many ways that storytellers render the tale and how it is put to use.[1] Near the end of scene 4, one character, Chunky, states that the previous scenes bring "us to our major / purpose here investigating legends from / the past in search of truths to live by / in the present" (14). The action then turns to the aftermath of the Spanish invasion, and the remaining scenes recount the tragic tale of Maria Xochiquetzal Feathered Blossom, a young Native woman, who, together with her children, drowns in the river after her Spanish partner has abandoned her for another. Set in sixteenth-century colonial Mexico, the play offers a conventional version of the Llorona tale while emphasizing the diversity of thought and stories within the cultural community. It also underscores the importance of understanding the roots of a storytelling tradition, which can shape our worlds in the present.

The works in this chapter are best characterized as representations of fairly conservative or static versions of the legend. I use the term *conventional* to identify productions that figure La Llorona's infanticide as a response to the dissolution of her relationship, for whatever reason, with her male lover. My explicit objectives concerning artifacts that represent La Llorona in this way is to document the endurance of the traditional tale and to illustrate the way that "tradition" is always historically relative. For instance, what is traditional to Chican@s was new to the Mexicas. In determining the function of tradition first, we can then determine the meaning it makes for us in the present.

The Sixth Omen: Raices of a Legend

In the beginning, there was a woman. Throughout the streets of Tenochtitlan, the capital city of the Mexicas (more commonly known as the Aztecs), a woman was heard weeping about the fate of her children prior to the Spanish conquest. James Lockhart's translation of the Nahua recounting of the sixth sign reads: "The sixth omen was that many times a woman would be heard going along weeping and shouting." Some say that she cried out, "O my children, we are about to go forever." Others heard her howling, "O my children, where am I to take you?"[2] As one of eight omens that began appearing ten years before the arrival of Cortés in 1519, the Native people attempted to decipher these "wonders" within the framework of their worldview.[3] The weeping woman, when taken together with the other signs, foretold of an undeniable end: "To the natives, these marvels augured their death and ruin, signifying that the end of the world was coming and that other peoples would be created to inhabit the earth" (León-Portilla, 11).

The Mexica-Aztecas' emperor, Motecuçoma, consulted the authority of his religious leaders to aid him in deciphering the portents and demanded to know if the priests had "heard the voice of Cihuacoatl [an ancient mother goddess], for when something [was] to happen, she [was] the first to predict it, even long before it [took] place" (León-Portilla, 14).[4] The priests' interpretation of the portents, along with Motecuçoma's response, sealed the fate of the empire and its people. When pressed by the emperor for information about the future of Mexico, the priests responded: "What can we say? The future has already been determined and decreed in heaven, and Motecuhzoma will behold and suffer a great mystery which must come to pass in his land" (León-Portilla, 14–15). The emperor reacts to the cultural readings of the priests by having them imprisoned and their wives and children killed.[5] From a Nahua perspective, the male priests translated the woman's cries as evidence of inevitable disaster for which preparations would be futile. By reading the omens as portents of doom, the priests inscribed the empire and its people into passive roles as victims awaiting the end.

Fray Bernardino de Sahagún translates Native accounts of the signs prior to the fall of the Mexica Empire in *Historia general de las cosas de la Nueva España* (1578), also known as the Florentine Codex, so named for its location in the Medicean-Flaurentian Library in Florence, Italy.[6] Written in Nahuatl, the native language of the Mexicas, and translated into Spanish, the history is divided into twelve books, the final of which focuses on the conquest of Mexico.[7] Although Motecuçoma believed the goddess Cihuacoatl, who could foretell the future, to be the likely source of the wailing, I argue that this story about the crying woman represents the first documented recounting of La Llorona as we know her: a figure whose Indigenous origins were later written over by the Spanish. The narrative also includes the primary elements in the lore: a woman, weeping for lost children, wandering, and water. Though water is not mentioned directly, Tenochtitlan was located in the middle of Lake Tetzcoco.

The arrival of the Spanish, and their military defeat of the Mexicas' empire, provides a new cultural environment that informs post-conquest readings of the woman's shouting in the capital city.[8] Now a lament bemoaning the fate of her people, the Native woman's outcry reinforces the alleged superiority of the Spanish and sanctions their domination of Native people through the appropriation and recoding of Indigenous texts. For example, while the eight omens may have, indeed, signaled the demise of the Mexicas' empire, the Spanish were certainly not named directly as the cause of this downfall. Through the co-optation of existing Native narratives, however, the Spanish wrote themselves into these stories, particularly the one about the "other peoples" prophesied to "inhabit the earth," which they then used as a tool to affirm their domination. As J. Jorge Klor de Alva reminds us in his foreword to *The Broken Spears* by Miguel León-Portilla, Mexico's premiere scholar on Mesoamerican cultures, this technique, not exclusive to the Spanish, was one familiar to most conquerors: "As is well known but quickly forgotten, the victors ordinarily write history. The losers are usually silenced or, if this is impossible, they are dismissed as liars, censored for being traitors, or left to circulate harmlessly in the confined spaces of the defeated" (xi). Although La Llorona's story as it has been handed down through generations and cultures serves as one example of a "confined space" that Klor de Alva cites, the defeated Mexicas are not altogether silenced as long as La Llorona wails.

The sound of a woman crying for her children in the months before Cortés' arrival signals for some the destruction of Mexica culture, through conquest and subjugation of the Indigenous people of Mexico, and intermarriage with the Spanish.[9] La Llorona, then, is ultimately a figure who "has lost her children, perhaps through no fault of her own" and who is, as Tey Diana Rebolledo asserts, "condemned to wander endlessly, reminding us constantly of our mortality and obligations" (*Women Singing*, 78). She is mother, sister, daughter, seer, and perhaps goddess, yet in all instances she is a woman who is condemned to either foresee or bemoan the fate of her children, biological in the tale but emblematic of the Indigenous people militarily, politically, and culturally displaced by the conquest.

It is my contention that European motifs were assimilated into or grafted onto Native stories about the gritona, the shouting woman. This view contradicts folklorist Robert A. Barakat and others who maintain that La Llorona stories have an Old World pattern "upon which native elements have been grafted" (290). Scholars, including Paredes and Limón, often cite Barakat's and Bacil F. Kirtley's work as indicating that La Llorona is European in origin, noting similar thematic elements in Euripides' *Medea* and Puccini's *Madame Butterfly*. Kirtley contributes the story of *die weisse Frau*, "The White Lady," as an additional European antecedent for La Llorona, stating that the "events of the 'La Llorona' story take place in an Europeanized milieu, and the characters' values, their responses, are thoroughly Spanish, not Indian" (161).[10] Kirtley and others maintain that Europeans introduced the narrative framework of La Llorona stories to Mexico. The conceit here is a European one, that colonizers are the source of the legend: "There can be little doubt that the foreigners confused their legend with a similar one of the Aztecs and, consequently, passed it on to the natives, who in turn added their own elements" (Barakat, 288). The opposite, however, is more likely the case, in spite of the fact that John Bierhorst, editor of *The Hungry Woman: Myths and Legends of the Aztecs* (1984), states that La Llorona does not appear in the contemporary Nahua storytelling tradition. La Llorona's failure to appear in these stories under her Spanish name is not surprising, for she appears under the names and semblance of her antecedents found in the pantheon of the Mexicas.

The assimilation of European ideas into the Native worldview, one that includes an understanding of a woman weeping for her children, would allow the Indigenous peoples of Mexico through the figure of La Llorona to account for and even explain the effects of European contact and conquest. Because of the dynamism of the tale, La Llorona and her story can be used to comment on the changing worldview of the Mexicas both pre- and post-conquest. I am not suggesting that the Spanish did not cultivate and contribute to the dissemination of the lore. They are largely responsible, especially in colonial Mexico, for infusing it with Christian ideas concerning divine judgment and damnation. According to Rebolledo, in La Llorona's history, she "brought together Indian and Spanish folklore and legends" (62). The two traditions since have become interwoven to reflect a distinct cultural mestizaje or mixed-bloodedness. As cultural theorist Rafael Pérez-Torres states, "At one point, there exists the need to distinguish one-self from the colonizing society. This involves a reevaluation of traditional cultural forms, a reclamation of a discredited heritage, an affirmation of the unique character of the colonized culture" (8–9). For Chican@s, then, La Llorona's story narrates the origins of an ongoing colonial project and serves as a space within a distinct cultural history to assert a national identity.

An accounting of La Llorona's history helps us to see the weight and endurance of this legend, as well as the various forces that helped shape it. According to González Obregón, stories about La Llorona began to surface around 1550. La Llorona has been with and a part of Greater Mexican cultural tradition for approximately five hundred years. As testament to the power of a Chican@ storytelling tradition that includes La Llorona, her stories endure into the present. Artist Carmen Lomas Garza depicts the act of storytelling and La Llorona in her 1989 painting *La Llorona*.[11] In the foreground of the scene, set at dusk, under the safety of a lighted backyard porch, a woman sits surrounded by children who, with their bodies leaning toward the speaker, appear to be listening intently. Wandering, dressed in black, with arms outstretched as if to snatch a potential victim, La Llorona appears in the upper right-hand corner. Garza juxtaposes the image of the female storyteller in the company of boys and girls with that of the woman mourning and searching for her lost family. The tension between the two scenes conveys the importance of family, community, and the transmission of the lore to a new generation.

The Scholarly Pursuit of La Llorona

Folklore was once the primary means used by cultural groups to convey their attitudes, beliefs, and concerns, but this form of transmitting cultural knowledge now competes with other methods. As such, La Llorona is no longer strictly confined to oral narratives, songs, or plays. From a weekly call-in radio show in Houston, Texas, called "La hora de la llorona" to a television program where she appeared under her English moniker, La Llorona permeates almost every genre of popular culture and even adorns many consumer products, as noted in the introduction.[12] Her presence in these areas remains largely unexplored and motivates my investigation to determine the various ways that the legend is constructed and circulated through these new sites.

Folklorists once monopolized the study of La Llorona. Stories about La

Llorona collected from cultural informants are housed in some of the largest folkloric collections in the United States, including the University of California–Berkeley's Folklore Archive, Utah State University's Fife Folkloric Archive, and the University of Texas–Pan American's Rio Grande Folkloric Archive. The latter purports on its Web site to have the "world's largest computerized collection of Mexican American folklore." More than any other discipline, folklore studies is primarily responsible for bringing La Llorona into the academy. However, scholars of these early studies fail to problematize their own cultural positions in relation to the native or folk communities in which they work. While this type of self-reflection was not common practice until fairly recently, we see this move explicitly made by the anthropologist-in-training featured in Don Daglow's *The Blessing of La Llorona,* discussed in Chapter 5. In addition to those works previously mentioned, the most frequently cited folklore studies, in both English and Spanish, relevant to La Llorona include Thomas A. Janvier, *Legends of the City of Mexico* (1910); Aurelio M. Espinosa, "New-Mexican Spanish Folk-lore" (1910); Betty Leddy, "La Llorona in Southern Arizona" (1948); Luis González Obregón, *Las Calles de México* (1922); Frances Toor, *A Treasury of Mexican Folkways* (1947); Soledad Pérez, "Mexican Folklore From Austin, Texas" (1951); Kirtley, "'La Llorona' and Related Themes" (1960); Hawes, "La Llorona in Juvenile Hall" (1968); Michael Kearney, "La Llorona as a Social Symbol" (1969); Paredes, *Folktales of Mexico* (1970) and "Mexican Legendry and the Rise of the Mestizo: A Survey" (1971); and Limón, "La Llorona, The Third Legend of Greater Mexico: Cultural Symbols, Women, and the Political Unconscious" (1990).[13] Each of these studies devotes considerable attention to La Llorona and the oral stories about her. And while some folklorists may take notice of other cultural forms used to represent La Llorona, they do not attempt to account for or consider the cultural work done by Mexican Americans or Chican@s to maintain and revitalize the lore through these productions.

Though I am not a trained folklorist, it is necessary to include the work of La Llorona folklore scholars in my own work to highlight the ways in which their studies shape or inform critical conversations in other disciplines. Two folklore studies, in particular, have inspired and influenced my work. In her initial study "La Llorona in Southern Arizona," Leddy cites Greater Mexican cultural productions that feature La Llorona, including, for example, José M. Marroqui's historical novel *La Llorona* (1887), Francisco C. Neve's play *La llorona* (1917), and a 1946 magazine article "La Llorona" (272).[14] In Kirtley's 1960 study, he mentions La Llorona's appearance in Gus Arriola's famous, long-running comic strip *Gordo* (1941–1985). Neither Leddy nor Kirtley attends to these or other cultural productions germane to the time period of both studies, such as the Mexican films

La Llorona (1933) by Ramón Peón; *La Herencia de La Llorona* (1947) by Mauricio Magdaleno; *El Grito de la Muerte* (1958) by Fernando Méndez; *La Llorona* (1960) by René Cardona; the play *La Llorona* (1959) by Carmen Toscano; and versions of the folksong "La Llorona" found throughout various regions in Mexico.[15] The absence of critical considerations of these popular artifacts represents the discipline's focus at that time rather than negligence on the part of the folklorists.[16] More important than what Leddy does not say is her observation that these other cultural productions "refresh" or revitalize the legend ("Southern," 272). Though almost sixty years have passed since Leddy's first La Llorona study, I see as my task to contemplate these other artifacts and/or texts, specifically Chican@ or Mexican American cultural productions that represent traditional versions of La Llorona's story, as well as those that move it in new directions or offer other interpretations.

Rather than a chronological arrangement, I have organized my discussion of the artifacts in this chapter, and throughout the book, to emphasize their shared characteristics beyond subject matter and to call attention to the cultural work done in and through these productions, regardless of when they were produced. Additionally, the categories of artifacts offered in this chapter, though distinct, have overlapping characteristics. As Mark Glazer did in his 1984 study, I sort traditional from contemporary renderings of La Llorona, but do so to delineate certain types of Chican@ and Mexican American cultural productions. Glazer's study identifies "contemporary dimensions" of oral folktales, such as the emphasis storytellers place on poverty, for example, distinct from those found in traditional renderings. These new dimensions provide evidence, in Glazer's view, "for the adaptation of a legend to both a certain locality and to a new period in a culture's history" (211). His conclusion meets directly with Rebolledo's own ideas about contemporary renderings of La Llorona, "whose children are lost because of their assimilation into the dominant culture or because of violence and prejudice" (77). Both suggest that the dynamic quality of the lore allows it to accommodate and reflect the changing cultural concerns of La Llorona's native community. The intersection of these two ideas demonstrates the way in which scholars in different disciplines reach a similar conclusion through the gathering of data from cultural productions—oral narratives and literature, respectively— generated by and produced for members of La Llorona's parent culture.

With this point in mind, I wish to foreground audience in my consideration of the artifacts discussed in the first four chapters. Most Chican@s who bring La Llorona into their productions assume of their audiences a certain level of familiarity with the legendary figure and her story. Denise Chávez, in her novel *The Last of the Menu Girls* (1986), and Roberta Fernández, in *Intaglio: A Novel in Six*

Stories (1990), both include references to La Llorona or "lloronas" without offering any additional information about the lore. The authors' use of the figure in
this manner indicates that she is firmly established within the culture as a point
of reference. Apropos to this point, folklorist Barre Toelken states in his consideration of an author's deliberate use of folklore in narrative construction:

> We may suspect, because of the considerable cultural power of folklore
> and the depth with which many people register their recognition of their
> traditions, that a sensitive writer will not use folklore materials lightly,
> but will be motivated by the conviction that the use of certain images,
> phrases, and structures will serve as a powerful emotional link between
> the responses of the audience and the emotional and moral issues in the
> literature. (335)

Though he is speaking exclusively about literature, his claim applies equally to
other cultural productions that include a folkloric component. Chican@ cultural
producers, then, incorporate La Llorona folklore to code their texts for specific
audiences. This is not to say that these artifacts do not have a wider appeal, but
I am interested in how La Llorona serves as a kind of cultural currency used to
exchange and reinforce certain ideas like those found in traditional and contemporary representations.

Traditional Artifacts in the Contemporary World

A cultural reading of the artifacts examined in this chapter reveals that these
representations of La Llorona closely resemble conventional accounts of her, like
Tony Sanchez's illustrations included in *The Weeping Woman: Encounters with La
Llorona* (1988) by novice folklorists Edward Garcia Kraul and Judith Beatty, and
Terri and Carlos Encinas' unpublished children's book that features illustrations
that are widely disseminated via the Internet and appear on Web sites and book
covers (figures 1.1 and 1.2).[17] Alternately, La Llorona is positioned in the folklore
as a bruja, siren, or harlot. Bernadine Santistevan offers these categories, along
with that of virgin, to visitors to her Web site The Cry, an online archive of all
things Llorona, including songs, drawings, cuentos, and a clip from Santistevan's film *The Cry* (2006).[18] There is even a link on the Web site to blog about La
Llorona. La Llorona and/or her story as featured in cultural productions can reinforce conventional ideas about sex, morality, gender roles, and heterosexuality.
Furthermore, the themes, motifs, tropes, and symbolism found in oral stories are
also present in other cultural productions featuring La Llorona.

FIGURE 1.1. *La Llorona,* by Carlos Encinas © 1995. Used by permission of the artist.

Categorically, traditional or conventional representations of La Llorona frequently, but not exclusively, focus on La Llorona as a despairing figure who has
lost both her man and her children. Renderings of this type usually position or
promote La Llorona as selfish, vain, vengeful, whorish, and, worst of all, a bad
mother, while excusing or ignoring the behavior of the man. Elements from the
originary portent (water, weeping, wailing, and children) are often included or
foregrounded within traditional renderings. The primary characteristic of these
productions is that they represent the lore and the various ways in which it is
put to use without critiquing, overtly, La Llorona, her story, or the misogyny at
the center of the tale. Because the image of La Llorona as a threatening figure
remains the most salient and persistent element in traditional versions, the majority of works considered for this study represent her in this way.

Many Mexican Americans and Chican@s centralize La Llorona's ability to in-
cite fear or her monstrous appearance. All of the following position La Llorona as
menacing: David Salas' graphic art image, which appears on T-shirts and postage
stamps (figure 1.3); Rueben Muñoz's commercial product line bearing his rendering of La Llorona on items such as a journal, coffee mug, and mouse pad; and
Albert Ramirez's installation from his Casa de Sade Web site. Others choose to

FIGURE 1.2. *La Llorona*, by Carlos Encinas © 1995. Used by permission of the artist.

represent La Llorona in the act reflected in her name—weeping: Stevon Lucero's painting *La Llorona* (n.d.); Simon Silva's painting *La Llorona* (n.d.); Jessica Abel's graphic novel illustration (figure 1.4); Francisco Muñoz's choreographed dance "La Llorona" (2002); and Daniel Lechón's cover art for Alfred Avila's book *Mexican Ghost Tales of the Southwest* (1994), which also includes Avila's own renderings of La Llorona. These works portray La Llorona gripped in agony or wandering while uttering her famous lament. Some, however, highlight the horror of the infanticide, as in the case of Sonya Fe's painting *La Llorona* (1998; mixedmedia, 18″ × 14″), in which La Llorona's children appear suspended beneath the surface of the river's edge, or Oscar Lozoya's photograph *Pecado de la Llorona* (2007), featuring La Llorona with her head upturned to heaven as she pushes her infant's head beneath the water (figure 1.5). Each of these productions draws on a common cultural understanding of La Llorona's seemingly static position within the lore as a cultural villain.

While there appears to be a consensus, at least in traditional renderings, regarding La Llorona's cultural status as a bogey-woman, the physical attributes assigned to her are as varied as the stories told about her. Known for her mutable manifestations, which range from ghostly hag to beautiful seductress, a number of cultural productions emphasize the latter, thus reinforcing her position as a sexual object and particular threat to men: Monica Alaniz's etching *La Llorona*, used to promote Women's History Month at the University of Texas, San Antonio, in 2004; Carmen León's cover art *La Llorona* for Alma Luz Villanueva's collection of short stories *Weeping Woman: La Llorona and Other Stories* (figure 1.6); and Gina "Genie" Perez's pencil drawing *The Forest Lady: La Llorona* (2002). In sharp contrast to these visions of a comely Llorona, Frank Romero, in his

FIGURE 1.3. *La Llorona*, by David Salas © 2005. Used by permission of the artist. The artwork appears on T-shirts and postage stamps available through Salas' Web site.

FIGURE 1.4. (above) *Bardín baila con la más fea,* by Jessica Abel © 2000. Used by permission of Abel and Max. The panel is part of a collaborative comic by Max, the Spanish cartoonist, who asked contributors to imagine a panel with Max's character Bardín dancing with La Muerte. La Llorona appears wailing in the background.

FIGURE 1.5. *Pecado de la Llorona,* by Oscar Lozoya © 2007. Used by permission of the artist.

FIGURE 1.6. *La Llorona,* by Carmen León © 1994. Used as cover art for Alma Luz Villanueva's *Weeping Woman: La Llorona and Other Stories.* Collection of Alma Luz Villanueva. Used by permission of the artist.

painting *La Llorona* (1985; oil on canvas, 50″ × 72″), depicts a nude Llorona with the head of horse standing beside a child who is trapped in a cage. All of these images correlate directly to descriptions of her found in oral tales.

An additional convention attached to the lore is La Llorona's position as a predator who seeks out wayward men or naughty children, as in Anaya's novel *Bless Me, Ultima* (1972), Helena Maria Viramontes' novel *Under the Feet of Jesus*

(1995), and José L. Cruz's DVD production *Haunted From Within* (2004), though in this case she also has the ability to possess other women to exact her revenge. From a young age children are taught, under specific gender constraints, that La Llorona will "get them" if they misbehave or wander off too far from home or from sight. As Rebolledo states, she "is known to appear to young men who roam about at night. They believe she is a young girl or beautiful young woman, but when they approach her (with sexual intent in mind), she shows herself to be a hag or a terrible image of death personified" (63). The tale teaches boys to see women as temptresses, embodiments of a malevolent sexuality that could cause them to lose their souls and control of their bodies, placing them in utterly passive relationships with more powerful, dominant partners. The cuento, therefore, affirms the sexual agency of women, while at the same time coding the behavior as dangerous to men because it threatens male access to and control over women's bodies. Girls are taught that sexuality, when acted on, can lead to despair and eternal punishment. For both girls and boys, the tale introduces the threat of a thieving mother who will take them away from the security of their "real" mothers and home. In Anaya's novel, La Llorona poses a significant threat to men. Antonio, the young protagonist, has nightmares about the feminine demon that wails along the shores of the river and *"seeks the blood of boys and men to drink"* (23). Here Anaya positions La Llorona as a vampire who desires Antonio's innocent soul, and he learns to fear her.

La Llorona stories are also put to use as a behavioral deterrent. We see the lore used as a threat to induce "good" behavior in young girls, as in Alicia Gaspar de Alba's poem "Domingo Means Scrubbing" (1989). Girls, playing "family" at dusk and innocently trading kisses in their roles as mother and father, are admonished by their grandmother, who shouts: *"La Llorona / knows what you kids are doing!"* (*Three Times*, 6.28–29). As poet and theorist Cordelia Candelaria asserts, "the tale teaches that girls get punished for conduct for which men are rewarded; that pleasure, especially sexual gratification, is sinful for women; that female independence and personal agency create monsters capable of destroying even their offspring [. . .] ("Letting La Llorona Go," *Arroyos*, 126).[19] Presumably because the girls' experimentation is a prelude to their loss of innocence or may even hint at lesbianism, the grandmother evokes La Llorona as a disciplinarian who will punish the girls for their behavior.

Felicia Luna Lemus combines La Llorona's role as a predator and her use as a behavioral deterrent in her novel *Trace Elements of Random Tea Parties* (2003), in which La Llorona acts as a kind of dominatrix to the novel's protagonist, Leti. Instead of representing a radical revision of the lore, La Llorona's role in the novel, aside from this new dimension Lumas adds, is quite conventional: she flies, wanders, threatens, cajoles, weeps, and eventually abandons the protagonist. The prominence Lemus gives La Llorona and the way in which she is put to use in a novel about young, queer, primarily working-class youths indicate the capacity of the lore to accommodate contemporary concerns about multiple cultural and sexual realities. Whereas traditional renderings of the lore assume, and reinforce, the heterosexuality of the subjects featured in the tale, by recasting the sexual dynamics of the legend, Chicana lesbians write themselves into Chican@ oral and literary traditions to, at times, radically alter the tale, as discussed in later chapters.

As this example suggests, social class is also a visible component in the tale. La Llorona's poverty often stands in stark contrast to her male lover's wealth. Folklorist John O. West observes that "the most frequent use of the story is aimed at romantic teenaged girls, to warn them against falling for a young man who [. . .] is too far above them to consider marriage" (*Mexican*, 76). The dynamic endurance of the folklore for centuries therefore reinscribes in generation after generation a negative sexuality for women, as well as, in some cases, a classist depiction of poor women. Hector Armienta's opera *River of Women* (2001), Ray John de Aragón's novella *The Legend of La Llorona* (1980), and Gilbert Hernandez's illustrated story "La Llorona: The Legend of the Crying Woman" in the graphic novel *Fear of Comics* (2000) emphasize poverty as a key factor contributing to La Llorona's tragedy. Her lack of economic resources is heightened when faced with the financial responsibility of supporting herself and her child or children.

Class disparity is particularly emphasized in nationalistic renderings of the Llorona tale, most notably casting the woman as a poor india and the male as a wealthy Hispano or criollo.[20] In Jose Antonio Gomez's photograph *A Dead Soul Who Cries* (2002), which does not feature La Llorona's lover, her identity as a Native woman is central to the piece and suggests a direct relationship between her cultural identity and the tragedy for which she is known. Works that foreground the nationalities of the woman and man at the center of the tale speak specifically to the post-conquest colonization of Mexico by emphasizing the subjugation of the Indigenous population. Such is the case in Silvia Gonzalez S.' one-act play *La Llorona Llora* (1996) and Angel Vigil's story "The Weeping Woman (La Llorona)," in *The Corn Woman: Stories and Legends of the Hispanic Southwest* (1994). In most instances, the woman is powerless to act against the man, so she murders their children to exact her revenge upon him. While the man seemingly escapes retribution for his abandonment of the woman and their children, the woman, like the colonialist legacy itself, haunts the man and the people of the town.

There is a wide range of artifacts within the category of traditional renderings of the lore, though all of these productions tell us that however one chooses to view La Llorona, she is, as Rebolledo asserts, a cultural icon "tied up in some vague way with sexuality and the death or loss of children: the negative mother image" (63). La Llorona serves as a cultural counterpoint to La Virgen de Guadalupe's maternal goodness, but La Llorona's betrayal of her own children aligns her with another Greater Mexican cultural figure. Some cultural readers will notice the undeniable parallels between La Llorona's story and that of La Malinche. In his essay "La Llorona, The Third Legend of Greater Mexico," Limón, as part of his larger argument about the legendary figure, makes the case that La Llorona represents a tertiary model of womanhood, along with La Virgen and La Malinche, for the people of Greater Mexico. Though countless books have been written about the Virgen de Guadalupe, and notable studies focus on La Malinche, such as Sandra Messinger Cypess' *La Malinche in Mexican Literature: From History to Myth* (1991) and the edited collection *Feminism, Nation and Myth: La Malinche* (2005), we have, until now, lacked a book-length, interdisciplinary study devoted solely to La Llorona.[21]

I, too, want to distinguish La Malinche (alternately known as Malintzin, Malinalli Tenepal, and Doña Marina) and La Llorona as separate figures in spite of the fact that the two are often conflated, "until in many areas they are transformed into a unitary figure" (Rebolledo, 63).[22] The conflation of these figures arises from their seemingly identical experiences, yet these women and their attendant narratives are two distinct entities, each representing something very different within criollo, Indigenous Mexican, and Chican@ cultures, and they will be treated as such in this study.[23] Though there are clearly similarities between the two, each represents a different historical moment. One foretells the future; the other is shaped by that future.

Nevertheless, the narrative details of Cortés' relationship with Malinche parallel those found in La Llorona stories ("handsome" stranger, beautiful woman, betrayal and abandonment) and contribute to the merging of these distinct figures. In this conflation, aspects of Malinche's life are mythologized, most notably her act of infanticide. Malinche was, in fact, a Nahua woman who was thrice given away: once by her family; again, along with twenty other women, as an offering to Cortés; and finally by Cortés to one of his captains, Juan Jaramillo. Since Malinche served as a "lover, translator and tactical advisor" for Cortés and supposedly conspired against her people to aid him in his conquest, some see her as the ultimate betrayer of her people, and her name has become synonymous with the most treacherous of deeds (Alarcón, "Chicana's Feminist Literature," 182). For example, during el movimiento, Chicanas who fought for their rights as women were called Malinchistas, betrayers to the causes of la raza.

Malinche's conflation with La Llorona arises primarily from the fictionalized fate of Malinche's children. People often mistakenly contend that when Cortés announced that he was returning to Spain with "his" children, Malinche murdered her children in an act of defiance and personal agency rather than allowing them to be taken from her. However, there is no historical evidence that this event took place. History records that Malinche and Cortés had one son, Martín, for whom Hernán gained "papal legitimacy" (Alcalá, 34). This fact is ignored, however, in favor of a more damning view, one directly tied to Spanish, Catholic, patriarchal, and colonialist efforts to undermine Malinche's power. Furthermore, because the children in most versions of the Malinche legend are almost always identified as male, their perceived worth as children is increased by their gender. History all but ignores the daughter Malinche had with Juan Jaramillo, the final man to whom Malinche was passed. As Rita Cano Alcalá points out, "María Jaramillo, who was an infant when her mother died, is largely forgotten by history and legend in spite of the fact that any real descendants of La Malinche in Mexico owe their lineage to her, and not to Martín Cortés" (34). Though Malinche does not murder her children, she loses them nonetheless: one to assimilation and the other to history. Yet rather than place blame at the feet of the colonizers, where it belongs, history favors the villainization of a remarkable woman.[24]

My decision not to include artifacts such as Trina Lopez's short film *La Llorona* (1994) or Gaspar de Alba's poem "Malinchista, A Myth Revised" (1989), which point to La Malinche as the source of La Llorona's story, is not meant to exclude, silence, erase, or ignore the narratives or the people who view La Malinche in this way. It is one of the parameters I chose for this study to make an already ambitious project manageable. My position on this issue also arises in part out of Chicana feminist rereadings of both figures. In the words of literary and cultural theorist Norma Alarcón:

> Insofar as feminine symbolic figures are concerned, much of the Mexican/Chicano oral tradition as well as the intellectual are dominated by La Malinche/Llorona and the Virgin of Guadalupe. The former is a subversive feminine symbol which often is identified with La Llorona, the latter a feminine symbol of transcendence and salvation. The Mexican/Chicano cultural tradition has tended to polarize the lives of women through these national (and nationalistic) symbols thereby exercising almost sole authority over the control, interpretation and visualization of women. (189 n1)

Within this polarization, Chican@s see Malinche as the mother of the mestizos, the site where European and Indigenous, conqueror and conquered, come together, creating the Chicano people. She is the woman who not only crosses borders between two cultures, but also bridges them. To write La Llorona's history as Malinche's is to take away their individual significance by blending perceived cultural asesina with traicionera, and the result minimizes the potential of both as symbols of resistance.

This distinction is made clear primarily in the works of Chicana artists. Rebolledo observes that "Chicana writers' responses to La Malinche/La Llorona are varied and complex," adding, "One thing is certain, nevertheless: in their writing these two figures are almost never confused—the identities of the two women remain clear and defined" (*Infinite Divisions*, 192). For example, Gaspar de Alba begins her poem "Malinchista, A Myth Revised" with a brief description of the traditional Mexican view of La Malinche: "Some say that the spirit of La Malinche is *La Llorona*" (16). While keeping them separate, Gaspar de Alba unites them through the act of betrayal perpetrated against them. Though La Llorona and La Malinche endure similar vilification, they emerge as distinct individuals who share a history of conflict with Old World, Spanish, Catholic patriarchy, which defines them in the present but has different implications for each, especially in contemporary renderings.

The boundary between traditional and contemporary versions of La Llorona's legend is neither rigid nor fixed. Therefore, a contemporary rendering might include some traditional elements. For example, in her poem "La Llorona, the Crying Woman" (2000), structured as a question-and-answer session, Anita Endrezze (Yaqui) writes La Llorona into the familiar position as a predator but with a notable twist. Endrezze locates La Llorona "in the modern, urban world" where her hunger for new victims equals her desire to translate her experiences into art (156). In a note for the poem, Endrezze speculates, "Perhaps she is now a poet or an artist" (156). La Llorona, then, does not wander near rivers or on the shores of lakes: she roams city streets looking for prey. The legendary figure has found new ways to kill by learning to transform herself into heroin and other drugs so that she may exact revenge for the violent rape of her daughter and infection of her son with tuberculosis, which led to his death. By day she creates her art; at night she creates the subject of her art—revenge. Making La Llorona the author or creator of her own narratives does not liberate her from the confined space of the lore, but it does give her a certain level of agency, without overtly critiquing the way in which La Llorona stories operate traditionally.

In contrast to the many traditional La Llorona artifacts, there are few artifacts that represent contemporary versions of the lore. Chican@s who offer contemporary versions of the legend emphasize loss, both literal and metaphoric, rather than some of the tale's other prominent elements or themes. While La

Llorona still searches, cultural producers represent Chican@s as either contemporary Lloronas or as her symbolic children, who have become lost as a result of
economic, political, racial, or social violence. For example, one of the Chicano
movement's most prolific poets, Abelardo B. Delgado, in "Today's Lloronas"
(1997), directly cites war, disease, gang violence, and racism for creating contemporary Weeping Women. Similarly, in Rosemary Catacalos' poem "A Vision
of La Llorona" (1984), the titular figure loses her son to gang violence and wanders through life hopeless and despairing. Though these Lloronas no longer carry
the burden of infanticide, they have still lost children for whom they search and
mourn.

Thus, La Llorona serves as a powerful means of articulating new threats.
Gaspar de Alba includes La Llorona in her poem "La Frontera" (1989) to reflect
on the dangers of immigration to the United States. She suggests that border
crossings by Mexicans entering the United States turn the women left behind,
who are faced with the uncertain futures of their loved ones on el otro lado, into
Lloronas. In *La Llorona on the Longfellow Bridge* (2003), Gaspar de Alba states
her explicit understanding of the relationship between La Llorona and la frontera: "To me, La Llorona *is* the border" (x). By equating the two, she exposes the
vulnerability of these undocumented individuals in a new cultural landscape and
makes visible the suffering of "silent lloronas" who mourn loved ones who have
literally, and perhaps figuratively, crossed over ("La Frontera," 5.14). Gaspar de
Alba's poem demonstrates explicitly the lore's capacity to accommodate contemporary political, social, and economic issues.

La Llorona's journey toward an urban landscape is often reflected in contemporary renderings. In these cases, La Llorona has moved beyond the boundaries of the river to wander along roadsides and university campuses. This movement parallels her native community's movement into these areas as well. As La
Llorona's narrative becomes "urbanized," objects within the urban landscape
replace elements found in traditional tales. For instance, in the absence of the
unfaithful lover, an equally oppressive or disabling force, such as bureaucratic institutions or corporations, is cited for contributing to La Llorona's despair. Gloria
Holguín Cuádraz's multi-genre piece "Diary of *La Llorona* with a Ph.D." (2001)
illustrates how education or its pursuit creates Lloronas of a different kind. Education, frequently offered as a means of liberating the mind, can trap the body—
in particular, women's bodies. The microenvironment of a college campus unveils or heightens the class, educational, cultural, and social disparities between
Chicanas or Latinas and other, often more privileged, groups. In this setting, Chicanas can become isolated from their peers and their own families, as in the case
of the protagonist in Susan San Miguel's short story "La Llorona of Leon Creek"

(1997), making them vulnerable to La Llorona's despair. However, the speaker in Cuádraz's work is not susceptible to La Llorona in this way: she *is* La Llorona. Though fulfilled intellectually, the speaker ponders the sacrifices she has made in her pursuit of a Ph.D., which includes complete devotion to her task rather than to a romantic relationship or children. *La Doctora Llorona* therefore weeps not for the children she has lost, "*pero / por los niños / que nunca tuvo*" (212). Instead of languishing in self-pity, the educated Llorona comforts herself with the knowledge that "There's a whole cadre of women — other educated *Lloronas* of the twentieth century, who had the historical audacity (and ovaries) to become thinkers. We are historical apertures, unwanted in our times, and adulteresses to our culture and class" (217). The speaker ultimately transforms her view of La Llorona in the same way that she has transformed herself.

A certain level of nostalgia permeates the work of cultural producers who reconceptualize La Llorona's loss, for not only has she lost us, her metaphoric children, we are losing touch with her. In Ricardo Sánchez's "Homing" (1976) and raúlrsalinas' "Un Trip Through the Mind Jail" (1980) both poets identify new threats in the barrio and their lives that have supplanted La Llorona. Police sirens replace La Llorona's wail in raúlrsalinas' poem.[25] Bruce-Novoa's cultural reading of the barrio "trip" reveals that La Llorona symbolizes the threat posed by the outside world to the members of the barrio community who venture beyond the safety of its cultural, geographic, and ideological boundaries. At one point, the boys gather in Zaragosa Park to tell La Llorona stories, and Bruce-Novoa contends that "the boys already know that they are unwelcome in the outside society; the folklore supports the view of the world as hostile" (40). La Llorona, fear, and external threats to the barrio community merge in both time and location, and the "boys run home, back to the very center of their original space, frightened by their own traditional explanation of the world; and in that center they find that Mexican folklore also can supply the remedy for those who stray, but have the sense to come home [. . .]" (40). But not all make it home. Those who do not become lost to drug use, prison, and violence. La Llorona stories, then, represent a time when they were young enough to believe that she posed the biggest threat in their lives. Her disappearance from their lives symbolizes not only a loss of innocence, but also what they have endured since her absence.

The poet Alurista brings us full circle to La Llorona's point of origin in "must be the season of the witch" (1971) to show us why we need La Llorona in our lives. In the modern world, industry and technology have devoured La Llorona's children "en las barrancas of industry" (26.6). The speaker implies that we have allowed ourselves to become victims because we have forgotten both "la magia de durango / y la de moctezuma" and La Llorona (26.16–17). Without this important cultural connection, we become lost to her and to ourselves. Though Alurista's speaker is not specific, the implication is that La Llorona serves as a protective force for both her literal and metaphoric children, who "sufren; sin ella" (26.21). The poem, in spite of its early date, anticipates some of the more radical reimaginings of La Llorona included in this book. More important, however, is his transferring of the site of suffering from La Llorona to her children. If, as cultural theorist María Herrera-Sobek suggests, "Many Chicanos identify themselves as orphans of La Llorona," we must continue to look to the weeping woman to avoid becoming lost under the weight of new oppressive forces that seek to subjugate or erase our cultural identities (*Corrido*, 57).

The inclusion of La Llorona in the oral narratives and cultural productions of Greater Mexicans represents not only her prominence as a cultural figure of femininity but her potential to evolve beyond traditional feminine constructions. Specifically, she is a figure of mourning that weeps for the losses Chicanas and Chicanos have sustained in contemporary mainstream American culture, especially women, who suffer gender as well as ethnic oppression. She is, at the same time, a figure of revolt against those same losses.

Because Chican@s are not a monolithic group with a singular view or set of beliefs—a point that advertisers attempting to tap into billions of "Latino" revenue dollars have yet to understand—I hasten to add that not all Chican@ cultural readers are going to agree on the interpretations of these representations or the use of these strategies. For example, Mario S. Garcia, in "Holding *La Llorona's* Feet to the Fire" (1998), sees the story as singular, conservative, and unchanging: she did something horrible, she deserved to be punished, punto. For Garcia, there *is* no other way to see her. Therefore, La Llorona is unworthy of reconsideration, revision, reworking, or, most especially, our sympathies. In fact, the title of his article, a reference to the torture inflicted by the Spanish on the last Aztec emperor, Cuauhtémoc, encourages the compounding and continuation of La Llorona's suffering. Motivated by greed, the Spanish tortured Cuauhtémoc to force him to reveal the location of hidden Aztec treasure. Because no such cache existed, Cuauhtémoc suffered but survived the torment. The allusion in the title therefore casts Garcia in the role of the Spanish torturers. Like Virgil, who admonishes Dante for his swooning, weeping, and initial pity for the damned they encounter in the *Inferno*, Garcia scolds his cultural "sisters," who in his view are reading La Llorona's story incorrectly, and vows to prevent them "fall[ing] victim to *Llorona's* deceptive cries" (1).[26] Garcia fails to consider why La Llorona and her story resonate for contemporary Chicanas in particular. He explicitly fails to problematize or reflect critically on his own male privilege and positioning as a savior who will "rescue" misguided Chicanas like Candelaria, who has inspired his indignation, from their own thoughts and reconsiderations of a figure who, in his opinion, is wholly contemptible. His purpose lies in promoting cultural adherence to a singular interpretation of the legend.

La Llorona continues to speak to Chican@s because she is the eternal mother who refuses to give up on her children. She will continue to seek us out wherever we may be: McAllen, Texas; Santa Fe, New Mexico; San Francisco, California; Chicago, Illinois; Minneapolis, Minnesota; Cambridge, Massachusetts; New York, New York; Bellagio, Italy. We, in turn, look to her to symbolize or articulate our contemporary reality. As the men and women at the conclusion of Huerta's play emphatically state: "We're here to tell the story / the only way we can!" (49). By continuing to imagine La Llorona, we revitalize the legend and create new conversations about our lives, cultures, and communities.

TWO

Revision and the Process of Critical Interrogation

There is honesty in images of suffering, no glamour, just truth.

—LIZZ LOPEZ

IN AN EXCERPT from Mexican writer Carmen Toscano's play *La Llorona* (1959), which was published as a dramatic dialogue in *Literatura Chicana: Texto y contexto* (1972), the character Fourth Woman says of La Llorona, "What merciless destiny drags her through the silent streets, / and over the most hidden paths. Everywhere, her white spectre makes / hearts tremble, everywhere one can hear her hideous lament" (103).[1] As in this version, the countless variations of traditional folklore show that La Llorona's merciless destiny is to wander and wail eternally in search of her murdered children's bodies. One of the most salient, and seemingly unchangeable, features of the legend is La Llorona's suffering. Rudolfo Anaya contemplates the fixity of her fate when remembering stories from his childhood. Unlike the heroines Snow White and Cinderella, who eventually free themselves from their tragic lives, "There is no happy ending to the story of La Llorona. She comes from a Catholic world, and breaking a taboo is not forgiven. She is condemned to search for her children forever" ("La Llorona," 53). In the traditional narrative, La Llorona's destiny has been meted out by divine judgment, and as a result we often have difficulty imagining her outside of the tragic context that defines her.

Reading for revisions involves identifying the means by which cultural producers engage critically the multiple sources (for instance, storytellers, structure, or conventions) from which the legend derives power without abandoning the lore altogether. These reconceptualizations are dependent upon audiences' prior knowledge of traditional lore and its features. As demonstrated in Chapter 1, repeatedly a woman, water, weeping, and/or wailing are incorporated in most cultural productions about La Llorona. Still, some folklorists, like Hawes, argue that there are no consistent elements in the legend. If we were to accept this premise, then a discussion of revision would be futile because any combination of narrative or visual elements that include La Llorona as a subject would simply constitute a variation of the legend. Studies of oral folklore do, in fact, substantiate the seemingly infinite variations of the legend, but the corpus of work produced by Chican@s on La Llorona and disseminated through other mediums suggest that revisions *are* possible. These reconsiderations are best exemplified through the Lloronas featured in the artifacts discussed in this chapter: *The Death of Speedy* (1989), a graphic novel by Jaime Hernandez; the poems "La Llorona" (1985) by Naomi Quiñonez, "El Río Grande" (1995) by Pat Mora, and "La Llorona, Crying Lady of the Creekbeds, 483 Years Old, and Aging" (1977) by Victoria Moreno; the novel *Rio Grande Fall* (1996) by Anaya; the short story "La Llorona's Final Cry" (1994) by Angel Vigil; the film *Chasing Papi* (2003) by Linda Mendoza; the television commercial, "La Llorona, Got Milk?" (2002); "La Llorona Loca: The Other Side" (1991), a short story by Monica Palacios; and *The Legend of La Llorona* (2002), a short film by Stephanie Saint Sanchez. Most of the Lloronas found in these works bear little resemblance to La Llorona in traditional narratives; those that do include familiar Lloronas use her and the lore in unfamiliar ways.

Despite the diversity of artifacts, only a limited number actually represent revisions of the lore. When they revise, Mexican Americans and Chican@s do not abandon conventional versions of the tale, for their productions are dependent upon or in conversation with them. Extensive revisions, such as abandoning the theme of loss or the act of weeping, would be incongruous with the legend's central figure and produce renderings that no longer fit the definitional criteria audiences use to read or recognize La Llorona. Those who revise the lore commingle conservative constructions of La Llorona with revisionist representations. This coexistence serves as a form of critique, one form commenting on the other to consider critically a single cultural source that informs a Chican@ worldview. Revisions are brought about also by changing elements of the tale: using the lore in new ways—for example, as a source of humor—or initiating a process of critical interrogation that changes how we feel about La Llorona.

These kinds of alterations to and reconsiderations of the traditional story are not supported by all Mexican Americans or Chican@s. Some, like Mario S.

Garcia, see these efforts as misplaced: "As scholars and as a society, we need to acknowledge *la Llorona's* crimes, not make excuses for them" (2). In his condemnation of La Llorona, he is willing to concede that the man is at fault for his behavior within the context of the lore, but Garcia sees the woman's "negative" agency, through the choice and act of infanticide, as the far greater transgression. He does not interrogate or even name those oppressive forces at work on women that make this horrifying possibility plausible or even desirable. Garcia's own view illustrates what is at stake in this argument: male authority and interpretive power. Yet the real "crime" is failing to interrogate the stories that inform our worldview, leaving unchallenged classist, sexist, or homophobic ideologies attached to and conveyed by artifacts like those featuring La Llorona.

Jaime Hernandez demonstrates the difficulties of successfully revising the story without abandoning its deterministic framework. Through his work, La Llorona becomes a cautionary tale, one that reveals how her name and fate are intertwined. A band in the Hernandez brothers' graphic novel series *Love and Rockets* takes the name La Llorona (figure 2.1).[2] On the surface, the tale serves simply as a cultural source for the name of a band, but Jaime reconceptualizes the legend for readers acquainted with the lore. Though their readership is not exclusively Chican@, Hernandez makes no overt attempt to accommodate those unfamiliar with the tale, offering only that the band's name is derived from "'*a pretty famous ghost to us Mexicans*'" (quoted in Carlson, 108). Naming a punk/ rock group La Llorona seemingly unshackles her from the constraints of the lore. It also repositions her geographically (on stage) and in the cultural imagination of her people.[3] Readers learn, however, that revision involves more than changing venues or reimagining her as something other than a despairing woman.

The band's choice of name proves to be a poor one. Although La Llorona, the figure, is liberated through the band's appropriation of her name, the band soon finds itself trapped in a contemporary version of the lore: they roam from gig to gig and wail on their guitars in the dead of night. Clubs and dives replace bodies of water as their haunting grounds. Furthermore, the band dynamic replicates, on the surface, the power dynamic attached to the lore. Three women and one man comprise La Llorona (figure 2.2). The man is the drummer, which means that though he is hidden, he provides the driving beat for the music. As in the legend, the woman (in this case, women) is foregrounded, while the man and his role in the tragedy are largely obscured from our view. We see this idea clearly in the cover art featuring La Llorona, with Monica, the lead singer, whose eyes are downcast and whose body is positioned in a Virgen like pose, with Hopey (Esperanza) and Terry flanking her at either side.[4]

Closer inspection reveals a more complicated visual representation of the tale.

FIGURE 2.1. "The Band, La Llorona" panel, by Jaime Hernandez © 2006. Reprinted by permission of Fantagraphics Books.

Hopey, who is looking away in the panel, has her arm around Monica in what appears to be both an embrace and a protective gesture. Terry, clad in leather with a cigarette dangling from the corner of her mouth, looks askance as if casing the locale for any potential threats. The image positions Monica as a person of value, one whose position eclipses the role of the lone male of the group, Zero, the drummer, who stands behind all three women, looking furtively over Monica's shoulder as if working in concert with the other members to watch the lead singer's back. Together they safeguard Monica, the voice of La Llorona.

Jaime makes no effort to speak for or offer any strategies about how to change the legend, though he does demonstrate successfully the way in which the lore can be used as a metaphor for other, contemporary cultural issues such as women musicians' struggles to find success in a male-dominated industry. Both popular criticism and praise have been heaped upon the brothers Hernandez for their representation of women in their graphic novels, but however one feels about their work, they repeatedly show the difficulties that women—especially Mexicanas and Chicanas—have when they try to break free from male-dominated ideas and attitudes about the roles women can or should play.

By suggesting a cause-and-effect relationship between the band's taking of the name La Llorona and their wandering in search of success, Hernandez highlights the potential dangers of configuring La Llorona, in her traditional role as a bogey-woman, as a source of personal inspiration for women. However, Gloria Anzaldúa, Alicia Gaspar de Alba, and Cherríe Moraga interpret La Llorona's "threat" differently, as I address in later chapters. Bringing to light these perils also reveals the scale and scope of the revisions necessary to fully reconceptualize La Llorona or her actions within the tale. The ostensible reluctance on the part of the brothers Hernandez to pursue more intensive revision should not be read as endorsement of the gender politics attached to traditional versions of the legend, for the artists are known (Jaime, in particular) for strong women characters who struggle to live and love on their own terms.

Men do participate in revisionings and reconsiderations of the legend in limiting ways, but women produced most of the artifacts examined in this chapter. La Llorona's power in the cultural imagination of her people, especially the way in which she is used to comment on and police women's behavior, makes her an ideal candidate for reconsideration by Chicana feminists. In a chapter titled "From Coatlicue to La Llorona," Tey Diana Rebolledo provides an analysis of Chicana writers' incorporation and revision of cultural materials and figures

FIGURE 2.2. "Individual Band Members' Profiles" panel, by Jaime Hernandez © 2006. Reprinted by permission of Fantagraphics Books.

in their writing. She asserts that this move is necessary due to the restrictive cultural roles offered to Chicanas: "Women's lives are particularly circumscribed by cultural values and norms that try to dictate how women should behave and who their role models should be" (*Women Singing,* 49). In their efforts to challenge existing views on La Llorona, the infanticide of the tale presents one of the major obstacles to achieving this end. Instead of sidestepping the issue, many Chicana cultural producers keep this as a focal point of their productions, but radically alter the context or expose mitigating or hidden factors that contributed to the infanticide.

Carmen Toscano's dramatic dialogue, excerpted from her play *La Llorona,* represents one of the earliest examples of the kind of interrogation later found in Chican@ cultural productions that revise the lore. Toscano creates tension between a traditional version of the legend and one that challenges its conventionality. Together, the women in Toscano's play problematize La Llorona's abject position by questioning the forces, such as male power and the male-dominated Catholic worldview, that contribute to the weeping woman's fate, and they begin to see her not as a figure of loathing, but as one who embodies the effects of colonization and/or domination. In this way, Toscano's characters initiate a revisioning of La Llorona that Chican@ cultural producers later sustain and advance.

Despite the early date of Toscano's play (1959), she establishes an interrogative model for contemporary writers such as Naomi Quiñonez, Pat Mora, and Victoria Moreno. These poets revise the folktale and/or our view of La Llorona by generating sympathy for her, imagining her outside of a Christian context, or absolving her of sole responsibility for the infanticide. Historically, Chicana poets have incorporated such traditional cultural figures as the Virgen de Guadalupe, La Malinche, and La Llorona to reflect a particularly women-centered aesthetic and set of cultural concerns; this choice can be explained in part by the fact that men either offered them limited roles or wrote them out of formative creative, intellectual, and national narratives, such as *I am Joaquín* (1967) by Rudolfo "Corky" Gonzales.

Cultural forms such as folklore, Native Mexican mythology, legends, and corridos informed Chican@ literary "sensitivity" and sensibility in the early part of the Chicano Civil Rights Movement (1965–1975), particularly in the way they figure prominently in the expression of Chicano Nationalism.[5] One of the most well-known and significant poems to emerge from this period is Gonzales' epic poem. In *Joaquín,* the poet constructs a Chicano past by creating a narrative around cultural figures and icons, primarily male figures from Spanish and Indigenous Mexican history, including the Spanish conquistador Cortés, the last

Aztec emperor Cuauhtémoc, the "outlaw" Joaquín Murrieta, revolutionaries Francisco Madero, Emiliano Zapata, and Pancho Villa, and artist Diego Rivera. As cultural theorist Alfred Arteaga maintains, "Being 'chicano' is a process of continual remaking, a discursive process that is always negotiated within the context of the circumscribing discursive practices of the United States" (75). In his careful weaving of a distinct Chicano history, Corky Gonzales writes Chicanos and their experiences into US discourse. Gonzales describes *Joaquín* as "a historical essay, a social statement, a conclusion of our *mestisaje* [sic], a welding of the oppressor (Spaniard) and the oppressed (Indian). It is a mirror of our greatness and our weakness, a call to action as a total people [. . .]" (1). While this was a history that Gonzales admittedly wished to share with all of his "hermanos y hermanas," women are subordinated within the context of the poem. Gonzales characterizes women both verbally and visually as hard-working, faithful, virginal, maternal, and devoted—ones who mourn and pray.[6] These roles are not inherently demeaning, but they do restrict Chicana opportunities for constructing a subjectivity beyond these stringent boundaries.

The only female figures named in the poem are the Virgen de Guadalupe and her Aztec precursor, Tonantzin. Within the context of the poem, the primary image Gonzales presents of women is that of mother. There is a direct correlation between the status of women in the poem and women's roles within the movement. During this period, the Virgen de Guadalupe was adopted as the banner symbol for la raza.[7] The brown virgin, who possesses aspects of the Aztecan goddess Tonantzin, brought together the colonizers' and Indigenous people's religious beliefs and reflected the dual heritage of the Chican@s. As mother, she symbolically went before her children to guide and protect.

Some of the primary Chicana feminist criticisms of *I am Joaquín,* the Chicano movement, and Chicano nationalism are the ways in which heterosexual male power and authority were centralized through mythopoetic male figures, realized in such personages as the titular Murrieta or Zapata. Moraga reflects on how gender roles were mediated and became fixed during this period, stating,

For a generation, nationalist leaders used a kind of "selective memory," drawing exclusively from those aspects of Mexican and Native cultures that served the interests of male heterosexuals. At times, they took the worst of Mexican machismo and Aztec warrior bravado, combined it with some of the most oppressive male-conceived idealizations of "traditional" Mexican womanhood and called that cultural integrity. (*Last Generation,* 156–157)

The foregrounding of male icons limited the participation of women, narratively and literally, to subservient roles.

Women, made virtually invisible or cast in very traditional roles were, like La Llorona, lost in the male-dominated movement and its conception of nationalism.[8] Although they played powerful roles in the struggle, their identities as women were subsumed by the masculine "o" in "Chicano."[9] Chicanas who attempted to voice their concerns as women or feminists were often considered vendidas (sellouts) or Malinchistas, divisive traitors who sought to fragment the movement. Poets such as Ana Montes in "La Nueva Chicana" (1971), Leticia Hernández in "Mujer" (1971), Mary Helen Vigil in "Mujer" (1972), and Anita Sarah Duarte in "The Brown Women" (1975) make visible the particular difficulties Chicanas faced during the movement toward the rise of Chicana subjectivity and feminism.[10]

In "I Throw Punches for My Race, but I Don't Want to Be a Man: Writing Us—Chica-nos (Girl, Us)/Chicanas—into the Movement Script" (1992), Angie Chabram-Dernersesian illustrates how Chicana poets such as Martha Cotera in "La Loca de La Raza Cósmica" (1978) and Phyllis López in "La Chicana" (1978) constructed a then emergent Chicana subjectivity, a counterdiscourse to the male-dominated epic (his)tory found in *Joaquín*. Citing such works as *With His Pistol in His Hand* (1958) by Américo Paredes, *Pocho* (1959) by José Antonio Villarreal, and *I am Joaquín* (1967), Chabram-Dernersesian documents how the male authors and historical figures dominate the writing and scholarship of this period. She then calls attention to how Chicanas employ similar methods but inscribe female voices, figures, and positions in their works. Chicana feminists draw upon a feminine cultural and political legacy through figures like La Llorona. Often, in this process, they recast these feminine symbols outside of their previous constructions to instill them with new meaning.

La Virgen, La Malinche, and La Llorona have become—whether through our acceptance, rejection, or reworking of their stories—central to the formation of Chicana feminist thought. Of the three feminine cultural symbols, La Llorona is the last to be significantly transformed by writers, due in part to the infanticide of the tale, which is horrifically tragic and not usually seen as an act of agency by storytellers. When considered within the context of traditional narratives, La Llorona's actions are seen almost exclusively as negative. Therefore, when Chicanas write La Llorona into their work, they often designate new meanings for prominent features of the lore. For example, according to Cordelia Candelaria, when speaking generally about infanticide, "insanity is automatically assumed [on the part of the mother] and usually proven to explain the horror" ("Letting La Llorona Go," *Arroyos,* 125). Candelaria critiques the way in which this assessment discounts other cultural and social factors that may have contributed to the murder. Maria Figueredo, on the other hand, sees the infanticide as an act of "self-mutilation," one committed in response to "some form of oppression that has been internalized"; in other words, the act is committed "in reaction against the pain and suffering of the oppression" (240). Through their revisiting and re-visioning of La Llorona, Quiñonez, Mora, and Moreno offer other explanations for what happened to La Llorona and/or her children. Most of the mitigating factors that these writers identify involve the diminishing of female power in Mexican and Chican@ cultures.

Naomi Quiñonez, in the poem "La Llorona" (1985), invites the reader to look again at La Llorona within the context of the traditional folklore.[11] Notably, the poem appeared not long after the publication of the feminist anthology *This Bridge Called My Back: Writings by Radical Women of Color* (Alarcón, ed., 1981), which brought together diverse conversations about feminisms and represents a Chicana feminist reconsideration of the legendary figure. To enable this process, Quiñonez offers a sympathetic encounter with the Weeping Woman that reveals the inherent complexities of her position in Chican@ culture as a person who both gives and takes life. The compassion that the narrator feels for La Llorona represents the major revision of the lore and is derived from the narrator's real-ization about how the legend has operated in her own life, wandering, as it does, through her existence. Though the narrator has been subject to visitations from the legendary woman, she does not fear her. "When La Llorona comes to me," the speaker says,

> vulnerability turns compassion
> the haunting melody of her song
> wanders as wounded and random
> as her legend through the rivers
> and alleyways of my existence. (1–6)

This lack of fear destabilizes the image of La Llorona as a menacing or horrific specter. Instead, she is presented as a "wounded" figure, a woman who endures great suffering as a consequence of her actions, a figure worthy of reconsidera-tion. Her suffering moves the narrator, and it courses through the speaker's veins, due in part to her identifying with and internalizing the legend as a part of her own history. Additionally, by directly referencing "rivers" and "alleyways," the narrator illustrates La Llorona's movement from a rural to an urban landscape, which reflects her dynamic and transitory nature.

From this initially sympathetic encounter with the Weeping Woman, the narrator subsequently relates a traditional version of the tale in which La Llorona, the "madre perdida" or "rejected mother / of desgraciados," forever searches for the children she has murdered (7, 11–12).[12] The narrator indicates that by accepting this static, despairing image of La Llorona, the "All-giving and all-loving / the all-forgiving part" of her own and La Llorona's being is negated (13–14). Specifically, if La Llorona is only remembered for what she became after she murdered her children, then her previous role as a life-giving, loving nurturer is erased. The narrator seeks to restore these aspects that are absent from the folklore, underscoring this point by locating La Llorona among other representations of female power:

> La madre bendita
> La mujer fuerte
> La puta madre
> La soldadera
> La india amorosa
> La mujer dolorosa[13] (16–21)

La Llorona remains distinct from these figures, for the infanticide included in the legend defines her. The task remains, then, how we, as the narrator states, can reconcile the actions of a woman who "sentences to death / the child she brings / into the world" (23–25).

Rather than reinforce the traditional view of the children's deaths as "murders," the narrator offers an alternate possibility. She argues that La Llorona "*sacrificed* her children / to haunt the weak / and comfort the living" (35–37; emphasis added). In this reading, La Llorona selflessly takes the lives of her children to save them from the violence of a world "that may destroy them / and will kill them" (31–32). Some may see this change in terminology as an attempt to dilute one of the tale's more horrific aspects, but the horror remains. It is simply shifted to a new site. Reconceptualizing the murders as sacrifices makes La Llorona a protector against social and political forces that would destroy her children. Her sacrifice suggests a divine intervention in the human world. She emerges as a holy woman, "mujer sagrada," whose offering is an act of faith, with parallels to the story of Abraham in the Bible and Agamemnon in Greek myth: both were asked to sacrifice their children to appease their deities (38).

As the narrator suggests, changing how we see La Llorona can result in liberation for her and us as well. Fundamental to this new view is an acknowledgement of female power: "La Llorona, the feminine / haunts us if we fear her / comforts us if we understand" (26–28). This image of La Llorona providing comfort restores her nurturing powers, so that readers can see her the way that the speaker does. The narrator assures us that La Llorona "makes her peace / with those who respect vulnerability / and draw from her strength" (40–42). Yet if we fail to sympathize with La Llorona or discredit her maternal or healing powers, the howling memory of her sacrifice will remain interminable. Thus Quiñonez does not ask us to abandon the traditional lore, but she does encourage readers to reconceptualize La Llorona's actions without altering the tale's conventional narrative, to see her as a good mother and woman of power who alone can carry the suffering of all children who are lost.

In "El Río Grande," Pat Mora does not ask her readers to reconceptualize La Llorona's actions, but she does encourage us to rethink the reasons behind her particular fate.[14] Each of the poem's three stanzas begins with the tentative supposition, "Maybe La Llorona is el Río Grande." The speaker conflates La Llorona with the land in an attempt to encourage readers to think about her in ways independent of the lore or to assign some other meaning to her story. Mora's poem does not offer a traditional version of the lore, yet the reconceptualization of the tale is dependent upon understanding what La Llorona represents symbolically, specifically the way in which her story is used to villainize women. The speaker also makes visible the positive aspects of Mexican women's lives, such as joy, freedom, and camaraderie, obscured by stories like La Llorona's.

Cultural readers know that we are being asked to reconceptualize La Llorona from the US side of the border, for in Mexico the same river is known as el Río Bravo. As a river, La Llorona "carries voices wherever she flows," but the voices she carries are distinct, for they are "the voices of women who speak only Spanish" (2–3). The suggestion is that La Llorona, as the river, is a figure with whom women can connect intimately, specifically by drinking her in: "women who scoop her to them in the heat, / lick her on their lips, their voices rising / like the morning star" (16–18). The Spanish-speaking women featured in the poem are strong and nourishing like the land. They also thrive independently of men, which means that these women pose a cultural threat to male power and authority: the women of the border are dangerous and transgressive in their self-sufficiency. The story of La Llorona is one way that men neutralize this threat. If La Llorona is el Río Grande, then she represents what happens when women of power are despoiled and polluted, like the river, by men.

In Victoria Moreno's "La Llorona, Crying Lady of the Creekbeds, 483 Years Old, and Aging," La Llorona's position is the result of numerous agents (including colonialism, poverty, social workers, and a lack of education) conspiring to ensure her suffering.[15] Due to the scope of Moreno's critique of the cultural, social, and political forces at work on La Llorona, I devote considerable attention to the piece. Moreno situates the Weeping Woman in an urban landscape complete with telephones and rivers that have been paved over, while at the same time providing her with a history that stretches back more than 483 years, as indicated in the title.[16] Moreno's revisioning of the story occurs not through relocating the Weeping Woman in an urban environment, but through the assertion that there is a hidden "truth" about La Llorona. The poem begins with lines of prose that recount the narrator's history with La Llorona and conventional versions, along with the uses, of her story: "Different versions and different reasons, each to tell us / a moral, to warn us" (4–5). The narrator emphasizes the endurance of the legend even in the face of the changing cultural and physical landscape:

> [. . .] We knew she would be forever with us, forever in our memories, crying for her dead children and for her children yet unborn that were to die.
>
> But creekbeds got scarce in the barrio, and so, La Llorona had to get a phone installed so we could reach her, so we could hear her, so she could let us know the truth. (11–16)

La Llorona's wails are no longer heard at night by the river. Instead, the narrator and her friends must seek out the Wailing Woman by telephoning her so they can hear her cry: "Once, we found out what her phone / number was and used to dial and listen to her cry, passing / around the phone from one to the next" (5–7).[17] By calling La Llorona and passing the phone from person to person, as one would pass along a story, the narrator revises, through a reversal, the direction of La Llorona's communication and methods for transmitting the narrative.[18] She no longer wails to us as she searches bodies of water; instead we must now find her, literally calling (to) her on the telephone. We cry out to her in a desire to know our cultural origins, and in La Llorona's reply, she imparts a new truth: she was and is not solely responsible for the loss of her children.

Shifting blame for her permanent separation from her children to new sites does not exonerate La Llorona, but it does illustrate that there were always mitigating factors. Moreno sees it as "a fate [La Llorona] had been accomplice / to" since the arrival of the Spaniards (10–11). The narrator identifies contemporary bureaucracy, racism, feminism, patriarchy, and classism as current issues contributing to La Llorona's loss. Each stanza begins with the line "they took away her children." This repetition reinforces the multiple sources of oppression at work on La Llorona and her children. The Weeping Woman imparts this new truth to those who now telephone to hear her wail:

> La Llorona
> they took away her children
> the welfare office came and stole away her children
> because she had no right, they said,
> to be a single parent, non-model American family [. . .] (17–21)

The narrator offers an image of a contemporary Llorona who is a poor woman with no legal rights and who fails to fulfill the mainstream cultural ideal about the nuclear family.

La Llorona's failure to achieve a white, middle-class maternal or familial ideal exposes the privileged economic, social, and political underpinnings of the "model" American family. The Weeping Woman and her children, then, represent the antithesis of that ideal. The assault on Chicana single-motherhood is compounded by the fact that La Llorona, from a social perspective, has few rights as a woman without a man. Clearly, it is La Llorona's failure to fulfill an Anglo cultural ideal that erases her from the modern landscape, not only as a multi-dimensional woman but also as a loving mother and human being. Moreover, this erasure underlines La Llorona's need for a phone line so people can find her because she, like her children, has become lost, or rather invisible, in contemporary culture.

Moreno revises the lore further by casting the welfare office in the role traditionally held by the lover. In conventional versions of the tale, the male lover poses not only a physical but an economic threat, which occasionally contributes to the fate of her children; for example, in some versions she kills her children to prevent their suffering from starvation. Also, as a male, often from a higher social class, the lover has the freedom to simply leave and take their children with him, leaving her with nothing. It is the welfare office that takes away her children because "she had no right, they said, / to be a single parent, non-model American family" (20–21). Moreno makes clear that outside forces beyond La Llorona's control, such as the social worker who "took away her children," have contributed to the creation of her despair.

In the second stanza, Moreno includes a feature of the conventional narrative: a man from a higher social class abandoning his mestiza lover. She translates this element into a contemporary drama. La Llorona has an affair with a married man who will not leave his wife or support any "illegitimate" offspring that might result from the relationship. Unlike the traditional tale, the children are eliminated before they are even conceived, since the woman is taking an oral contraceptive at his behest. Their conception is prevented because of her acquiescence to the

demands that he makes on the woman and her body. Yet the lines could be interpreted also as alluding to an abortion. Therefore, from a conservative view of
women's reproductive rights, infanticide remains a component of the narrative.
However one chooses to interpret the lines, Moreno revises the traditional tale by
erasing the children from the equation *before* they come into being. La Llorona
is then left weeping for the children she was discouraged from having. In this
stanza, she is a completely passive and subordinate figure, as revealed by the use
of "she" in contrast to the capitalized "He." Although the capitalization demonstrates the disparity in their authority, it also reinforces male power.

Moreno makes clear that it is the man's selfishness and self-righteousness that
leads him to take away La Llorona's unborn children and condemn her for her
sexuality:

> they took away her children
>   (all unborn)
> because He was married and she was on the pill and
> He didn't care to fool with divorces and didn't care to
> have any bastard children and asked her
> not to have his. (22–27)

The double standard employed here does not condemn the man for his behavior.
The man (or in this case, men, as indicated by "they") denies La Llorona motherhood because he does not view her as his legitimate partner. Her usefulness to
men lies in her ability and willingness to provide them with extramarital sex.
Though this type of sexual subjugation is not an overt feature of the lore, embedded in the story is the idea that La Llorona's body was valued for what it could
produce, pleasure and progeny, for one man. The erasure of the children from
the narrative before they are conceived does not minimize La Llorona's feelings
of loss and despair, a point illustrated by Gloria Holguín Cuádraz in "Diary of
La Llorona with a Ph.D," discussed in Chapter 1.

The issues of class and ethnicity figure prominently in conventional, nationalist renderings (upper versus lower class, and Spanish versus criolla/mestiza
or india), yet Moreno uses both issues in the third stanza to emphasize the gap
between white, middle-class feminist professional women and many Chicanas.
The value ascribed to white feminists of placing a professional career over family
increases the disparity between the two points of view. According to the narrator,
women from outside the Chican@ community attempt to diminish the worth
that Chicanas place on directly overseeing the lives of their children. At the same

time, these women are soothing their own guilt about enrolling their children in daycare in order to pursue professional careers:

it was way-out-of-style to long for large families
and staying home with one's babies and breast-feeding truth
and love and all that rot, especially if you were a professional
and should know better, and one was only allowed to have two
anyway, and only if one let the day-care raise them. (29–33)

Their criticisms are also class based, for they assume that all women have equal access to the education and job training that allow women to enter the workforce as professionals.

Moreno's narrator underscores the idea that those outside of the community have very little sense of Chicanas' needs and desires: some women want to stay home, and their choice of professional career can be that of mother. Stanza 4 continues with this theme as "they" ask La Llorona, "how are you PROTECT-ING yourself?" (35). The suggestion is that "one could be *attacked* by pregnancy at any minute / and torn to shreds" (36–37). Here the women, female outsiders, discourage pregnancy. In writing their economic and political concerns across Chicanas, white, middle-class feminists effectively erase Chicanas and their children from the landscape, creating barrios full of Lloronas. Within the narrative, white feminists assume the place and function of the man featured in the tale.

Moreno's narrator turns her critical lens toward capitalism and bureaucratic institutions in stanzas 5 and 6, arguing that these oppressive systems have enough resources to impose antifertility measures on Chicanas but not enough to build their children a world. The emphasis in stanza 5 is on the damaging mind-set of cultural materialism. Instant gratification, serving oneself in the now, disallows the construction of a future for children. Again, class plays an important role in this revision. Because capitalist culture wages war against the poor, La Llorona "had to struggle just / to stay alive" (42–43). She therefore becomes a powerful symbol of the lower and working classes whose daily lives are consumed with feeding, clothing, and housing themselves and their families.

The narrator's criticism continues into the sixth stanza as politicians spewing bureaucratic rhetoric also become responsible for taking away La Llorona's children. Although they may preach about families and clean cities, what they really want to do is clean cities of Mexicano and Chicano families. La Llorona's children-to-be are taken from her without her knowledge through the implementation of a covert, forced sterilization program.[19] Antifertility drugs are slipped into the water to supposedly fight disease, "to insure a society that was *clean* and / *scheduled* and *sterile* [. . .]" (47–48). Through the reference to clinical sterility, the narrator suggests that the Anglo desire to eradicate disease originates with white fear over the growing Chican@ population and perhaps the intermingling of whites and Chican@s. White culture displaces its xenophobia and discomfort onto the bodies of Chican@s as a fear of dis-ease.

The final stanzas bring the narrative full circle and assign an explicitly Indigenous identity to La Llorona. The narrator closes with an image of what happened to La Llorona when she encountered modernity:

> And the Aztec Lady crying down the creekbeds
> ran into a concrete wall and, puzzled blank,
> stopped her wailing for her children
> and just stared, realizing that
> > hope was gone. (52–56)

Concrete has been poured over her river, indicating that her avenues for reaching Chican@s and her territory of protest have been eliminated. She appears, in effect, doubly damned by God for the infanticide and by Anglos who prevent Chican@s from hearing her. Her cries as a Mexican Indian woman are silenced in the face of geographic and cultural change. She must, then, find a new way to reach her children.

Not until the final stanza do readers discover that the narrator has assumed the responsibility of conveying La Llorona's truth. She takes on La Llorona's mourning cry

> and, screaming down the streets at night,
> carried on the insane truth, the pain
> knowing that
>
> they took away her children. (58–61)

The concluding scene of the narrator screaming in the night announces that the narrator has taken up La Llorona's cause. Instead of letting La Llorona's legacy die in the concrete urban world, the narrator intervenes in the tale in an attempt to ensure that the Weeping Woman's loss, and poor or working-class women of Mexican descent, will not be forgotten. Her chances of success are limited by the fact that she faces the same debilitating and oppressive forces as La Llorona. Still, the narrator does not let this diminish her desire to let people know that "they took away [La Llorona's] children" (61). The ending of the poem represents a continuation of the story, but not of resistance to the forms of oppression at work on La Llorona. Although the speaker continues to disseminate the lore, she does not directly challenge these forces. The poem does, however, represent an important step in using the legend to formally identify and critique the oppressive forces at work on Chican@s that contribute to the making of modern-day Lloronas. The final line of the poem challenges the reader's complacency. After Moreno reveals obscured truths about La Llorona, the question remains: What will we do with this information? The cultural producers included in this chapter respond to that question by revisiting the lore to search for their own answers.

Chicano author, playwright, and cultural critic Rudolfo Anaya and author Angel Vigil provide two equally startling hidden truths about La Llorona. Anaya's devotion to La Llorona matches that of other artists and writers, including Anzaldúa, Moraga, and Gaspar de Alba, to name a few. In "La Llorona, Magic Realism, and the Frontier," from *Beyond Bounds: Cross-Cultural Essays on Anglo, American Indian, and Chicano Literature,* Robert Franklin Gish traces La Llorona's appearance throughout Anaya's oeuvre, beginning with *Heart of Aztlán* (1976) and continuing through the novels *Bless Me, Ultima* (1972) and *Tortuga* (1979), his short story collection *The Silence of the Llano* (1982), and the novella *The Legend of La Llorona* (1984).[20] Though not included in Gish's study, La Llorona also appears in Anaya's epic poem *The Adventures of Juan Chicaspatas* (1985) and throughout Anaya's detective series featuring Sonny Baca, a character that first appears prominently in Anaya's novel *Alburquerque* (1992), which also includes La Llorona. To add to the astounding number of texts across literary genres, including children's and juvenile literature, that involve La Llorona, Anaya has also written an unpublished play called "The Season of La Llorona" (2003), the essay "La Llorona, El Kookoóee, and Sexuality," and a libretto centering on La Llorona. In each production, Anaya refines his view of La Llorona so that readers may trace literally, and literarily, the evolution of his thinking about the legend.

While Anaya often positions La Llorona traditionally as a predatory spectre, he also openly challenges conventional interpretations, particularly in his later work. His most prominent revision of the lore occurs in the Sonny Baca mystery *Rio Grande Fall* (1996). The narrator, when speaking of Baca's former antagonist, describes her relation to a conventional version of La Llorona's story but emphasizes the tale's use as a behavioral deterrent. Baca later reflects on a different version of the story, one told to him by his grandmother, who revealed that in an effort to drive La Llorona mad, her husband killed their children. While the man's role or complicity in the children's deaths is understood, it has, by and large, remained unstated. In the grandmother's story, he is the single source of the tragedy. This revelation absolves La Llorona of the infanticide, but in the novel, the grandmother's story represents a minority opinion with little power to change prevailing views about the legendary figure. Ultimately, the community has no desire to challenge popular versions of the story.

Like Anaya, Vigil offers a new revelation about the Weeping Woman in his story "La Llorona's Final Cry" (1994). Through an act of compassion, La Llorona finds redemption, but, as Vigil demonstrates, the community featured in the narrative is unwilling to uphold or accept this new view. Two naughty children, who stay out late one night playing down by the river, court an encounter with La Llorona. She obliges them and begins to drag them away when suddenly she hears a woman crying in anguish. The children identify the woman's screams as belonging to their mother, who is frantic about not being able to find them. La Llorona identifies with the woman's pain and sends the kids back to their mother, saying, "Go. Go home. I can't bear to think of another woman suffering as I have over my own two lost children. Your mother's cries are too much for me to bear. [. . .] This is my eternal punishment for what I did. Now go. Go home. Your mother is calling you" (187). La Llorona claims responsibility for her actions and places another woman's needs before her own. In what represents a notable revision of the lore, she is released from her suffering and ascends to heaven. After the children return home safely, the father translates their experience and explains the consequences of La Llorona's decision to release them: God has forgiven her. His status as a male authority, one with the ability to decipher God's actions, makes his interpretation of the event definitive. However, while God releases La Llorona from the suffering that defined her, the community is not so willing to do the same.

In La Llorona's absence, the community discovers that they miss her and can no longer rely on her stories as a means of transmitting cultural knowledge. They then begin to make up new stories about her, all the while knowing that she has been redeemed. Her individual fate is deemphasized, and forgotten, in favor of more traditional cuentos. The implication is that regardless of any new truths revealed about La Llorona, the people will resist letting go of conventional constructions that position her as a bogey-woman. They both want and need for her to suffer, so that they might alleviate their own misery.

Humor and the Dismantling of a Tradition

The focus of this chapter, thus far, has been on cultural productions that feature repositionings of La Llorona without radically altering the story or its grim tone. Because the folktale is used to inspire fear, either for recreation or as a behavioral deterrent, its use as a source of humor may strike some as a substantial challenge to its social and cultural status. Historically, satire or parody has served as a way to expose the faults or flaws in dominative ideologies or cultural texts. For this reason, humor is one of the most serious forms of criticism we have. While inviting us to laugh, satire also requires critical reflection on the part of audiences to determine our/its position in relation to the subject or form under interrogation. As Guillermo E. Hernández notes in *Chicano Satire: A Study in Literary Culture* (1991), "Audiences thus react favorably or negatively to the texts or performances of comics and satirists because of their familiarity with specific normative paradigms encoded in cultural conventions" (113). Thus reading humor is an act of cultural reading. Cultural productions about La Llorona that include humor represent some of the most radical revisions of the lore outside of those that choose to abandon both the structure and conventions of traditional tales. Some may bristle at the thought of finding any humor in La Llorona's story or using it as a source of humor. I know I did. The idea of laughing at a woman condemned to suffer for eternity was more than distasteful; it seemed malicious.

I once asked my students if they had ever heard of a Llorona story that was not scary. One student wanted me to clarify my question, asking, "What other kind of La Llorona story could there be?" At the time, I could not conceive of a humorous use of La Llorona or her story, so I offered other emotions that might be elicited by the story, such as sadness, sympathy, pity, and so on. What I have found since then is that, for the most part, cultural producers who use humor do not take away La Llorona's inherent ability to frighten, nor do they invite us to laugh directly at her; they ask us to laugh at our fear or the conventions of the tale. Complicated rhetorical and cultural moves are involved in this process, and not everyone will find the use of humor effective or even palatable. Regardless of how we feel about the infusion of humor into the legend, we cannot deny that these productions participate in disseminating the lore on new fronts. As cultural readers, our obligation is to determine how revisions of the tale's somber tone, for instance, open new paths of discussion about it and encourage us to see La Llorona and her story in new ways. Hernández makes a similar observation, stating, "The observer who analyzes cultural expressions must decipher a complex interplay of evaluative possibilities that require abilities and qualities that are already familiar to literary scholars: knowledge of cultural traditions, theoretical soundness, ample reading, sensitivity to subtlety and nuance, and discernment of major trends" (113). Humorous scenarios that feature La Llorona do not necessarily diminish her symbolic power. In fact, the opposite is the case: humorous revisions can reinforce her power in the narrative and take power away from oppressive individuals and institutions that play a role in her subjugation.

American Indian cultural theorist Vine Deloria Jr. (Standing Rock Sioux)

once stated in his discussion of Indian humor: "One of the best ways to understand a people is to know what makes them laugh" (146). Conversely, knowing
what people do not find funny or refuse to poke fun at can be equally informative.
People of Mexican descent hold certain images sacred. The Virgen specifically
comes to mind. Few would argue for the sanctity of La Llorona, but most would
agree that she is not a figure who immediately lends herself to humor. When
Yolanda López created her now famous Guadalupe series featuring images of the
Virgen in tennis shoes or as a working-class abuelita sitting at a sewing machine,
some people were shocked and outraged that she would reimagine such a revered
image in her art. Yet the Virgen's place in Greater Mexican culture as the passive venerated mother makes her an ideal subject for reconsideration. In López's
work, the Virgen serves as the source and site of criticism about cultural models
available to women. At the same time, according to Amalia Mesa-Bains, the Virgen becomes a means of transforming these restrictive roles: "This repositioning
becomes both satire and provocation, while retaining the transfigurative liberation of the icon" (137). Mesa-Baines goes on to state that the art in the Guadalupe
series "does not simply reflect an existing ideology; it actively constructs a new
one" (137). The same can be said of cultural producers who infuse humor in their
works featuring La Llorona. Her set position as a cultural villain makes the lore
an ideal subject for parody. These repositionings of La Llorona create alliances
among women, initiate a process of making her a speaking subject, liberate her
from the infanticide, change her sexual orientation, and dismantle a centuries-
old tradition of using her story exclusively to inspire fear.

The film *Chasing Papi* (2003) is one of the more recent works that attempts
to use La Llorona as a source of humor. The endeavor is hampered by the filmmaker's efforts to make La Llorona accessible to those familiar and unfamiliar
with the tale at the expense of integrating the lore in a meaningful way into the
narrative. Cowritten by Nueva Mexicana Laura Angélica Simón and directed
by first-time feature film director Linda Mendoza, *Chasing Papi* focuses on the
romantic life of a marketing director for a perfume company, Tomás Fuentes
(played by Eduardo Verástegui), the titular Papi.[21] All women, young and old,
find Tomás irresistible, especially the three very different women he claims to
love: Lorena, Cici, and Patricia. Puerto Rican–born actress Roselyn Sanchez, best
known for her work in telenovelas, plays Lorena, a sexually repressed, poetry-
loving activist lawyer in Chicago who has no sense of her own physical beauty.
Columbiana Sofi Vergara plays Cici, a Miami-based, street-smart cocktail wait-
ress who aspires to be a professional dancer. Christian singer Jaci Velasquez, born
in Houston, plays Patricia, a spoiled rich girl living in New York with her parents,
who are trying to find her a rich man to marry.

The film establishes La Llorona as a figure that women can call upon to punish unfaithful men, presumably by frightening them to death. Audiences are invited to see the deaths of philandering men in this way as funny. The first time La Llorona appears on screen is after Cici warns Tomás that La Llorona will get him if he ever cheats. Cici morphs into a ghostly pale Llorona in a tattered white dress and lunges at Tomás. Audiences see La Llorona (played by Laurie Carrasco) from Tomás' point of view. Below her image, the following definition appears: "La Llorona: A spirit in Latin mythology who haunts naughty children. See also Medea, Bloody Mary." No other explanation about La Llorona is given in the film.[22] The emphasis on "naughty" children is one of the confusing aspects of the definition because if audiences are unfamiliar with La Llorona, they are to use Medea and Bloody Mary as points of reference. Although killing figures prominently in some stories about all three, what remains unclear is how La Llorona functions within the film. The definition might lead some to believe that a murder of, or an injury to, a child is going to be played for comic effect, which does not prove to be the case in the film. But the definition illustrates the difficulties, even for Latin@s, of mediating La Llorona lore for a wide audience.

In the film, La Llorona neither weeps nor wanders. Instead, the Llorona that audiences see resembles the one who appears in the recountings of men who have had the unfortunate experience of crossing her path. Audiences are not encouraged to laugh at La Llorona, specifically; instead, we are supposed to laugh at the effect she has on one man's physical and psychological well-being. After Cici's initial threat, every time Tomás feels overwhelming guilt about dating three women at once, La Llorona appears. When she does, a woman in Tomás' presence, not always one with whom he is involved romantically, transforms into La Llorona.

According to the definition of La Llorona offered in the film, Tomás' multiple love interests are simply evidence of his "naughty" behavior and the overactive libido of a juvenile male. Audiences are led to believe, based on the number of times we see La Llorona, that Tomás is besieged by guilt. Her appearances affect his performance at work, cause him to faint, and lead him to believe he is hallucinating. None of these experiences are enough to inspire him to resolve his romantic quandary, in part because he does not see dating three women as a problem, even though the affairs are taking a toll on his health. The women are the ones to force the issue after all three, independently, decide to "surprise" him in Los Angeles. At his house, they discover each other's existence, yet rather than leave Tomás, they try to force him to choose between them. Tomás, who is being treated by a physician for exhaustion, mixes tranquilizers and alcohol in attempt to cope with this personal catastrophe. As a result, he passes out, but before doing so, as the women hover over him, the last thing he sees is each woman's face alternately morphing into the guise of La Llorona. Once he passes out, La Llorona disappears from the film.[23]

From the outset of the film, audiences are encouraged to laugh at Tomás' sexual antics. Mendoza's use of animation during the opening credits sets a light tone, and the sequence provides audiences with Papi's chulo-making history at the hands of the many women who helped raise him and establishes his sex appeal across gender and generational lines. The animation sequences are also used as transitions between some scenes early in the film, giving the film and its subject matter—women competing for the attention of one man—a comic book feel, calling to mind Betty and Veronica of *Archie* comics fame. The famous working-class blonde and spoiled, rich brunette, respectively, were constantly battling for the affections of Archie, the redheaded namesake of the series. The fluffy tenor of the film does not inspire serious consideration of how women contribute to the making of Papi Chulos by fawning, catering, forgiving, supporting, and loving these men, who in turn create Lloronas. In the cast commentary Roselyn Sanchez warns that a "Papi Chulo" is dangerous. Her comment simply hangs for a moment on the DVD audio track, and no one else picks up on or adds to it. The assessment is simply passed over, yet the point she makes is an important one that is addressed half-heartedly through the film's use of La Llorona as a figure of vengeance.

The studio selected the film for its "universal themes" and opportunity to present characters that audiences do not normally see [read: Latinas] in a screwball comedy. The film was generally panned, with one reviewer calling it an "insipid comedy" and another seeing it as an "unfocused frenzy."[24] Others took offense at the recycling of Latin@ stereotypes by Latinas. While I agree with most of these assessments, the film's use of the legend gives it some compelling cultural resonance. After Cici recounts La Llorona's story to Tomás, he begins to see the world around him, the women in his life, and his own actions through the lens of the lore. As a result, it retains its moral component, with one key difference: La Llorona comes to the aid of her fellow sisters who have also suffered heartache caused by men. The revision of the tale's social function makes La Llorona the exclusive domain of women, but neither the threat of nor her actual appearance is enough to correct or curtail the womanizing behavior of men like Tomás. Therefore, the revision is an interesting one, but its possible implications are not fully explored in the film.

Whereas *Chasing Papi* includes La Llorona as a part of a humorous backdrop for a slapstick comedy, the "La Llorona, Got Milk?" commercial focuses exclusively on the figure and invites us to find humor in a reconfiguration of the legend.[25] In 2001 the California Milk Processor Board (CMPB) asked Latino students at the Art Center College of Design in Pasadena to submit ideas for "Got Milk?" commercials that would reflect Latin@ cultures and traditions. The invitation represented another in a long line of efforts to promote milk consumption in Latin@ communities. Over the years, the marketing of milk to Latin@s, or rather Hispanics, has vexed advertisers, leading them to take approaches different from those like the humorous "Got Milk?" ads used to sell in the "general market," a term that Arlene Dávila in *Latinos, Inc.: The Marketing and Making of a People* (2001) identifies as "a euphemism for Anglo" (97). Advertisers' perceptions of Hispanic women as "more emotionally expressive, family-oriented, and feminine" led them to appeal to the presumed nurturing instinct of Latin@s in the promotion of milk consumption (97). Dávila notes that "While the general market ad revolves around comic scenes of milk scarcity, prompted by 'Got milk?' the Hispanic campaign features a grandmother cooking traditional milk-based desserts with a caption that reads: 'Have you given your loved ones enough milk today?'" (98). Market research in other campaigns revealed that Hispanic women were responsible for most of the shopping in their households. Fearing that "Hispanics would not get the humor of the original ad," advertisers attempted to instill and then exploit Latinas' anxieties about being good mothers by equating the consumption of milk with love (98). This fear could then be easily eliminated during routine shopping excursions to the grocery store or bodega by buying some milk. One milk billboard ad included in Dávila's study features a child safely and lovingly encircled in the embrace of her caring, refined grandmother, reinforcing visually the idea of the good, family-oriented Latina nurturing her family through consumption.

In 1999, the CMPB made a specific attempt at reaching Latin@ teens through a "Got Milk?" ad campaign that featured both Spanish and English dialogue. The group was chosen for its tendency to set cultural trends and because they represented an opportunity for the CMPB to create lifelong milk consumers. Many of the teens in the focus groups organized to review the ads found the spots funny, according to journalist Rick Wartzman, but they were also critical of the fact that there were not enough Latin@s cast in the ads, and that they failed to address aspects of their often bicultural lives. Their assessment demonstrated a heightened awareness of their own representations through these outlets, as well as their savvy as cultural critics of the media. Older Latin@s were also critical of the ads. Although they certainly "got" the intent, they did not find the premise of the commercials, being deprived of milk, funny, for it reminded some of their impoverished childhoods or suggested an inability to provide for their own families.[26]

The goal of the 2001 campaign was to reach teenaged consumers whose milk consumption was in decline. The only stipulation the CMPB placed on the students was that the ads had to include the theme of milk deprivation, the focal point of the long-running commercial series; the rest was left to their creative imaginations. Tania Sosa-Lane, José Rennard, David Delgado, and Ali Alvarez developed the idea for a Llorona milk commercial in which La Llorona weeps for milk, presumably instead of for her lost children. The ad was groundbreaking for several reasons: it was developed by Latin@ students; it was a Spanish-language ad that aired on English-language television; and it featured a figure from Greater Mexican lore. Oscar-nominated Mexican cinematographer Emmanuel Lubezki, who worked on such films as *Like Water for Chocolate* (1992), *Meet Joe Black* (1998) and, more recently, *Y tu mamá también* (2001), directed the spot. The result, according to one Hispanic news outlet, was a "darkly comical spin on a revered Hispanic legend."[27] Most of the media responses to the commercial focused on the "innovation" of drawing from cultural sources to sell products to a specific cultural community, which, as Dávila's study reveals, hardly represents a novel approach. No commentators reflected critically on the actual content of the commercial or interrogated the revision that served as the source of the humor.

A revisioning of La Llorona's story appeared to be the perfect means of meeting all of the objectives set forth by the CMPB, for who better than the perpetual weeper to lament over an empty carton of milk? The ad appears to be a visual replication of a traditional version of the legend, an idea reinforced in the opening shot of La Llorona dressed in her signature white gown, wandering through a house, weeping. She roams down the halls of the home and into a bedroom where a man and a woman are sleeping. Lying on the man's chest is an open copy of a gilded, leather-bound book entitled *La Leyenda de La Llorona*. La Llorona then proceeds through the wall into the kitchen, where she opens the refrigerator and spies a carton of milk. She immediately ceases to weep, smiles ear-to-ear, and utters, "Leche." After taking an enormous bite of pan dulce, she lifts the carton to her lips. Upon discovering that it is empty, she weeps once more. The ad ends with La Llorona slamming the refrigerator door and the familiar tag line, "got milk?" The ad's humor comes from the substitution of milk for La Llorona's lost children, a replacement that transforms her from a Weeping Woman to a llorona, or crybaby. The joke in the commercial is dependent on the audience's prior knowledge of the legend. Without this information, the production loses much of its impact, as demonstrated by the reaction of Anglo viewers who thought the ad was a promotional tie-in to a film about a ghost.

The CMPB spent $2 million to air the commercial on English-language television stations, first in California and then in other states. The ad generated buzz among consumers, although to a lesser degree among non-Latin@s, but responses were mixed. Many viewers, including teens, may have indeed found the commercial funny, yet I am certain that more than a handful of others, myself included, shared Gabriela Lemus' reservations about using La Llorona to sell or promote anything. Lemus, policy director for the League of United Latin American Citizens in Washington, was quoted as stating, "My grandmother used to say 'La Llorona is coming to get you.' [. . .] I don't know if I'd buy milk from someone who was trying to kill me."[28]

The ad also caught the attention of other producers and manufacturers, particularly after it was covered by such news outlets as CNN, the *Los Angeles Times,* and the *Wall Street Journal,* which ushered La Llorona and her crying for milk into the national spotlight.[29] In an interview on the National Public Radio show *All Things Considered,* the executive director of the CMPB, Jeff Manning, stated that "Amongst Hispanics—they were actually stunned that the advertising or marketing worlds would have unearthed this legend of La Llorona, and they loved the idea."[30] Manning's comment gives credit to the advertisers and marketers for "unearthing" the legend, making them akin to anthropologists. However, the Latin@ students who selected the legend as the subject of their ad did so because La Llorona is at the forefront of their cultural imagination, not buried beneath it. According to David Delgado, one of the students involved in the project, La Llorona's status as a cultural icon made her an ideal choice for their ad: "Superstitions and legends such as La Llorona are prominent in the Hispanic culture. We wanted to take a scary childhood story and put a funny spin on it—one that would appeal to all teens."[31] The students' choice of subject is also notable, when we consider the following assertion from Dávila:

> Looking at Hispanic marketing is [. . .] particularly revealing of the relationship between culture, corporate sponsorship, and politics, and moreover can illuminate how commercial representations may shape people's cultural identities as well as affect notions of belonging and cultural citizenship in public life. (2)

As featured in the commercial, La Llorona becomes an assertion of the cultural identity of Mexican@s and Chican@s within the larger subset of Latin@ consumers. The students' objective was to "take the scariness out of [the legend] and put a joke into it," but they may have had an additional aim, especially when we consider the ways that Latin@s are perceived by advertisers and have traditionally been represented in their campaigns.[32]

When featured in advertisements, "the Latina icon," as Dávila illustrates, "is mostly a mom who is young, light-skinned, long-haired, 'soft-featured,' and beautiful [. . .]" (131). More specifically, the Latina mother in these productions inherently embodies selflessness, setting aside individual concerns in favor of tending to her family: "In advertisements she is most of all the caretaker and guardian of the family, concerns that she keeps always in mind as she selects any product, from soap to yogurt" (131). The depiction of Latina motherhood in this way is not necessarily demeaning or negative, though it certainly is limiting. In casting La Llorona as the ad's central figure, the students followed the long-standing tradition of featuring a Latina mother in product promotion, but they replaced the ideal mother with one known for infanticide. Nevertheless, the actress who plays her shares many of the aesthetic qualities of Latina icons: she is young, light-skinned, long-haired, soft-featured, and beautiful.

In terms of commercial effectiveness, numerous blogs attest to the ad's popularity, but it was not projected to significantly impact the sale of milk in the Latin@ youth market.[33] The ad ran in English-language markets, so Spanish speakers were not its only intended audience, and while it may not have inspired young Latin@s to run out and drink milk, the commercial did serve to disseminate the lore to a wider audience in the cultural mainstream.

Ironically, in the end, the politics behind the making of the commercial serves as an interesting element of an ultraconservative version of the lore, with the CMPB occupying the role of the lover. According to José Rennard, another student involved in the production, "The CMPB displayed great insight and courage in producing this commercial and running it on English language TV."[34] Despite their "courage," no doubt when the CMPB is done using La Llorona to promote milk consumption, it, too, will abandon her as they move on to the next hot strategy, trend, or consumer group.

Comedienne, author, and multimedia artist Monica Palacios, in her short story "La Llorona Loca: The Other Side" (1991), also revises the tale's somber tone by introducing humor in a story within a story. More specifically, she changes the gender dynamics of the relationship at the center of the tale so that "el otro lado" refers to both the United States and an alternative to heterosexuality. Through this revision, as Rebolledo notes, Palacios "revitalizes the archetype, turning the Llorona myth into a funny but fatal lesbian romance" (80). Yet Yvonne Yarbro-Bejarano sees Palacios' reimagining as explicitly "lesbianizing the signifiers of Mexican culture" (193). The major revisions to the lore include the use of humor, the recasting of the affair at the center of the tale, and the substitution of a crime of passion for infanticide, so that in the end, La Llorona Loca weeps for her lost love.

The author reconfigures the sexual power relations in the traditional folktale to focus on the struggles of the protagonist, Caliente, the Llorona figure of the story, and her lover, La Stranger, while maintaining many of its elements, including a love affair, infidelity, murder, a haunting, and a body of water. In casting La Llorona in a lesbian romance, Palacios parodies the heterosexual romance featured in most versions of the story. Palacios not only satirizes male power, but also white, middle-class feminism and self-help groups. Another source of humor in the story comes from Palacios' inclusion of modern details like caffeine addiction and professional networking, which make the narrative a reflection of contemporary life. Palacios also subverts audiences' expectations about the tone of La Llorona stories and the authority of academic folkloric collections.

The narrative is structured in two parts: the narrator's story about La Llorona and a story found in one of the premiere folklore archives in the United States. The story that precedes the "folkloric account" provides the speaker's childhood history with the legend of, in this case, "La Llorona Loca—the crazy crier," and her desire to learn more about the woman at its center (49). Palacios' narrator associates the story she tells with La Llorona's legend from the outset and positions herself as a caretaker of Llorona lore, a scribe who puts her own stamp on it. For example, La Llorona murders her children not in an act of revenge or grief but as a result of waking up one morning in a really bad mood. As a child, the narrator tells us, she heard from her mother stories of La Llorona Loca, who murdered her children one day when she "woke up on the wrong side of the bed" (49). While we know what contributed to her actions on that fateful day, the result of the story is still the same for La Llorona. This "new" information, infused with humor, does not prevent her from wandering in a traditional, long white gown, but the speaker does speculate that the legendary woman has on "low heels" because, after all, "she's searching" (49). These small details illustrate that the conventional "truth" about this story, along with La Llorona's choice of footwear, represents merely one version of the events.

Palacios' narrator also wonders about the portions of La Llorona's life not addressed in traditional cuentos. Yet instead of concerning herself with a protracted version of La Llorona's history, the narrator wants to know other important details from La Llorona's life, such as her astrological sign, her knowledge of "networking," and whether or not the Weeping Woman was attempting to wean herself from caffeine when the tragedy occurred. Her need to find the answers to these questions motivates her to search through the University of California's extensive collection of La Llorona stories in its folklore archives, where she discovers a version of the legend she has never heard. Chances are, neither have most Chican@ readers.

In spite of these humorous considerations, the tale, as a parody, maintains recognizable features of a conventional, traditional narrative. In the archival story, La Llorona is marginalized within the community after her abandonment and homicidal act à la the traditional folklore, but the Weeping Woman of this version is a lesbian. The protagonist, Caliente, as she is known prior to her death, is a beautiful, voluptuous woman who attracts the attention of both men and women in the Mexican town where she resides. Though Trujillo assigns La Llorona a specific name, which seemingly signals a re-turning of La Llorona in the lore (a strategy discussed in Chapter 4), the name is metaphoric rather than literal. The townspeople see Caliente ("hot" or "fiery") as a beautiful sex object and comment specifically on her "chi-chis" (breasts). Her sexuality also becomes the subject of town gossip. Relying on stereotypes of lesbians, they gossip about Caliente and speculate that she "wears spurs—on her houseslippers" or is a "PE teacher," simply because she does not seek the company of men (49). However, Caliente does not collapse under the weight of these insults and continues to live her life as she sees fit.

The narrator introduces other established elements of a traditional Llorona narrative, such as the dashing stranger who comes to town and captures the heart of a town maiden. This feature is quickly revised to maintain the subversive features of the rendering. A dashing stranger does come into town, wearing a cowboy hat and leather chaps, and does, in fact, capture Caliente's heart, but readers discover that the "cowboy" is actually a "cow*girl*," La Stranger. The reorientation of the sexual politics in the "folk story" erases the male's position and authority in the lore, as does the fact that she shows the couple successfully eluding the "macho Mexican dudes" who chase them in a rage (50).

In contrast to renderings of the tale that focus on La Llorona's despair and unhappiness, the narrator discloses that Caliente, who escapes with her lover to "el otro lado," lives happily for quite some time in Bakersfield, California. The two are even married in Tijuana, Mexico, by a curandera, which serves to legitimize their union in a manner often denied La Llorona, whose lover abandons her to marry a woman from his own social class. However, because this ultimately *is* a La Llorona story, their happiness does not last.

As in the original tale, it is infidelity that initiates the tragedy, but La Stranger does not abandon Caliente; instead, she tells her face-to-face that she has been having an affair with a woman named Trixie while Caliente has been attending her "Latina: I Am Woman—You Are Scum" support group. La Stranger mocks this group and Caliente's attempt to fortify her identity as a Latina feminist. Caliente responds by biting her lover, who then suggests that they form a "feeling circle" to discuss the issue. Here we see Palacios' parody of a feminist self-awareness group, for in spite of its intention to heighten Latina awareness, Caliente has not learned from it even enough to be aware of what is going on in her own relationship. La Stranger's infidelity is not her only mistake, for she also underestimates Caliente's rage and chooses to tell her lover about the infidelity at their favorite spot down by the river.

Further revising conventional versions of the tale, Palacios eliminates children from the narrative, and Caliente focuses her rage on her lover, pushing her down in the river and holding her head under water until La Stranger drowns. Caliente, like La Llorona, murders what she loves. Similarly, Caliente feels remorse for what she has done and begins to cry. She then faints into the river and dies herself, adding a slapstick dimension to the tragedy being parodied here. At this point, the narrator comedically interjects an aside to the reader: "I'm sorry to bring you down folks, but that's life" (51). Or perhaps more accurately, that's the legend.

Continuing with her comedic rendering of the story, Palacios has Caliente's and La Stranger's bodies discovered by a group of women returning home from a "sexual healing weekend." Caliente's ghost, "dressed all in white and wearing clogs," makes her presence known to a man wandering on the shore of the river by his village, but her cries are mistaken for "really loud Carly Simon music" (51). Through humor, Palacios satirizes the dominant culture's gender conventions and new age feel-goodism to demonstrate that Caliente's attempts at transformation have made her, even in death, indistinguishable from an Anglo woman. At the same time, her use of humor, while entertaining, functions as comic relief for the dramatic tension of the narrative and serves to humanize both women in the story. Additionally, by providing Caliente with a female lover, Palacios delimits new sexual boundaries to produce a contemporary lesbian La Llorona story that, as the narrator states, few know. Palacios does not upend the lore. She works within its structure, going so far as to adhere to the conventional outcome to critique infidelity as a social problem that contributes to the making of Lloronas, even the lesbian loca ones.

The Legend of La Llorona (2002) by writer, director, producer, and actor Stephanie Saint Sanchez represents the most radical revision of the lore included in this chapter. Her production reveals La Llorona's "true" identity, the actual events behind the story, and, perhaps the most shocking detail, that the story is a fairly recent phenomenon. Like the students who created the milk commercial, the filmmaker uses humor in her version of the tale but does so as a form of sociopolitical critique. Saint Sanchez asks the audience to see the "specific normative paradigms," as put forth by Guillermo Hernández, of her satiric rendition of the folktale, not in an effort to make fun of us, but to reveal instead how "facts" have been twisted through the telling of the legend to convey a particular kind of "truth." The short film is a "totally true account of [. . .] shocking events as told by the chainsmoking chica de muerto herself."[35] Audiences learn that La Llorona was an inventor who in the afterlife has turned to stand-up comedy to disseminate her social and cultural message. The tone of the film is humorous, but Saint Sanchez does not abandon the more serious issues attached to legend. Rather, she reconfigures them through a dismantling or debunking of traditional versions of the tale. Corporate theft, murder, religious hypocrisy, popular culture, and class conflict figure prominently in her version. Perhaps the most shocking discovery is that a woman named Maria Tortilla (played by Mela Carmela) concocted the Llorona cuento, fairly recently, in order to hide her criminal activity.

The film is structured, like Palacios' narrative, in two parts. The first part is a recounting of the lore, one representing literally the folkloric tradition, and the second part is offered as a corrective to this tradition. In the opening shot, audiences see an angel statue wrapped in lights and hear the voice of a woman chanting the familiar rhyme signaling the conclusion of an oral tale, "Colorín, colorado, este cuento se ha acabado." As the camera pulls back from the angel, we see a kind-looking grandmother kissing her granddaughters good night before sending them off to bed. The angel and children, Xo and Siouxsie, convey an innocence that Saint Sanchez juxtaposes with the vanity and sadism of the grandmother. Xo and Siouxsie beg their grandmother for another story, specifically a Llorona story. The grandmother agrees only after the girls resort to flattering her ability to tell the best Llorona story. Xo instructs her grandmother, who has started her version of the story, to "Make it good." Siouxsie interjects, "And scary." The grandmother, through tender and endearing words, agrees to do both. When she begins anew, Siouxsie once more interrupts, insisting that the story be "super scary." The grandmother quickly loses her temper, and a harsh tone immediately replaces her loving one. At this point, viewers may begin to suspect that the grandmother is not what she appears to be.

This view is confirmed when the grandmother takes sadistic delight in recounting La Llorona's suffering, particularly the part involving the deaths of the children. She is downright gleeful that the woman was able to live such a good life after disposing of her children. Her attitude is explained later in film when viewers discover that the grandmother is actually Maria Tortilla, the originator of the tale, which explains why she can tell it, as Xo states, "more better" than anyone. The film posits that conventional versions of the traditional lore are veiled accounts of the "actual events" in the life of a woman named La Llorena. As the grandmother concludes her version of the folktale with La Llorona's legendary lament, "¿DONDE ESTAN MIS HIJOS?" the camera cuts from the grand-

FIGURE 2.3. Stephanie Saint Sanchez as "La Llorena." The misspelling of
the name, or pochoism, is part of the humor. Photo by Jeanie Low
© 2006. Used by permission of Stephanie Saint Sanchez.

mother's living room to a comedy club "somewhere in Texas." La Llorena (played
by Stephanie Saint Sanchez) repeats the line, shouting, "¡DONDE ESTAN MIS
HIJOS?!" Llorena challenges the veracity and authority of the tale when she asks,
"Can you believe that?" Llorena attempts to set the record straight by telling her
audiences how she came to be "misrepresented" in folktales (figure 2.3).

    Saint Sanchez uses elements of the lore, particularly the man, children, and
her famous wail, in ways that do not undermine the social or moral messages
often conveyed by the folktale. Her usage does, however, shift these messages to

new sites. For example, as in the traditional tale, a man does play a significant role in Llorena's life. He is not her lover, but a customer who has her fired from her job at Blockbuster® video. The humor of this scenario lies in the identity of the customer: Academy Award®–winning actor Gene Hackman.[36] The actor has Llorena fired after she fails to recognize him and insults the film *Hoosiers* (1986), in which the actor had a starring role. Llorena likens the experience of watching the film to banging one's head against a brick wall. While the loss of a job is not funny, Llorena tells it in a humorous way through exaggerated facial expressions and by hitting a microphone against her head. Hackman's status as a celebrity, along with its attendant cultural power, makes him an ideal stand-in for the privileged lover in the tale. Llorena's unemployment leads to the introduction of another element from the lore: the children.

In Saint Sanchez's version, Llorena demonstrates how this feature has been twisted around to create sympathy for two thugs *posing* as children. Llorena explains that after she was fired, she sat at home, watched television, gained fifty pounds, and earned her degree in TV/VCR repair, but decided to become a "snackologist," a person who develops new snack food taste sensations. Within weeks she developed her "creation," sour cream and cilantro Fritos®. Before she could sell the recipe for millions of dollars, she describes how two little people pretending to be children stole it from her. Llorena continues narrating her own version of events by explaining that the thieves worked for an unidentified woman. The henchmen had orders to dispose of Llorena by tying her up and throwing her in the bayou. Although Llorena confesses to throwing the criminals into the bayou instead, she claims no knowledge of their ultimate fate. Her actions in this scenario are meant to represent a "clear" case of self-defense.

The final element Saint Sanchez revises is La Llorona's legendary lament, "¿Donde están mis hijos?" Llorena discovers that Maria Tortilla, the head of a snack food empire, is behind the theft of the recipe. Before Llorena can confront Tortilla, a car strikes the snackologist dead while she is crossing the street. As in traditional versions of the lore, Llorena ascends to heaven but is immediately sent back down to earth. Her punishment is the result of her failure to bring her sour cream and cilantro Fritos® to heaven with her. When she admits to no longer having the recipe, she is sent back to wander in search of what she has lost, forever crying, "¿Donde están mis Fritos®?" The stolen corn chip recipe, like the milk in the commercial, replaces the role of the children in the traditional tale, yet in this instance, the effect is a potentially more humorous one because the substitution is not the only revision to the story. The whole story is exposed as an elaborate hoax created to hide greed, which inspires heinous acts on par with child murder.

A confrontation between Llorena and Maria Tortilla brings the narrative full circle and serves as the means for delivering the film's social criticism. After hearing Tortilla's villainous laughter, Llorena leaves the comedy club stage and materializes in Maria's living room. Llorena challenges Maria, asking "¿Donde están mis Fritos®?" Maria replies that she ate them, and then orders Xo and Siouxsie to attack Llorena. The girls begin to beat Llorena with enormous, oversized crayons, while Maria applauds, cackles, and shouts, "Harder! Harder!" Saint Sanchez demonstrates the way in which greed proves far more insidious than the woman featured in traditional versions of the legend, for it can inspire individuals to concoct and use a story about male power and oppression, as represented by the unmistakably phallic crayons, to beat up on other women. In this case, Maria Tortilla benefits from the demonizing of men and women through a lie she has turned into a cultural truth. Though Saint Sanchez admits to putting La Llorona "in a modern situation and [having] fun with her," the conclusion carries a strong social message.[37] Played for laughs, the end is a satirical look at how we beat up on La Llorona to hide our own faults and transgressions.[38]

Cultural producers use revisions to lay a foundation to interrogate and make visible the cultural, political, and social forces at work in the folktale. The critical questions raised by these revisions represent an important step in reading productions that recover lost elements of La Llorona's life or demonstrate how the lore can be used as a site of resistance to dominative or other oppressive ideologies and practices. Cultural readers should keep in mind that the subsequent conversations and critical analyses emerge from the considerations made in Chapter 1. The most radical revisions and reconsiderations of La Llorona are done, and best understood, with the knowledge of how she operates within her folk community. La Llorona serves as a reflection of our fears and cultural concerns. Conversely, she carries with her a hope for a better future. In the cultural productions discussed in the next two chapters, La Llorona emerges as a champion for her people who teaches us how to resist and survive in the most hopeless of situations.

THREE

Infamy and Activism

La Llorona as Resistance

The official version was a lie. I knew that from the same bone that first held the memory of the cuento. Who would kill their kid over some man dumping them?

—CHERRÍE MORAGA

MIL MASCARAS, SANTO (El Enmascardo de Plata), Perro Aguayo, El Demonio Azul. In the hearts of old-school Mexican wrestling fans, these names epitomize the theatrics, thrill, and drama of the lucha libre. Many a night I spent in front of the nine-inch black and white television nestled in the opened window of the only bedroom of my Big Grandpa and Grandma's shotgun house. Aluminum foil wrapped around the antennae jutting out into the night air presented our only hope of receiving a clearer picture, which we never got. We watched channel 39 through the onscreen snowstorm as Mil Mascaras lunged, slammed, and clotheslined his way through an evening of *Houston Wrestling*. I remember my grandmother bouncing on the bed in excitement as she shouted orders for Mascaras to "¡Tirelo!" or "¡Termínelo!" Regardless of the TV reception, I could always make out Mascaras on the screen because of the mask's accent color lining the cutouts for his eyes, nose, and mouth. Along with trademark colors, a cape, or a signature finishing move, a mask offered wrestlers a way to distinguish themselves in the sport. It also generated mystery and allowed wrestlers to reinvent themselves, but most of all it provided anonymity, permitting them to move in the "real" world undetected, a bit like a comic book superhero.

With few exceptions, the sport showcased the exploits of male wrestlers enacting, in a world of good versus evil, small-scale battles with legendary outcomes, where good most often prevailed. On occasion we saw matches between little people or women, but it was clear that these were preludes to or intermissions for the "real" shows featuring men. For many, the prominence of lucha libre in the cultural landscape is equal to or greater than La Llorona folklore, though both are reflections of a Manichean world with little or no room for moral ambiguity.

Another, more subtle correlation between the two is best understood through the verb *luchar*. In addition to its more familiar meaning, "to fight," it also means "to struggle" or "to dispute." It is in this space of struggle and dispute that artist Lizz Lopez weds lucha libre with La Llorona in her painting *La Llorona* (2002), and where I begin my discussion of La Llorona as a symbol of resistance. As explained in the introduction, the cultural knowledge required to read the artifacts in each chapter is cumulative, but the strategies are not mutually exclusive. While an understanding of how cultural producers revise the lore will aid readers in determining La Llorona's function in many of the representations discussed in this chapter, not all of the artifacts are revisions. Reading for resistance involves, in part, identifying the ways in which cultural producers, as critical and cultural readers of the lore, imagine La Llorona as a figure that resists oppression directly or inspires others to do the same, as in Lopez's painting *La Llorona*, Pat Mora's poem "Llantos de La Llorona" (*Agua Santa*, 1995), Sandra Cisneros' short story "Woman Hollering Creek" (1991), Helena Maria Viramontes' short story "The Cariboo Cafe" (1985), and Cherríe Moraga's play *The Hungry Woman: A Mexican Medea* (2001). In several of these works, La Llorona acts as an agent of transformation or as a means of liberation for women, but the most radical repositionings involve abandoning traditional elements of the lore or changing the outcome to challenge its social conventions and the dominating forces at work in it: forces most often cited as heterosexual Mexicanos and Chicanos, Catholicism, and other patriarchal institutions.

In light of extant conversations about "resistance" in literature, I wish to clarify my use of the term. Barbara Harlow, in her definitive work on the subject, asserts that "Resistance literature calls attention to itself, and to literature in general, as a political and politicized activity. The literature of resistance sees itself furthermore as immediately and directly involved in a struggle against ascendant or dominant forms of ideological and cultural production" (28–29). Although the cultural producers in this chapter represent direct efforts to engage with the figure of La Llorona in the kind of struggle Harlow identifies, I recognize that my understanding and application of the term closely resembles Ralph E. Rodriguez's ideas concerning a "contestatory literature," one that "employs varying narrative strategies to critique, resist, and oppose racism, sexism, homophobia, and/or classism" (67). Chicanas who position La Llorona as a figure of resistance rely on the existing narrative strategies attached to the lore to contest and oppose the oppressive forces Rodriguez identifies. In his analysis of this shift in contemporary Chican@ writing, "Chicana/o Fiction from Resistance to Contestation," Rodriguez theorizes that "the term 'resistance literature' is used most appropriately when discussing armed liberation movements that have direct links to territorial claims, where there is literally a battle for terrain and governance at stake" (64). However, I do not believe that we can minimize the importance of the territorial battle taking place in the cultural productions that feature La Llorona as a resistant figure: as she is featured in the productions of Chicanas, she is a revolutionary engaged in a cultural battle for the liberation of women's minds, bodies, and spirits. La Llorona both epitomizes and represents, in all of these productions, the articulation of a contemporary struggle or lucha. At times she haunts the cultural landscape of our imaginations, reminding us of the necessity and consequences of acting out against oppression, but she also teaches us how to use our voices, whether wailing in protest or shouting in liberation, so that we may actively shape new cultural and social realities.

These repositionings of La Llorona are generated exclusively by Chicanas. Tey Diana Rebolledo's culturally based study of Chicana literature, *Women Singing in the Snow*, offers one explanation for this occurrence. Though her analysis is confined to literature, she observes in the chapter "From Coatlicue to La Llorona" that "Chicana writers choose, define, and image [*sic*] their myths and heroines," including such figures as the Mexica goddesses Coatlicue and Tonantzin, and folkloric figures like La Llorona to "create new role models for themselves" or imbue existing models with "different (sometimes radically different) traits and characteristics" (49). The creation of these new or revised models is necessitated by the limitations or constraints that traditional figures often place on Chicana identity, casting women into fixed binaries of virgin/whore or creator/destroyer. Chicanas are recasting feminine cultural symbols to modernize traditional narratives, but they are also addressing contemporary issues such as exploitation, domestic abuse, and political persecution, as well as concerns about Indigeneity, sexual alliance, and the consequences of their activism.

However, Cordelia Candelaria's assertion that La Llorona's eternal torture serves "as grassroots propaganda intended to reinforce the patriarchy" provides us with additional insight as to the exclusivity of Chicana productions ("Letting La Llorona Go," 130). Most versions of the conventional tale conclude with La Llorona weeping and wandering, while the male lover lives, never suffering the consequences of his actions. His life reaffirms for men the security of the patriarchy, thereby continuing the subordination of women. Rather than favor a "masculinized understanding of the tale," Candelaria understands La Llorona's actions in the context of the traditional tale as an endeavor "to will her own destiny by electing a tragic fate rather than allow herself and her children to live under inescapable tyranny" (131). Candelaria is not alone in her view of the male as the primary source of oppression in most Llorona tales, though often the man is also representative of other dominating patriarchal institutions such as the law and the Church.

Not all Chican@s, however, are ready to empathize or even sympathize with La Llorona's plight, or to see her as a figure with agency, so while in some cases she inspires others to wage war, in others she is the one against whom war is waged. The speaker in Candelaria's poetic triptych that begins with "Go 'Way from My Window, La Llorona" (1984) engages in an act of resistance not by embracing La Llorona, but, as the title indicates, by sending her away.[1] Candelaria positions this rejection before the radical recuperations in the successive poems (discussed in the following chapter) to reveal the community's reluctance to see La Llorona as something other than helpless or passive.

The poem assumes cultural knowledge of the lore on the part of the reader, for it begins with a haunting that reflects the stage in La Llorona's life in which she is an established figure of suffering. Yet Candelaria's narrator does not fear an encounter with La Llorona, nor does she engage her with understanding or compassion; instead, the speaker verbally accosts La Llorona, telling her, "Get lost, lady! ¡Andale! / Far away and forever. ¡Vete!" (1-2). As readers learn, this belligerent response stems from the speaker's own painful family memories, filled with "beatings and blood" (21). La Llorona, as presented in the poem, "becomes connected more specifically to evil, sickness, and violence" — in this case, domestic violence (Rebolledo, 77). In commanding the spectre to vanish, the speaker wants La Llorona gone forever, so she cannot return

> Like sinks of dirty water swallowed by the drain
> To rise again in cesspools, not like
> A fat black cucaracha swept away
> Returns with crowds at midnight. [. . .] (3–6)

In rejecting La Llorona, the speaker sends away a vital means of reconciling with a past that still informs her present, thus compounding her own anguish. By ordering La Llorona out of her life, the young woman engages in an act of resistance to expose the physical abuse of women that accompanies patriarchal dominance. The speaker cannot see La Llorona's infanticide within the context of the lore as an act of resistance.

As a prevailing image of terror from her youth, the narrator also blames La Llorona for affecting her youthful view of the world, conflating the horror of the folktale with the violence in her own home. The speaker learns to see her parents through the Llorona legend, which mirrors her father's tyranny and her mother's passivity. She also holds contempt for her mother, who endures bloody bouts with her spouse and lives in a marriage based "in sickness and in sickness" (18). From the narrator's point of view, La Llorona's story not only contributes to her mother's situation, it also facilitates the abuse, for she perceives La Llorona's story as one of tragedy, not hope:

> And the reality of your unreality
> Turned me into the taste of moldy brine
> At the bottom of a jar,
> Into Goneril seeing her father
> As all fathers with all mothers.
> Married forever in sickness and in sickness
> Till death parts them in sickness
> And in loudness at midnight[2] (13–20)

The narrator believes that La Llorona's story gives men permission to abuse their wives and encourages women to stay in bad marriages in order to avoid La Llorona's fate. She specifically blames La Llorona for "scaring" away her childhood and giving her nightmares that spill over into her daily life (9). The speaker feels that she has been victimized by La Llorona and made into a passive observer forced to watch the bloody beatings followed by the inevitable reconciliation between her parents. Demonstrating an ongoing cycle of abuse, these reconciliations signal the next violent outburst, what the speaker calls a "forever sickness" (22).

Wounded by the poverty and violence of her past, the speaker addresses the grieving phantom as a "¡Brujamala!" whom she wants out of her life (7). She condemns her mother and La Llorona for not doing more than simply weeping and continuing their tragic lives; she wants them to find a way to end their suffering and that of their children. This call for agency indicates that the speaker cannot see the redemptive aspects of the folklore, nor does she comprehend that La Llorona does not weep for herself but for all children who are lost due to violence, sickness, and evil. Indeed, La Llorona weeps for the narrator and others like her so that they may take comfort in knowing that she too has suffered yet still manages to retain the hope of recovering her lost children. Nevertheless, the narrator, who rejects this legacy, sends La Llorona away:

> Go!   Follow your babies
> Llorando into the roiling waters
> Del Rio de las Animas Perdidas.
> Let them stare you clear-eyed into Hell. (23–26)

Exorcising La Llorona from her life will not end the speaker's pain, for to send
La Llorona away is to banish hope. Additionally, in damning La Llorona, the
narrator is callous toward the hellish life of weeping and wandering that defines
La Llorona's existence, and she turns away from compassion for herself as well.
Exacerbating La Llorona's condition is the fact that people in her own cultural
community, like the narrator, reject her as a figure of comfort, choosing to see her
only as a horrific figure that haunted their childhoods. Candelaria illustrates our
continuing need for La Llorona and the legacy she imparts to us in the present.
As Rebolledo states, "Although La Llorona represents ambiguity, guilt, and loss,
and inspires fear of the unknown, she is nevertheless part of us—a dark part we
need to come to terms with" (79). Sending her away prevents us from confronting this darker part, which includes the way La Llorona's story is used to uphold
a legacy of violence against women.

In order to read La Llorona as a figure of liberation, we must first address
her established position as a cultural villain, most notably as a result of the infanticide. We must reflect critically on the literal and symbolic meanings of the
act—not to absolve her of the murders, which would take away her radical act
of resistance, but to determine those oppressive forces acting on her which she
acts against. Most often when mothers kill their own children, according to Candelaria, "insanity is automatically assumed and usually proven to explain the
horror" ("Letting La Llorona Go," 125). But this explanation does not account
for the culpability of abusive men or oppressive institutions, nor does it assign
agency to La Llorona's harrowing decision.

Agency, most often, is what La Llorona seemingly lacks, for she wails, wanders, and weeps while futilely searching for the unrecoverable. Artist Lizz Lopez
challenges and dismantles this idea of futility in one of the most arresting renditions of the lore (figure 3.1).

Lopez visually represents La Llorona as a figure of resistance by outfitting her
in the mask of the luchador(a). The mask simultaneously codes the woman as a
fighter and protects her identity, though it also locates La Llorona, which only
may be the pseudonym under which she fights, in a male-dominated arena. In
this space, La Llorona, like most fighters, is defined by her exploits, most notably
the alleged infanticide, a dominant motif in the piece. Though not represented

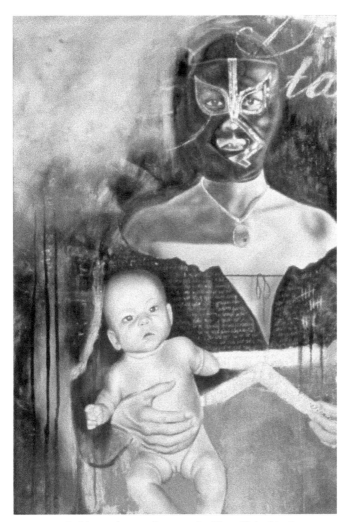

FIGURE 3.1. *La Llorona* (2002, oil on wood, 28″ × 36″), by Lizz Lopez
© 2005. Collection of Susanne Longo. Used by permission of the artist.

literally, Lopez offers clues to the identity of La Llorona's opponents: patriarchy, and those who uphold the view that progeny are the exclusive property of men.

Lopez learned of La Llorona's legend from her mother and grandmother, who imparted a traditional version of the lore.[3] Many of the elements found in conventional La Llorona stories are present in the painting: a woman holding a child stands in the foreground, and a river stretches out in a haze behind them. La Llorona appears positioned behind or housed in glass, where she is preserved and on display in a climate-controlled environment much like an artifact one would expect to find in a museum. Condensation runs down in rivulets on the left-hand side of the glass. While the moisture provides an additional means of including water, it also calls to mind La Llorona's tears. In the upper left-hand corner of the painting, in the fogged part of the glass, a face appears to be staring off into the distance. The blood staining the front of the woman's dress alludes to the infanticide, as if she has recently wiped her hands on her dress or is bleeding from her breasts. Therefore, the face in the corner may be that of La Llorona's recently murdered child. But the rendering is far from conventional. Lopez, born and raised in San Antonio, Texas, is known for creating new iconography in her work. In this instance, she takes La Llorona and transforms her from a traditional figure of suffering into one of resistance.

Details of the painting that facilitate our reconsideration of La Llorona include her necklace, the child, and the mask. An ornate necklace featuring a large blue stone, which could crudely represent the "family jewels," adorns the woman's neck. The lavish necklace seemingly conveys the wealthy status of the woman or of her lover, but the stone, whether aquamarine or blue topaz, is only semiprecious. It therefore conveys the woman's limited worth, a value determined by the man and based on her ability to bear children like the one perched on her hip. The blue of the pendant matches the color of the river and appears to be another method of alluding to the water in traditional versions of the tale, a view substantiated if we identify the stone as aquamarine, translating literally to "water of the sea." However, the brilliancy of the color suggests that the gem is topaz, a term derived from the Greek word "topazos," meaning "to seek." Instead of representing La Llorona's endless wandering, the stone conveys the necessity of our search for a new understanding of La Llorona as a figure with a great power.

The child, whose female genitalia are clearly visible, confirms further that La Llorona is embattled with the patriarchy. La Llorona holds the baby, who is facing outward, against her blood-stained dress. The girl's left arm, from above the elbow down, appears malformed, yet upon closer inspection, the existing stump resembles a circumcised penis. In the context of the painting, Lopez imparts the idea that to do harm to a child, even if that child is female, is to do harm to the patriarchy, because children are viewed as the property of their father, thus confirming Robert Barakat's assessment that "the act of infanticide is in reality an act against the man [. . .]" (291). Moraga, however, sees the child murder included in the lore not as a reprisal against one man but against men in general. Consequently, the infanticide becomes a "retaliation against misogyny" (*Loving*, 145). La Llorona's power to act directly against men necessitates her confinement and public punishment. Staring out at us from the painting, La Llorona implores those of us who judge her, who live in glass houses as the adage goes, to throw stones and release her from her prison. Whether through figurative imprisonment in static versions of the lore or literal confinement in depictions such as Lopez's, La Llorona's "containment," as presented in the artifacts discussed below, represents a widescale and systematic undertaking to curtail female power.

In contrast to Lopez, who purposely conceals La Llorona's identity in both a protective gesture or to represent visually the way in which the actual woman behind the legend is effaced, Pat Mora, in "Llantos de La Llorona: Warnings From the Wailer," documents a detailed personal history of La Llorona and gives her a voice with which to author her own account of conquest and the role it played in the shaping of her story. "Llantos" is one of four poems included in Mora's "Cuarteto Mexicano," a series of talk show interviews with famous Chican@ female figures: Coatlicue offers rules, Malinche gives tips, the Virgen de Guadalupe provides counsel, and La Llorona bequeaths warnings.[4] Malinche, once again filling the role of cultural translator, aptly seizes on the spirit of Mora's quartet in her fourth tip: "Alter the altared women" ("Malinche's Tips," 66). Mora gives voices to these famous figures so that they may dispense their learned insights on dealing with the world of men, who either alter or altar women as a means of containing their power.

La Llorona's unveiling of the process by which she became the woman of legend represents an act of resistance against her Native community, Spanish colonizers, and later, more specifically, men and their systematic efforts to silence or criminalize the behavior of resistant women who refuse to adhere to socially prescribed gender roles. Mora's poem can also be interpreted as a re-turning, a strategy discussed in Chapter 4. I have chosen to examine it here because of its emphasis on the need to resist stories of domination and the methods for doing so. Instead of the more traditional translation of La Llorona as "Weeping Woman," Mora chooses "Wailer," which connotes a type of protest reflected in both its meaning and Mora's interpretation. Throughout the poem, La Llorona repeats, "ay, ay, ay," not so much as a lament, but as a means of challenging her own past as narrated by men and upheld by the community with whom, as disclosed, she has had a long-standing antagonistic relationship. Each stanza concludes with the imperative "Oye," commanding us to listen to her instructional strategies for resisting multiple forms and sources of oppression.

Mora emphasizes La Llorona's Native identity, established through her mother who is identified as a Mayan figure of legend. Instead of assigning the wailer a Mexica heritage, as many others have, Mora locates La Llorona among the Maya, the people who gave Malinche to Cortés as tribute, to illustrate that

the oppression of women did not begin with the arrival of the Spanish or that it
is an act exclusive to men. The first three stanzas of the poem are set in a Mayan
community before the time of conquest. La Llorona begins her exposé with the
statement: "Every family has one" (1).[5] The ambiguity of "one" is not clarified in
the stanza, but we do know that as a child La Llorona wailed at the people who
"sneered" in judgment of her family "as if they were / below them in some hole /
of quivering vermin" (4–7). Though the basis of this disapproval is not identified
explicitly, something about her family's status or its individual members causes
people to click their tongues in disapproval. La Llorona's early understanding of
her family's own marginalization prompts her to observe, "Agua santa can come
from our eyes" (8). Her wailing is made sacred, and with her own tears, she is
baptized into a Native world filled with its own biases and social prejudices.

The community's antagonism is also visible in the second and third stanzas, where Mora draws a correlation between La Llorona and the Mayan figure
X-tabai, said to seduce men by calling them into her home in the tangled roots
of the ceiba tree. La Llorona identifies X-tabai as her mother, implying that the
legendary figure we know is directly descended from another folkloric figure.[6]
Mother and daughter are condemned by the community for their beauty and
perceived ability to "start fires" in and "below" the hearts of men (16, 18). As a
result, readers may conclude that the preternatural loveliness often attributed
to X-tabai and her sexual availability are the sources of the community's un-
favorable view of the family. In other words, the community disapproves of the
women's sexual agency.

The tendency on the part of X-tabai and La Llorona to wander in the night
"near / sighing rivers and streams" with "hair and voices rising" only exacerbates the community's negative opinion of the mother and daughter (19–20,
21). La Llorona advises others, when faced with moral judgments circulated
through vicious rumor, to "Sing to confuse the gossips" as a demonstration of
one's strength and to prove the ineffectiveness of idle talk on one's self-worth
(22). Singing therefore becomes an act of resistance and a show of strength. La
Llorona emphasizes the necessity of identifying and then capitalizing on one's
perceived strengths. For instance, the people believe that La Llorona and her
mother, as seductresses, are waiting to squeeze the life out of innocents and married men "like snakes" (31). As a result, fear becomes a tool that affords mother
and daughter independence, though at the cost of their personal reputations.
Nevertheless, La Llorona advises: "Know your own strength" (33). Her recom-
mendation is more than simply a call for positive self-reflection; it asks us to
consider what we would be willing to endure in order to survive.

Self-sufficiency and resistance as strategies of female empowerment emerge explicitly in stanzas 4 and 5. According to La Llorona, the community introduces the element of child murder into their stories about her after the arrival of the Spanish, when "rumor says" that she began "having babies" (35, 36). The transformation of La Llorona's story following European contact parallels José Limón's observation about the invaders' contributions to the lore, which include "the motifs of (1) a woman with children (2) betrayed by an adulterous husband, their father, (3) a revengeful infanticide, and (4) anguished repentance during which she cries for her children" (408). La Llorona, however, suggests that she and her mother were criminalized by the people as a means of assuaging their own culpability in the colonial onslaught that resulted from the aid the Mayas offered Cortés and his troops, a gesture initiated by the presentation of Malinche as a gift. Furthermore, La Llorona's account reveals how her own community sought to elide the brutality of raping Native women by describing these crimes only as "conceptions" (37). Emphasizing the outcomes of these sexual assaults instead of the means by which Native women were impregnated serves to suppress the accountability of the community and the colonizers, leading La Llorona to observe: "Children are not bastards / though sometimes their fathers are" (45–46). At this point, La Llorona's criticism focuses almost exclusively on men.

After the births of the first mestizos, rumors begin to circulate about La Llorona drowning her own children. Her "crime," in the eyes of the community, escalates from sexual treachery to child murder. Rather than refute the claim outright, "ay, ay, ay," La Llorona adds to the rumors by suggesting that perhaps she begins "to like the feel / of a dagger, long and thin" (53–54). However, she imagines plunging the dagger into their little hearts not in an act of revenge, but as a tender mercy to prevent them from enduring other more painful "piquetitos" (58). Candelaria believes that the concept of a tender mercy, as identified in biblical folklore, "suggests that, within a thoroughly corrupt power structure, even an act of compassion may be brutal because it, too, partakes of the surrounding context of corruption. The tale can thus be 'read' as political euthanasia, a woman's conscious attempt to save her beloved and cherished children from their parents' awful fate" ("Letting La Llorona Go," 130). Re-reading the infanticide as a revolutionary act of salvation helps explain La Llorona's refusal to dispel the accusation within her own recounting. In fact, she cultivates the community's view of her as a murderess, stating, "Maybe I grow the dagger / gleaming like my nails in moonlight" (59–60). While the infanticide becomes further evidence, from the community's perspective, of the perceived immorality of La Llorona and X-tabai, La Llorona knows that it adds to her reputation as a woman capable of anything, which explains her suggestion, "Be resourceful. Grow what you need" (61). In this case, she is nurturing a reputation as a woman to be feared.

La Llorona contrasts her version of events with the prevailing story about her, calling it "his story" (63). Her assessment of the conventional narrative is that it is a "watery / or bloody mess" (72–73). In it, the infanticide is a response to the man's abandonment of his Native consort for a thin, light-skinned, silent, and virginal "princess," who makes his "parents smile" (65, 64). The accusation of infanticide is revealed as an attempt to deflect attention away from the man's abandonment of La Llorona in order to receive his inheritance or to uphold the family's reputation. La Llorona does not refute the allegation of infanticide, though she does acknowledge, "Perhaps I want to hurt the father" (62). Yet the reasons for her desire are far more substantive than his abandoning her for another woman. Because a woman's worth is derived by her purity and the color of her skin, La Llorona recommends encouraging "any man looking for a virgin / vessel to bear his own child" (70–71).

Her critical interrogation of the story about her does not, in her opinion, diminish the cultural or social value of the lore, for as she asserts, "Not all stabbings at the truth / are fatal" (83–84). In her recounting, however, she does clarify or revise certain elements of the existing lore. For example, instead of calling for her lost hijos, as she does in the traditional tale, La Llorona tells readers that she wails for her daughters, "Hijas mías," for it is they who, like her, will inherit a particular kind of struggle in a male-dominated world (78). By aligning herself with Malinche, specifically, and other "madbad ghostwomen / roaming in the dark," and exposing the systematic way that she and her mother were ostracized, La Llorona demonstrates a history of punishing women who fail to conform to cultural or social ideals (80–81). La Llorona, like the other talk-show subjects, uses her own experiences in an effort to create a new legacy for women by teaching them to be self-sufficient, resourceful, and defiant by wailing in protest. Therefore, La Llorona reminds her audience: "Sometimes raising the voice does get attention" (82).

As a solitary act, according to Anzaldúa, "Wailing is the Indian, Mexican and Chicana woman's feeble protest when she has no other recourse" (*Borderlands*, 33). She surmises that historically wailing "may have been a sign of resistance in a society which glorified the warrior and war [...]" (33). Indeed, Mora's La Llorona, alone, has few avenues for striking back at her community, colonization, or the men and women who shaped her legend, but as La Llorona states, she has learned to be resourceful. In addition to cultivating a fearsome persona that seemingly substantiates claims about her character made in the lore, she issues forth a call. In the final stanza, La Llorona proffers joining our raised voices in protest with hers, "for there's much to bewail" (97). Moreover, she reminds us to "[n]ever underestimate the power of the voice" (100).

Her self-identification at the end of the poem as a desert woman who knows about endurance signals both the extent of her transformation and her fortitude, for she has traveled a long way from her family's home in the Yucatán jungle.[7] Yet in spite of her wanderings and evolution over the years, though no longer in her original form, she has survived and has not forgotten where she came from or what she and her "lost" daughters have endured. La Llorona's warnings underscore the necessity of interrogating the lore so that we might understand how stories like hers uphold and reinforce patriarchal dominance.

Sandra Cisneros and Helena María Viramontes show us in their short stories what answering such a call can accomplish. Viramontes' treatment of La Llorona predates Cisneros', but the popularity of the latter, evidenced through the many critical analyses done of her work and its appearance as a mainstay in anthologies, has impacted the views many readers have of La Llorona. In some cases, "Woman Hollering Creek" serves as an introduction to La Llorona lore in fiction, which may lead people to believe that Cisneros was the first to position the legendary woman as a figure that inspires opposition to male domination. However, as my work makes clear, "Woman Hollering Creek" represents part of a larger initiative to imagine the subversive potential of La Llorona and her story.

Again, I am not the first to argue that La Llorona is a figure of resistance in "Woman Hollering Creek," or any other cultural production for that matter.[8] In fact, Anzaldúa and Limón were the first to introduce me to this possibility. The latter prompted my direct consideration of La Llorona as a "most potent symbol of resistance" through his critical appraisal of previous folkloric studies conducted about the lore ("La Llorona," 410). By calling attention to a primary element of the narrative, the water (a river, her tears), Limón poses the tantalizing possibility of La Llorona's recovery of her lost children "because their death by water is ambiguous, for it is also the water of rebirth" (426). Limón encourages a closer look at La Llorona as a model of resistance in order to tease out the other subversive possibilities embedded in or attached to the legend.[9]

Limón makes a case for thinking about La Llorona "as an important part of Greater Mexican women's symbolic repertoire for responding to domination," but he also criticizes those who interpret La Llorona "as a symbol through which women are further dominated" (419). Rather than a response to cultural productions that use the lore as a symbol of domination, Limón's position on the matter is a response, in part, to folkloric studies filled with "historically unwarranted stereotypes" about Mexican motherhood, specifically those that seek to "translate" cultural meaning independent of an actual community (410). But the fact remains, as evidenced by the cultural artifacts discussed in this chapter, that La Llorona's story *can* be put to use within her own cultural community as a tool of patriarchal domination. Sonia Saldívar-Hull, in *Feminism on the Border: Chicana Gender Politics and Literature* (2000), makes a similar observation about Cisneros' incorporation of La Llorona folklore in the story, where "ideological manipulation through mass media—the romance novel, the fotonovela (photo novel), and the telenovela (soap opera)—as well as through the male constructions of woman in the folk figure of La Llorona collude to keep women submissive" (106). While I agree completely with Saldívar-Hull's argument, I believe that Cisneros includes the lore as both a symbol of patriarchal domination and to emphasize the importance of women as an interpretive community with the power to read the legend in a way that undermines male power.

Community forces figure prominently in the shaping of Cisneros' protagonists' life on both sides of the border. In Mexico, Cleófilas Sanchez has other women with whom she shares her interest in romance novels and local chisme. Although she enjoys these diversions with her friends, they do not reflect critically on the content of the cultural productions they consume. In other words, Cleófilas has no interpretive community of women to help decode the darker "misogynistic plots" included in these cultural artifacts (Saldívar-Hull, 123). Having grown up in a house full of brothers without a mother, Cleófilas does not have a strong female presence in her life to teach her about actual relationships with men. Therefore, she constructs ideas about love on her own, and her view is strongly influenced by Mexican telenovelas. She and her like-minded friends idealize the lives of the women on TV and attempt to copy their lives without seeing the unrealistic or distorted views of love presented in each: "*Tú o Nadie.* 'You or No One.' The title of the current favorite *telenovela*. The beautiful Lucía Méndez having to put up with all kinds of hardships of the heart, separation and betrayal, and loving, always loving no matter what, because *that* is the most important thing [. . .]" (Cisneros, 44). Consequently, she believes that "to suffer for love is good" and that pain is sweet (45). After she marries Juan Pedro, her mundane life fails to resemble what she has seen, and she becomes disillusioned, but neither her family nor her community of women friends in Mexico have prepared her for the misery she will experience.

When Cleófilas is uprooted from her home in Mexico and taken to Seguin, Texas, she is notably disempowered, for she neither speaks the language nor knows how to drive a car, and she is completely isolated from her family and the neighborhood community. Her only friends are the abandoned women Soledad and Dolores, whose names in translation mean "Loneliness" and "Pain." Her isolation, along with her idealized notions of marriage and love, makes her vulnerable to a narrative of female disempowerment. She then becomes a battered wife whose husband begins to control every aspect of her life: financial, emotional, physical, psychological, and sexual. As a result, Cleófilas comes to see him as a "rival," "keeper," "lord," and "master" (49). Alone in a new country where she has no money of her own and is single-handedly raising a child she can barely care for, she feels as though she has little recourse and that she is without the power to change her life. Because she is without coping mechanisms or reading strategies, Cleófilas becomes steeped in a misery that rivals La Llorona's, and she begins to believe that the woman said to wander along the shores of the nearby Woman Hollering Creek is summoning her.

Although readers may make the connection between the name of the creek and the protagonist's own pain, Cleófilas herself cannot until she learns about its history. She asks the people of the town, but they either do not know or care, for "it was of no concern to their lives [how this creek] received its curious name" (46). The most anyone will tell her is *"Pues, allá de los indios, quién sabe"* (46).[10] Their indifference to the creek's name suggests the deterioration of the legend and the townspeople's separation from an Indigenous past and present naturalization in the United States. Later, when the creek becomes swollen with water just as she has become swollen with a child and tears, Cleófilas, whose life in no way resembles the idealized one she imagined, begins to wonder if La Llorona is calling to her: "Is it La Llorona, the weeping woman? La Llorona, who drowned her own children" (51). Although Cleófilas is uncertain how to interpret La Llorona's presence, she begins to open her eyes to the large-scale abuse of women:

> It seemed the newspapers were full of such stories. This woman found on the side of the interstate. This one pushed from a moving car. This one's cadaver, this one unconscious, this one beaten blue. Her ex-husband, her husband, her lover, her father, her brother, her uncle, her friend, her co-worker. Always. (52)

After her revelation, in an act that calls to mind La Llorona's drowning of her child, Cleófilas submerges a glass beneath the soapy water in the sink where she is washing dishes, which causes her to shiver. At this critical moment, Cleófilas understands that men who are closest to women pose the most immediate threat.

Though Cleófilas has made the connection between the oppressive forces at work on women like La Llorona and those in her own life, she cannot break free from her abusive relationship until she completely relinquishes the romantic idealism that keeps her in a loveless marriage and tells her that to suffer for love is good. She finally rejects this view when Juan Pedro, in a fit of rage, hurls one of Cleófilas' romance novels at her, striking her in the face. Symbolically, her romantic view of suffering has been literally thrown in her face, tainting her view of the telenovelas she once loved: "Cleófilas thought her life would have to be like that, like a *telenovela,* only now the episodes got sadder and sadder. [. . .] And no happy ending in sight" (52–53). Her realization, which occurs while she is holding her child down by the creek, is an important step because she can now see her own victimization and wants to break free from it, even though she does not know how. She cannot yet see the liberating effect of La Llorona's type of agency because she views her only in the context of the conventional, disempowered narratives she was told as a child.

Significantly, it is through the intervention of women that Cleófilas is able to extricate herself from her husband's tyranny and from the Llorona narrative into which she has been inscribed. Although the neighborhood community fails Cleófilas, an active female community of women, represented by Graciela and Felice, comes to her rescue at a women's health care facility. Graciela, whose job as a sonogram technician requires her to see literally what lies beneath the surface, reads the narrative of suffering written across Cleófilas' body in black and blue bruises and understands the imminent danger that she and her unborn child face. Graciela's suspicions are confirmed by Cleófilas' outburst of crying and pleas for help, prompting Graciela to take action. A secular, female Grace literally intervenes in Cleófilas' life and arranges for "Happiness" to transport the would-be Llorona back to Mexico. While we cannot overstate the importance of Graciela's reading or interpreting of Cleófilas' cries for help, Cleófilas demonstrates the initiative to ask for help and sock away money in preparation for a possible getaway.[11]

What she is not prepared for is her encounter with Felice. On the way out of town to the bus station, Felice and Cleófilas cross over Woman Hollering Creek, and when they do, Felice lets "out a yell as loud as any mariachi" (55). Felice's grito is an affirmation of her life: she drives a truck, swears, critiques the social and cultural value placed on women's virginity, and is most likely a lesbian, all of which make her a woman unlike any Cleófilas has ever known. More importantly, Felice demonstrates for Cleófilas that a woman can use her voice to yell. Instead of the traditional male mariachi outfitted in his traje de charro, riding to the woman's rescue, Felice helps save Cleófilas and in the process provides her a model of female empowerment.

Felice takes the meaning of the creek literally, and to her, a woman hollering is a sign of liberation, not of suffering. When Felice revisits the subject of the creek's name, she tells Cleófilas that it is not important whether it is pain or rage that makes the woman holler, suggesting that giving voice to one's experiences is what matters most. As she takes in this new liberating view, Cleófilas notices a "gurgling out of her own throat, a long ribbon of laughter, like water" (56). Before Cleófilas had been filled with sorrow, but now laughter and relief bubble up from her lungs, for she is delivered from her husband's oppression—and not by God or men, but by women.

Some may question why, in a story about female empowerment, Felice helps deliver Cleófilas back to a seemingly oppressive situation with her father and brothers. However, the Cleófilas who returns is not the same starry-eyed girl who left. More importantly, she does not return alone. In addition to her children, she also brings back a new conception of womanhood. Cleófilas starts out primed to become a Llorona-like figure and almost does, but in this "overtly feminist revision of a powerful cultural plot," Felice teaches her how to wail; consequently, Cleófilas' narrative offers "the possibility of social change through communal female solidarity" (Saldívar-Hull, 117). She understands that La Llorona's wail is one of protest or triumph as well as one of sorrow, and it is this understanding that she shares with her father, brothers, and girlfriends.[12] Cleófilas' revisioning of La Llorona "offers the possibility of seeing La Llorona as a powerful woman who *encourages* new alternatives to old discourses. Instead of a stereotypical view of Mexican women as passively accepting male violence, we get resistance and action through Cleófilas' contact with a society of women" (Saldívar-Hull, 120). Filled with a new sense of agency, Cleófilas, after living through her own experience, truly comprehends that there is no joy in suffering for love. In the end, she uses her voice to articulate her own tale of misery so that others can benefit from her story in the same way she has from La Llorona's.

Cisneros' feminist configuration of La Llorona's story explicitly shows readers the importance of Mexicana and Chicana solidarity in the formation of an interpretative community that reads La Llorona's story as one capable of inspiring resistance to patriarchal dominance and abuse. Though Cleófilas finally understands what can lead a woman to drown her children, La Llorona's presence in her life does not inspire her to do the same. Instead, she escapes with her life, along with her son's, and learns to holler both at her oppressors and in liberation.

The protagonist of Viramontes' story "The Cariboo Cafe" faces similar circumstances. While she, too, eventually uses her voice to shout back at those who seek to compound her suffering, this washerwoman, far from her home in Central America, has no community to turn to for help. When the oppressive government in her home country "detains" her six-year-old son Geraldo for alleged "criminal activity," the mother finds herself at the center of a Llorona narrative as she alternately searches for and awaits the return of Geraldo.

Viramontes uses a tripartite structure for the story that allows her to build her contemporary vision of La Llorona slowly: the first part focuses on a sister and brother, Sonya and Macky; the second, on the cook/owner of the Cariboo Cafe; and the third, on a Central American washerwoman. The little boy, Macky, emerges as the focal point in the lives of the other characters, whose narratives become intertwined through a set of tragic circumstances. Elements and motifs found in traditional Llorona narratives, such as children and loss, appear in the first two parts, but they do not become recognizable elements of a Llorona tale until part 3, narrated by the washerwoman. La Llorona is mentioned by name only once in the story, and as Deborah Owen Moore notes, the legend "functions in a retroactive manner, forcing the reader to refocus on the subtle specifics that have been woven into the narrative" (283). I agree with Moore's observation, but aside from the washerwoman's uttering of La Llorona's name, Viramontes offers her readers no outline or explanation of the legend; therefore, the process by which this "refocusing" is done remains ambiguous except to those familiar with the tale. For instance, cultural readers acquainted with the lore will recognize that the author absolves La Llorona of the infanticide by making the government responsible for Geraldo's death. Although exonerated of the crime, a defining characteristic in the traditional tale, the mother still blames herself for sending her son alone to the corner store on the night he was "arrested." So while she may not be guilty of the infanticide, she still carries the burden of guilt, and wanders and wails for her son. By shifting the responsibility for the child's death onto the government, Viramontes takes away La Llorona's one avenue of resistance, killing, to show the washerwoman's complete lack of power against absolute governmental oppression.

The tripartite narrative is like a river, especially in the way that the characters' lives are pushed along by unseen forces, moving them toward confluence at the Cariboo Cafe. Regardless of their differences, together they live in a highly militarized world, where the Immigration and Naturalization Service (INS), the police, governments, and armies—all male-dominated institutions—wage wars. Viramontes substitutes the lover found in traditional tales with these male-dominated entities to show how women and children have the least power to resist systemic oppression and often become casualties in wars such as these.

Men and/or the institutions through which they wield power are responsible for the scene that unfolds at the Cariboo Cafe. As recounted in the first part of Viramontes' story, Sonya and Macky become lost because the young girl fears her father's reprisal for losing her apartment key, which happens when Lalo, a fellow classmate, wrestles Sonya to the ground during lunch break "so that he could see her underwear" (65). The Mexican immigrant family does not have legal residency, so Popi designs rules to provide protection even when he is not physically present and to help the family avoid detection by the INS agents, who later arrest workers at the cafe.[13] His rules are both evidence of and the means by which he exercises control over his family. Lalo's physical domination of Sonya indirectly places the girl and Macky in danger through his efforts to establish a reputation among his young male peers. When faced with the realization that, through no fault of her own, she cannot comply with her father's rules, Sonya is uncertain which is worse: losing her key or having to explain to her father how she lost it. Her duty to safeguard Macky, along with her desire to avoid telling her father about the loss of her key and evade his punishment for as long as possible, leads Sonya to make a decision that causes the children to become lost. Wandering in the urban landscape, they become vulnerable to police, the INS, and other predators. Believing "the zero-zero place" to be a temporary haven, Sonya leads Macky in the direction of the cafe and, unknowingly, toward the Llorona/washerwoman who saves Macky's life by pulling him out of the path of an oncoming car as the siblings are crossing the street.

In the second part of the story, the point of view shifts away from the siblings and onto the cook. Viramontes casts him as a woman in a reversal of the Llorona narrative. Like the washerwoman, the cook is alone and mourns for his child, lost to the violence of war, illustrating Moore's assertion that both parents are "like La Llorona, looking for [their] lost children" (284). An additional similarity between the two parents is that the cook also does not know the whereabouts of his son's remains. His suffering defines his life, and the two remaining legible letters, "OO," from the sign that once read "CARIBOO CAFE" can also be seen as numbers, reminders of all he has lost, particularly his wife Nell, who named the cafe. When Sonya and Macky enter his restaurant in the company of the washerwoman, the cook sees Macky as a surrogate for his own dead son, a move he has made in the past with Paulie, a junkie, whose age is that of JoJo's had he lived. The cook decides that Macky was "a real sweetheart like JoJo" (70). Notably, the cook has little regard for Sonya, who, in the cook's view, acts "like she owns [Macky]" (70). His judgment of the girl and regard for Macky reveals the way that possession of the boy, or what he represents, is a focal point of the struggle for all the characters. As Ana María Carbonell observes: "The La Llorona narrative converges for all three of these characters [Sonya, the washerwoman, and the cook] in Macky, the young undocumented boy who, on a mythical level, represents La Llorona's endangered child" (59). Viramontes draws parallels between the cook and the washerwoman, uniting them in their grief and their affection for Macky. However, as parents who have lost their children, their responses to the boy's appearance in their lives separates them and makes them opponents.

At the heart of the story lies a moral dilemma involving the safety of the siblings. If readers sympathize with the washerwoman, we must reconcile this sentiment with the fact that she abducts a child from the street, thus depriving another mother of her child. Regardless of how readers perceive the washer-woman's intervention in the lives of the siblings, the fact remains that she does save them from wandering alone in the street. She feeds them, delouses and bathes Macky, and gives them a place to sleep. In this way, she is nothing like the predatory Llorona who seeks to harm living children. Nevertheless, she is in possession of another woman's child, thus illustrating Saldívar-Hull's point that Viramontes refuses to allow readers to "be lulled by a romanticized scene of ma-ternal nurturing" (151). Reading the washerwoman through the lens of the lore allows us to see fully the extent of her torment and that her actions are the result of political oppression, guilt, and grief. When the opportunity presents itself for her to reunite with her murdered child, she transforms from a passive victim to a woman of action.

One way Viramontes helps readers to anticipate this transformation is through the first-person narration of part 3, which begins with a third-person omniscient account of the events in the woman's home country. Her voice emerges out of this context as she tells her story of loss. By giving her a voice, the author gives the woman an authority on par with the white cafe owner. This power is in sharp contrast to her powerlessness in her home country. Women there are particu-larly vulnerable to brutality and violence, as the washerwoman makes clear, ex-plaining, "we try to live as best we can under the rule of men who rape women then rip their fetuses from their bellies" (75). The woman does not name her home country but the references to the Contras and the atrocities she witnesses at the storage containers, where she initiates her search for Geraldo, are a clear reference to the tactics of the death squads that terrorized Central America dur-ing the 1980s. Whether in El Salvador, Guatemala, or Nicaragua, these militias practiced genocide disproportionately in Indigenous communities, which were turned into towns full of Lloronas.

Men, not La Llorona, are responsible for the murder of children, quelling any thought of resistance with terror. Illiterate, poor, and powerless, the Central American mother is devastated by the abduction of her child, whom she sent to a corner market to fetch a mango. Her grief unites her with other women who have become isolated from their own people due to their fear of sharing a similar fate. Wailing becomes their recourse in the face of overwhelming poverty and governmental tyranny. As the grieving mother explains:

> The darkness becomes a serpent's tongue, swallowing us whole. It is the
> night of La Llorona. The women come up from the depths of sorrow to

search for their children. I join them, frantic, desperate, and our eyes become scrutinizers, our bodies opiated with the scent of their smiles. Descending from door to door, the wind whips our faces. I hear the wailing of the women and know it to be my own. (72–73)

When her son is taken, the woman joins the ranks of these suffering mothers, who are completely powerless. Their voices merge into one so that when "[t]he Salvadoreña gives her testimonio," she "becomes the modern-day wailing woman of Chicana/o folklore, who in this version represents all women who are victimized by conquering races and classes" (Saldívar-Hull, 149). She represents literally the effects of an ongoing colonial and capitalist project that seeks to subjugate brown bodies.

With few avenues for recourse, the washerwoman turns to God and her nephew Tavo for help. Her choices reveal that she is willing to align herself with men so that she might call upon their authority to aid her plight. As she pleads her case to God, her guilt, coupled with her anger at God, surfaces: "It is such delicate work, Lord, being a mother. This I understand, Lord, because I am. [. . .] It was only a matter of minutes and my life is lost somewhere in the clouds. I don't know, I don't know what games you play, Lord" (75). God seems indifferent to her suffering and that of the other mothers who live in a world so dangerous that they cannot send their children unattended even half a block away. Tavo, on the other hand, offers his aunt help and sells his car to help finance her escape from the war-torn country so that she can start a new life in the United States. The woman, though, expresses reluctance about leaving, fearing that "Geraldo will not have a home to return to, no mother to cradle his nightmares away, soothe the scars, stop the hemorrhaging of his heart" (75). Tavo's presence in the story demonstrates that men can serve as allies in the liberation of women. Ironically, his pregnant wife is the one who wants her husband's aunt to leave. Because the wife reads the washerwoman's life through the lens of a traditional Llorona tale, she perceives the arrival of the political refugee as a "bad omen" and fears that she may harm the baby once it is born (76). This fear, as Carbonell notes, "further connects [the washerwoman] to the destructive Llorona figure who murders other people's children out of spite or envy" (61). The expectant mother's fear is seemingly substantiated by the fact that from the time Geraldo is taken, he fills the washerwoman's every thought, and when she arrives in the United States, her only desire is "to watch the children playing in the street" (75). In her role as a Llorona, she continues searching for her son beyond the borders of her home country.

The woman soon transforms from passive observer to active participant in determining the course of her life. When the Central Americana spots Macky on the street, she perceives him to be her son Geraldo. Ultimately she convinces herself of his identity, believing that God would not "play such a cruel joke" (76). The mother describes how the opportunity to save Geraldo moved her to immediate action, illustrated by her jumping the curb, dashing into the street, and avoiding being hit by the car. While her actions are instinctive, they are also an indication of her transformation into a woman with an objective and a willingness to act. Without a thought for her own safety, she dashes into the street to retrieve Macky, wholly prepared to fend off her ever-looming enemy oppressors should they present themselves.

The washerwoman undermines the male divine authority that punishes La Llorona eternally in the traditional tale by reducing God to a mere mortal, thinking, "But God is a just man and His mistakes can be undone" (76). She takes away God's power over her life. More importantly, though, her recognition of God's fallibility empowers her to believe that she can set her situation right without divine intervention. For a moment the woman worries that the child she has saved is not her own son, but the memory of Geraldo is so painful that she pushes the thought from her mind. Her narrative intersects with that of the cook when she takes Macky/Geraldo for a meal at the Cariboo Cafe to celebrate their reunion. As she begins to move past the pain of Geraldo's death, which has defined her life, her love for a living child is reawakened, and she reflects, while looking at the boy: "It's like birthing you again, mi'jo. My baby" (76). Later at a hotel, with her "son" safely tucked in bed, instead of using her voice to wail, she uses it to lull Macky/Geraldo to sleep. As she peacefully rests for the first time in years, she loses control of the narrative and another voice intervenes.

Three-quarters of the way through the section, a third-person speaker narrates events leading up to the conclusion at the Cariboo Cafe. The fact that neither the washerwoman nor the cook narrates this segment of the story indicates a loss of control on the part of both characters. While the washerwoman relinquishes herself to joy, the cook wraps himself in his grief, both reactions elicited by encounters with Macky. When the mother and two children return to the cafe, the narrator describes the woman's altered appearance: "She looks so different, so young. Her hair is combed slick back into one thick braid and her earrings hang like baskets of golden pears on her finely sculpted ears" (77). The cook "can't believe how different she looks" and thinks that she is "[a]lmost beautiful" (77). His recognition of her transformation represents a crucial moment in which two Lloronas could join forces against bigotry and male violence. Yet he fails to see the woman as a potential ally due to his privilege, prejudice, and despair.

The cook's abandonment by his wife Nell and the death of his son JoJo in the Vietnam War are meant to complicate the reader's assessment of his actions when the woman and children return to the cafe. Their presence exacerbates his grief by bringing back memories of Nell and JoJo, who is "crumbled up" in some unknown part of Vietnam (77). Instead of sympathizing with her, he remembers the news bulletin from the night before and calls the police, because "Children gotta be with their parents, family gotta be together, he thinks. It's only right" (77). While motivated by his love and longing for his son, his decision to call the police sets in motion the conflict between the two grieving parents.

Despite his convictions about the importance of families being together, the cook is not motivated to reunite the siblings with their parents by principle. His decision to call the police is a retaliatory act against the washerwoman, who has angered him by returning and making him cry for both his wife and child. Although the cook holds little regard for the police, seeing them as a nuisance that impinges upon his economic livelihood, he still has them at his command. When he calls, they dutifully arrive at his establishment to serve as his support in this conflict, though he cowers behind the counter as the situation in the cafe quickly escalates into a violent confrontation.

The washerwoman's first response when she sees the police "opening the screen door, their guns taut and cold like steel erections" is to flee these authoritarian males and whisk her son to safety (78). For her there is no difference between the police and the soldiers, who use their steel phalli to dispense death. As she attempts her escape, her movements are slowed by the memory of Geraldo's actual fate, involving mutilation and castration, and her guilt about sending her son out alone. The recollection reveals the depth of her torment. After Geraldo's disappearance, each child she heard in her home country pleading in the night became her own son reborn. For years she could only listen as these surrogate children were mutilated and murdered day after day. Her rescuing of Macky presents an opportunity for her to reunite with a living child. The mother is brought out of these thoughts by the sound of crying in the distance, yet for the first time in years, it is not her own.

The resurfacing of this painful memory about Geraldo's torturous end inspires her to stand and fight. She vows to never let go of her son, "For they will have to cut her arms off to take him, rip her mouth off to keep her from screaming for help" (78). In this battle, her voice proves to be her most powerful weapon. When she opens her mouth to scream, she channels her own pain along with all the other mothers who have lost children into a resounding, roaring howl that shakes the cafe walls. Her pleading howl for help indicts the community members who fail her by refusing to help her save "her children." Her unanswered plea harkens back to the original portent of the woman heard shouting in the streets of Tenochtitlan and anticipates Cleófilas' cry of liberation. Realizing that no one will respond to her cries for help, she takes control of her life and her story by wresting them away from the third-person narrator. She fights, physically and with words, out of the Llorona tale into which she has been written and resumes her first-person narration even as a gun barrel is placed at her head, insisting, "I will fight you for my son until I have no hands left to hold a knife" (78–79). No longer afraid, passive, or a traditional Llorona, she holds fast to Geraldo's hand, vowing never to let go. She continues to narrate her story even after being shot in the head, another act of deadly male penetration: "And then I hear something crunching like broken glass against my forehead and I am blinded by the liquid darkness. But I hold onto his hand. That I can feel, you see, I'll never let go. Because we are going home. My son and I" (79). Rather than being a tragic end to her painful life, her death is a triumphant one of her own making that facilitates her return home and a permanent reunion with her actual son, Geraldo.

Ultimately, the washerwoman wins her lucha against numerous oppressive forces not by abandoning the Llorona narrative that defined her life, but by using it subversively: first to recover her lost child, and then by rewriting it as a tale of resistance. Her "victory" leaves a mark on the landscape, represented literally in the blood that stains the cafe floor, and serves as a competing narrative to traditional Llorona tales and other authoritarian or patriarchal narratives used to oppress women. While the washerwoman transforms her Llorona narrative into a story of liberation, the cook becomes entrenched in a traditional tale. Though he remains geographically fixed, in telling and retelling the same story presumably to anyone who will listen, he is transported back through time, which is reflected by the shift in verb tense from past to present. Because his part of the story is narrated after the incident, we see he is still leading the same lonely life and still grieving for his lost son. His storytelling allows him to revisit Macky, who reminded him so much of JoJo, but when the story ends, he loses the boy all over again. As a traditional Llorona, the emasculated cook is trapped in a cycle from which he cannot break free. He is also haunted by the washerwoman. Refusing to acknowledge his role in the violent conflict, he chooses instead to blame "that crazy lady and the two kids that started all the trouble" (69). Unlike the washerwoman, he does not see that organized bands of armed men and those that control them are to blame. In spite of his efforts to eliminate any trace of the event, the floor stain serves as a constant reminder, for both the community and the cook, of his role in the woman's death and the likely deportation of the children along with their parents. The zero-zero place marked by murder, overdose, feces, and other forms of putrescence becomes a living hell that everyone manages to escape except the cook, who continues to haunt the CariBOO cafe.

La Llorona and the Imagining of a New Nation

Written in 1984, "The Cariboo Cafe" effectively demonstrates how people can become trapped in their own Llorona stories.[14] However, knowledge of how these stories coerce and oppress undermines their power and provides one path toward social and cultural liberation. Viramontes theorizes the subversive power of La Llorona's story by manipulating the conventional elements found in traditional tales to produce a different outcome. Her Chicana feminist repositioning of La Llorona prefigures, in fiction, Anzaldúa's consideration of La Llorona in *Borderlands/La Frontera: The New Mestiza* (1987), which publicly initiates her long-standing dedication to the cultural figure.

Anzaldúa's theorizing of La Llorona and her story occurs in three phases. The first, which appears in *Borderlands,* includes La Llorona as one example of how stories about female figures are used to bolster the authority of the patriarchy, inspire shame, and institutionally oppress Indi@s, Mexican@s, and Chican@s. Anzaldúa introduces La Llorona by identifying her, along with La Malinche and La Virgen, as one of three symbolic mothers who can serve as "mediators" in the lives of Chicanas (30). Her interpretation of these figures calls attention to the fact that "the true identity of all three has been subverted" to reinforce the virgin/whore dichotomy, which benefits the patriarchy by restricting the roles of women to categorically absolute, and either idealized or vilified, social positions (31). Concerning La Llorona, Anzaldúa argues that her story is used to "make us a long-suffering people" (31). In other words, the tale is used to inspire submission to the religious, national, or cultural authority of others.

Anzaldúa turns our attention to an "Azteca-Mexica" past and suggests that La Llorona's real identity is best understood through her association with the Mexica goddess Cihuacoatl, a deity she cites as La Llorona's direct antecedent, a point I discuss at length in the following chapter. A description of the goddess from the codices appears as the epigraph for the section in *Borderlands* that includes this assertion. According to Anzaldúa, the Mexicas justified their highly militarized empirical objectives by shifting attention away from an emphasis on harmony and the female mother goddesses, including Cihuacoatl (Snake Woman) and Coatlicue (Serpent Skirt), to disharmony and male deities, such as Huitzilopochtli, the god of war. This move "subverted the solidarity between men and women" and reflected the male domination that characterized the empire (34). Her interpretation of the Mexicas' systematic disempowerment of women is both critical and cautionary. Mexican patriarchal oppression did not begin in the colonial era, as Anzaldúa maintains. Therefore, when turning to the past as a basis for a contemporary Chican@ identity, we must not romanticize our Indigenous history or view the empire in an idealized state, for doing so only serves to replicate and reinvigorate male domination.

While Anzaldúa did not originate the conversation about the link between La Llorona and Mexica goddesses, she did use this relationship as evidence of the Azteca-Mexicas' efforts to erode female power and restrict women's creative energies by turning powerful goddesses into weeping mortals. Through her Indigenous-based methodology, Anzaldúa demonstrates a process for Chicanas to create counternarratives of empowerment. By reimagining cultural figures, like La Llorona, used to oppress mujeres mestizas, they can narrate resistance to, for example, the colonial legacy and patriarchal authority. Though Anzaldúa says relatively little about La Llorona in *Borderlands*, we cannot emphasize enough the importance of the discussion about the legendary figure that she helps to focus.[15]

Praxis best characterizes the second phase of Anzaldúa's work with La Llorona. Believing that men disseminated and wrote certain dominant "myths" associated with women, such as "the stories of Coatlicue, la Llorona, la Chingada, la Virgen de Guadalupe, and Coyolxauhqui, the moon goddess," Anzaldúa set about rewriting the stories of these figures to unleash their symbolic power (Keating, 219). As a part of this larger objective, in a 1994 interview Anzaldúa named three planned projects involving La Llorona: a children's book, *Prietita Encounters La Llorona;* a collection of cuentos in novel form, *La Prieta;* and a theoretical text to serve as a sequel to *Borderlands, Lloronas, mujeres que lean y escriben.*[16]

These endeavors reflect Anzaldúa's history with the legend and her belief, from an early age, that La Llorona's story was a potent oppositional narrative. She cites La Llorona as the "first cultural figure" she was introduced to as a child: "My grandmothers told me stories about her. She was a bogeyman. She was the horrific, the terror, the woman who killed her children, who misplaced her children. She was used [. . .] to scare the little girls into being good little girls. If you were a bad little girl la Llorona was going to come and get you" (229). While Anzaldúa's recounting emphasizes the way her family used the lore as a behavioral deterrent for girls, she developed her own view: "To me she was the central figure in Mexican mythology which empowered me to yell out, to scream out, to speak out, to break out of silence" (229). Viramontes' and Cisneros' stories parallel Anzaldúa's view of La Llorona as a speaking subject with the ability to empower generations of Chicanas, many of whom grew up believing that La Llorona's fate was unalterable. For Anzaldúa, La Llorona served as muse and a figurative mother whose story told the history of Chicana oppression and, at the same time, announced our liberation. Anzaldúa would later address directly the progression of her own work involving La Llorona: "I've recuperated la Llorona to trace how we go from victimhood to active resistance, from the wailing of suffering and grief to the grito of resistance, and on to the grito of celebration and joy" (Keating, 180). Her devotion to La Llorona shows us that when using cultural figures to "describe Chicana thought and experience," we can and should imbue them with new meanings to reflect our changing concerns (238).

Sadly, because of Anzaldúa's untimely death in 2004, we can, for now, only imagine the third phase of her work with Llorona. Based on the title of her *Borderlands* sequel and preliminary descriptions of the project, her plan was to "use the cultural figure of the serpent woman, la Llorona, through all the chapters, through all the theoretical writing" (Keating, 229). Rather than being simply a unifying element for the work, La Llorona was to serve, presumably, as its theoretical foundation. By identifying La Llorona as "serpent woman," Anzaldúa appears to have been in the process of positioning La Llorona as an alternate aspect of Cihuacoatl and Coatlicue that, taken together, would form a female trinity to rival that most patriarchal of affiliations: the Father, Son, and Holy Ghost.

Thus far, this chapter has focused exclusively on the work of Chicanas in the repositioning of La Llorona as a figure of resistance. The reason is clear: Chicanas represent the majority in these efforts and have taken up the task of critiquing the real-world consequences of La Llorona's story and others like it. However, Chicanas and Chicanos can unite ideologically by assuming joint responsibility for La Llorona and how she has been put to use historically. A cooperative project such as this could serve as the foundation for wider social activism to change or challenge conventional ideas about gender and gender roles. For Chicanos this means accepting responsibility for the role they have played in shaping La Llorona's story. In his essay "'I'm the King': The Macho Image," Rudolfo Anaya provides an example of this kind of accountability: "Blame men, the pillars of the morality of the community, if [La Llorona] has been given a bad rap" (71). Anaya cites La Llorona's story as one of the many cultural sources used by both men and women to foster a negative kind of machismo. His assertion emphasizes the importance of Chicanas acknowledging our own culpability in this effort and the ways that we contribute to our own oppression by leaving stories such as La Llorona's unchallenged.

Chicana poet, playwright, artist, and theorist Cherríe Moraga does more than challenge conventional interpretations of La Llorona in her play *The Hungry Woman: A Mexican Medea*.[17] Moraga sets her characters the task of dismantling a heterosexist, homophobic patriarchy. Goddesses from the pantheon of the Mexicas oversee the characters' resistance movement, which involves re-imagining La Llorona's sacrifice as an attempt to create what Anaya refers to as "a new humanity" (70). Through her characters, Moraga creates a continuum, one that begins in the Mexica past and reaches into a "fictional" dystopian future, mapping the ongoing patriarchal project to deny or erode female power. Medea represents another in a long line of female figures—namely Coatlicue, Coyol-xauhqui, Cihuateteo, and La Llorona, all present in the play—that have been transformed by men's seizure of power. Moraga establishes that the figures are all part of the same oppressive story, and she presents Medea's imprisonment as an example of the fulfillment of patriarchal domination in Aztlán, the setting of the play.

Regarding La Llorona specifically, Moraga does not include a version of the legend, nor does the Weeping Woman appear physically. Instead, she is named in conversations, and her piercing wail is heard at crucial moments. Her haunting of certain characters suggests, initially, that Moraga writes La Llorona into her familiar role as simply a ghostly presence, yet La Llorona's purpose is far greater than this. Her role in the play is to confer her legacy and that of all the goddesses on Medea, not to doom her, but to provide her a path of resistance and secure her liberation from her prison/narrative, the same story that trapped La Llorona and her predecessors. The legendary figure's ability to serve in this capacity reflects Moraga's belief that La Llorona's liberation from narrative confinement is central to the Chicana's and Mexicana's own liberation. Moraga writes: "Maybe somewhere in me I believe that if I could get to the heart of Llorona, I could get to the heart of the mexicana prison and in the naming I could free us . . . if only just a little" (*Loving,* 150). Through the association between Medea and her predecessors, Moraga suggests that the outcome of Medea's story can facilitate the release of all these female figures that are narratively confined. The play therefore represents Moraga's attempt to reach the heart of that prison and to imagine Medea's release and Chicanas' as well.

The play is set in a "muy 'Blade Runner-esque,'" futuristic world after an ethnic civil war that has divided the United States into smaller nations, including the Mechicano Nation of Aztlán (*Hungry,* 7). In this postwar world, "any one, regardless of blood quantum, who shared political affinities with these independent nations was permitted to reside within their territories; however, the right to hold title to land was determined differently within each nation" (6). In Aztlán that determination is made by Native blood quantum. Moraga describes how "after the revolution, a counter-revolution followed in most of the newly-independent nations" (6). Following this internecine conflict, gender hierarchies separate men and women, who had previously joined forces. Because this division is based on heteronormative ideas about gender performance, almost all queer people from each of the newly formed nations are sent into exile in Phoenix, "the dumping site of every kind of poison and person unwanted by its neighbors" (6). Though once a key figure, along with her husband Jasón, in the initial revolt that helped to establish Aztlán, Medea is exiled because of her relationship with her female lover, Luna. Her banishment from Aztlán represents, ultimately, the failure of the Mechicano Nation, for as Moraga reminds us in another work, "No progressive movement can succeed while any member of the population remains in submission" (*Last Generation,* 162). The residents have renamed the city Tomoanchán, which is translated in the play as "we seek our home," but this act of naming only underscores the depth of their exclusion from the Aztlán they helped make a reality (I.iii.24). Following a brief prelude, the play begins with Moraga's protagonist, Medea, a curandera of Yaqui ancestry, housed as an inmate in a psychiatric ward for "murdering" her son.

Whereas "[i]n the late sixties and early seventies," according to Moraga, "Chicano nationalism meant the right to control our own resources, language, and cultural traditions," *The Hungry Woman* offers audiences a different glimpse of a fully realized Aztlán (*Last Generation,* 151). Male dominance and the privileging of Native identity over all else characterize the nation. After the creation of Aztlán, men seize power and create gender hierarchies to limit women's authority.[18] Indian identity carries with it the greatest cultural currency in the nation, for Native blood quantum determines access to land and the right to rule. Therefore, a male resident who can confirm that he is descended from Indian ancestors has access to tremendous political and economic power in Aztlán. For men who lack Native lineage or whose bloodlines are diminished, marriage to an Indian woman serves as a means of gaining power. When women's bodies are exploited for the purposes of male authority, there can be no harmony or balance. Replacing oppressive whites with oppressive brown men solves virtually nothing and only replicates the dominating structures that the revolutionaries in Aztlán sought to overthrow. Moraga invites audiences to imagine a different Aztlán, a place where everyone can take up residence regardless of blood quantum, sexual alliance, gender performance, age, or religious practice. In her own envisioning of a new Aztlán, Moraga writes, "A new Chicano nationalism calls for the integration of both the traditional and the revolutionary, the ancient and the contemporary. It requires a serious reckoning with the weaknesses in our mestizo culture, and a reaffirmation of what has preserved and sustained us as a people" (*Last Generation,* 174). Figures from the past and present join forces to create a new Nation, outside of existing structures, that will resist, challenge, and perhaps even overthrow heterosexual, patriarchal domination in the Mechicano Nation.

In Medea, Moraga merges European and pre-Columbian myth and brings both into the present. Numerous folkloric and literary studies emphasize the similarities between La Llorona and the Medea of ancient Greek mythology. For instance, Rebolledo states that "La Llorona was a syncretic image connected both to Spanish medieval notions of *ánimas en pena,* spirits in purgatory expiating their sins, and to the Medea myth" (63). Though the Greek Medea, La Llorona, and Moraga's Mexican Medea all have conflicts with powerful patriarchs and are attached to an element of tragedy, they are not simply different names for the same figure. Understanding their distinctions helps to establish a wider history of female disempowerment that stretches beyond geographic and cultural boundaries. Moraga's choice of names for her protagonist allows her to wed the political themes associated with the Greek figure Medea, namely her role in her husband's ascent to power and subsequent exile, to the thematic concerns associated with stories about La Llorona that reflect a Chican@ nationalist perspective; that is, a Native woman betrayed by her Spanish or criollo husband. Medea's husband's name, Jasón, an Anglo-sounding name "Hispanicized" through the addition of an accent mark, is meant to reflect his European ancestry and his lack of any Native claim to power through direct bloodlines. The latter underscores the political motivation of his marriage to Medea, who is of Yaqui ancestry, as well as the reason behind Jasón's ascendance to power; his desire to marry a young Apache woman to replace Medea; and his efforts to gain custody of his mestizo son with Medea, Adolfo/Chac-Mool, whose own bloodline Jasón hopes to use to his political advantage.

Moraga reinforces Medea's Indigenous identity through her devotion to and her association with Coatlicue and the Cihuateteo, figures cited by Rebolledo, Thomas Janvier, and Betty Leddy as antecedents to La Llorona. In the play, the Cihuateteo—related in the Mexica tradition to Cihuapipiltin, goddesses of the cross roads—serve as the chorus and intervene directly in Medea's story.[19] According to Mexica belief, women who died in childbirth, known as Mocihuaquetzque, "were the only Aztec women to achieve afterlife in the place of the warriors" and as such were venerated (Rebolledo, 63). In death, these women were known as Cihuapipiltin, and at certain times of the year the figures, whose faces were "whitened with chalk," descended to earth and were said to appear at crossroads, so parents warned their children: "'Go not forth; the Cihuapipiltin arrive on earth; they descend'" (Sahagún, I:19). Those who fell under their spell seemed possessed: "one's mouth was twisted; one's face was contorted; one lacked use of a hand; one's feet were misshapen—one's feet were deadened; one's hand trembled; one foamed at the mouth" (I:19). Because these women, in death, were made equal to or in some cases given status above that of men, their authority serves as a physical reminder of the power Medea has been denied. A Cihuateteo statue that appears as part of a museum exhibit in the play represents visually another example of the patriarchy's attempts to contain female power. Medea's own liberation from her particular kind of prison is foreshadowed when Luna "steals" the statue and presents it to Medea as a gift, which serves as a physical reminder of the larger narrative of which they, as women, are all a part.

From the first scene, Moraga establishes the theme of female power central to the play with an altar dedicated to Coatlicue, "the Aztec Goddess of Creation and Destruction" (I.Prelude.9, stage directions [s.d.]). The image of the goddess that gave birth to the celestial beings adorns center stage in the prelude, and the description of it in the stage directions calls to mind the actual statue of her unearthed in 1824 in Mexico City (figure 3.2). Despite her gruesome appearance (a necklace of human hearts and hands, taloned feet, and a skirt of snakes), for many Chicana feminists, Anzaldúa especially, Coatlicue represents a source of Indigenous female power, both creative and destructive, diminished historically by the emphasis on male deities.[20] While "[t]he feminist version of Coatlicue owes a lot to the Chicana feminists who set out to rescue the goddess from her Aztec imprisonment," as theorist Jean Franco points out, in Moraga's play Coatlicue is not idealized; instead, she, along with other female figures from the Mexica past, is a captive (216). Her story serves as the starting point for our understanding of the current state of female oppression in Aztlán. The post-apocalyptic Cihuateteo who attends the statue states: "This is how all stories begin and end" (I.Prelude.9). Moraga parallels the stories of the goddess and Medea through the Cihuateteo's proclamation, "So, too, begins and ends this story," suggesting that the outcome of the narrative into which Medea has been inscribed is set literally in stone (I.Prelude.9). Later, Medea turns away from the goddess she once honored and blames the Earth Mother for her part in ushering in an age of male domination that extends from the past and into Medea's own dystopian reality.

The story of Coatlicue's impregnation and birthing of the god of war, Huitzilopochtli, is the source of Medea's view that Coatlicue has betrayed not only her own daughter, Coyolxauhqui, the moon goddess, but also her figurative Indigenous daughters. Like La Llorona, a male figures prominently in Coatlicue's loss of her child. Similar to a version of Coatlicue's story found in the Florentine Codex, the Cihuateteo narrate their own tale of the goddess' impregnation:

CIHUATETEO EAST: A long time ago, before the Aztec war of the flowers, before war, Coatlicue, la mera madre diosa, was sweeping on top of the mountain, Coatepec, when she encounters two delicate plumitas. She stuffs the feathers into her apron, thinking later she might weave them

FIGURE 3.2. *Coatlicue,* Museo Nacional de Antropología e Historia,
Mexico City. Photo credit: Werner Forman/Art Resource, NY.
Used by permission of Art Resource.

into a cloth for her altar. But suddenly, secretly, the feathers begin to ges-
tate there by her womb, y de repente, Coatlicue, goddess of Creation and
Destruction, becomes pregnant. (II.Prelude.55)

According to the myth, Coyolxauhqui then made a case to her star god brothers
and sisters, Centzon Huitznahuas, that their mother should be killed for the
"dishonor" and "shame" she had brought upon them by becoming pregnant in
an unexplained way. She leads the "Four Hundred" in an attack against their
mother and, depending on the version, either kills Coatlicue or is struck down

before she can commit matricide. In both versions, Huitzilopochtli kills his sister. The war god emerges from his mother fully formed and dressed for battle: "he pierced Coyolxauhqui, and then quickly struck off her head [. . .] her body came falling below; it fell breaking to pieces; in various places her arms, her legs, her body each fell" (Sahagún, III:4). He also dispatches his siblings who organized against their mother and then tosses the severed head of his sister into the night sky, forever separating mother and daughter.

Moraga parallels the relationships between Coatlicue, Coyolxauhqui, and Huitzilopochtli to that of Medea, Luna, and Adolfo/Chac-mool.[21] Medea's lover, Luna, whose name is the Spanish word for "moon," serves an alternate representation of the moon goddess, Coyolxauhqui. Moraga's substitution of a female lover, Luna, for the female child, Coyolxauhqui, privileges the broader issue of gender alliance over that of maternal fidelity and allows Moraga to address heterosexual oppression as a part of patriarchal oppression. Thus, in relation to the Llorona legend, Luna/Coyolxauhqui represents a broken or lost bond between women. Moraga reads Coyolxauhqui's actions not as a revolt against the mother, but instead as an attempt to prevent or organize against future oppression, which her mother helps bring about: "As we feministas have interpreted the myth, Coyolxauhqui hopes to halt, through the murder of her mother, the birth of the War God, Huitzilopotchli [sic]. She is convinced that Huitzilopotchli's birth will also mean the birth of slavery, human sacrifice and imperialism (in short, patriarchy)" (Loving, 147). Though Coyolxauhqui fails in her attempt, her presence in the night sky serves as both a reminder of her fate and what has yet to be accomplished in terms of organized female resistance against male domination. In the final scene before the epilogue, Medea turns away from Coatlicue and pledges her devotion to Coyolxauhqui. By transferring her affection from the "treasonous" mother to the "hija rebelde," Medea allies herself with a female resistance movement to overthrow or thwart her oppressors (II.viii.92).

As messenger and architect of a kind of resistance, La Llorona plays a key role in Medea's actively taking up this cause, but she also helps to prepare Adolfo/Chac-Mool for his role as sacrificient. When Adolfo changes his name to Chac-Mool, his choice of names associates him directly with the ritual of sacrifice and foretells his fate. Chacmol is the term assigned to a vessel that adorned the tops of temples. The figure, depicted in repose, balances in his lap a plate or bowl in which sacrifices to the gods were traditionally placed. In the play, the character Chac-Mool serves as both the vessel for an offering and the offering itself. To prepare the boy for his destiny, La Llorona shares her story with him. Chac-Mool, who does not fear La Llorona, states: "I felt like she / was telling me her side of the story, like I was the only one that heard / it like that" (I.vi.38). His teaching and nurturing by a community of women may explain his openness to listening and hearing the message included in La Llorona's version of events. Since the time Chac-Mool left Aztlán at the age of five to go into exile with his mother, the strongest influences in the young man's life have been women: Medea, Luna, and Mama Sal, Medea's mother. But their influence is not enough for Chac-Mool to relinquish his desire to participate in the initiation rites of manhood practiced in Aztlán. As a young man, the lure of patriarchal power is too great a force for him to resist.

La Llorona also prepares Medea for the final stages of her own lucha. The Cihuateteo appear and herald the arrival of La Llorona, whose "ominous and chilling wail, fills the air" (II.i.63, s.d.). Imitating La Llorona's cry, the Cihuateteo "pierce and slash themselves" with maguey thorns (II.i.63, s.d.). This scene of self-mutilation prefigures both Chac-Mool's and Medea's deaths, for when a mother kills her child, as Moraga cites elsewhere, she is, in fact, killing a part of her self (*Loving*, 146). Through this blood ritual, the Cihuateteo initiate Medea into their legacy: "They encircle MEDEA with the ghostly white veil of La Llorona. It is a river in the silver light. MEDEA and the sound of the children's cries drown beneath it" (II.i.63, s.d.). As a figure of resistance, "La Llorona goes counter to the patriarchy, which says the nuclear heterosexual family is the most important thing, wife and children under the control of the patriarch, the man" (Keating, 191). Therefore, in order to free herself of patriarchal control, Medea must ally herself in body and spirit with women. The Cihuateteo's placing of La Llorona's veil symbolizes Medea's initiation and marriage to a sisterhood of power, one broken when Coatlicue "betrayed" Coyolxauhqui. Medea's lesbian plural marriage to these female figures stands in defiance of the patriarchal authority and heterosexism that characterize Aztlán—and the same powers Jasón calls upon to gain control of his son.

After the "patriarchs who stole [Medea's] country" grant Jasón custody of the boy, Medea realizes that her son is lost (II.ii.71). This understanding, coupled with another profound loss, moves Medea to action. Earlier in the play, after Jasón first announces his intent to gain custody of Adolfo, Luna makes love to Medea and speaks a creation myth about an insatiable woman, the hungry woman named in the title of the play, into her lover's body.[22] Medea becomes pregnant, but this new hermaphroditic being is delivered stillborn. Rather than a personal or biological failure, the new entity, which looks like Luna, does not survive because there is no place in the world, not even in Tamoanchán, the place of queer exile, for this kind of new gender. Facing the loss of both of her children, Medea solidifies her resolve to sacrifice Chac-Mool by poisoning him with powerful herbs.

In an effort to save Chac-Mool from becoming like his father, Medea kills him. She refuses to contribute further to the oppression of women, queer folk, and other disenfranchised groups who reside in Tomoanchán. Seemingly Llorona-like, Medea poisons Chac-Mool, but she does not throw his lifeless form into a body of water. Moraga purposely disassociates Medea's act from water so that cultural readers will see her as a figure distinct from La Llorona, even though they share a similar history. Medea, however, does not seek the cleansing or restorative powers associated with the water in a Native or any other context. Instead, with the help of the Cihuateteo, she creates an altar of corn stalks on which she places Chac-Mool's body. The scene calls to mind a sacrificial ritual practiced by the Mexicas to honor the corn goddess, Chicomecoatl, who required a female sacrificient. The female aspect of corn, the goddess Chicomecoatl, along with the goddesses associated with water and salt, Chalchuihtlicue and Huixtocihuatl, respectively, were honored highly among the Mexicas. These natural resources were seen as "the livelihood of the people" for "through them [the people] can live" (Sahagún, I:22). Each year the Mexicas sacrificed a young woman, who was also decapitated and flayed, to make a blood offering to the corn goddess to ensure fertility, renewal, and sustenance. The young woman's sacrificial blood, and its life-giving and sustaining qualities, ensured the continuation of the people. Medea replicates this ritual through her sacrifice, but in offering her male child, she interrupts a traditional renewal. The offering, made in this way, represents a violation of the ancient ritual, yet one powerful enough to create something new.

Intertwining La Llorona's story with that of Medea's allows audiences to see other possibilities in the legend. Anaya, who believes La Llorona's legend "has been too narrowly analyzed," offers an alternate interpretation of it: "Perhaps *La Llorona* realizes the child has to die to be reborn a better male. That is, the consciousness of the child has to be reshaped to fit the time. Consciousness is evolving, and in this case the mother (*La Llorona*) is a key player in that new consciousness. Put another way, *La Llorona* is creating a new humanity" ("'King,'" 70). Similar to the Llorona that Anaya envisions, Medea facilitates Chac-Mool's transformation into a new kind of man, one who does not derive his power from the subjugation of disenfranchised groups or from stories about women weeping and wandering. In the final scene of the play, which takes place at the prison, Chac-Mool reappears after his death as a man with the determination and ability to set his mother free from the oppression that has clouded her life. This concluding scene features Chac-Mool offering the same cup of deadly herbs to his mother to drink that she gave to him.

Some may criticize Moraga for handing over the final scene in the play to

Chac-Mool, who orchestrates his mother's "release" from the narrative that imprisons her. But the final scene is the culmination of events that Medea set in motion. Chac-Mool simply performs the last act that initiates a new cycle and unites diverse Mechicano people in the same cause. As such, no solitary individual liberates Medea from her literal and metaphoric prison: Medea frees her mind; Luna, her spirit; and Chac-Mool, her physical body. Medea represents the realization of Moraga's search for "a whole woman [she] can shape with [her] own Chicana tongue and hand. A free citizen of Aztlán and the world" (*Last Generation,* 76). Medea is delivered from her imprisonment through a collaborative, community effort involving friends, family, and other spiritual allies like La Llorona. In bequeathing her legacy of resistance to Medea, La Llorona helps the exiled and imprisoned curandera to usher in a new age. The effort, however, is a collaborative one involving a diverse community of men and women, queer and straight, with the potential to change Aztlán. Moraga gives no hint at the success of this new project, though audiences are encouraged to imagine a Mechicano Nation that no longer relies upon blood quantum, sexual alliance, or gender performance as the basis of residency and citizenship. The nationalism Moraga seeks "is one that decolonizes the brown and female body as it decolonizes the brown and female earth. It is a new nationalism in which la Chicana Indígena stands at the center, and heterosexism and homophobia are no longer the cultural order of the day" (150). To this Moraga adds, "I cling to the word 'nation' because without the specific naming of the nation, the nation will be lost [. . .]" (150). As a Chicana Indígena who fought for the creation of Aztlán, Medea attempts to dismantle the nation in its present state by refusing to allow Jasón, and other men like him lacking in Native ancestry, to exploit Native women and their children for political gain.

In the end, audiences are asked to look upon Medea cradled in the arms of her son in a reverse pietà. The scene asks for our compassion for the sacrifices that mother and son have made on behalf of the people of Aztlán. While we may read this ending as tragic, the final scene of the Cihuateteo dancing commemorates the addition of a new warrior woman to their ranks. Medea, who dies as a result of giving birth to a new kind of man, transcends time and space to take her place among the goddesses.

By reimagining La Llorona as a luchadora with the power to serve as an agent of change or liberation for women, Chican@s imbue the figure with new cultural meaning and demonstrate our continuing need of her as a presence in our lives. We must not abandon La Llorona in her search for renewal. If we do so, we face losing a story that can help us, both men and women, narrate our liberation from oppression on both familiar and new fronts. As Anaya points out, we must "Blame ourselves if we do not reinterpret the old myths and give them new meaning for our violent time. There's hope in new interpretations, a hope that will bring new understanding to our roles as men and women" (71).

The cultural productions analyzed in this chapter show us how recontextualizing or reinterpreting La Llorona's story can bring about a new understanding, not simply concerning gender, but also a host of other cultural, social, and political issues. Whereas the majority of cultural productions included in this chapter subvert La Llorona's traditional meaning found in conventional versions of the legend by positioning her as a figure of resistance, in the following chapter cultural producers move La Llorona outside of the lore's narrative confines by re-turning her to the past and toward new cultural possibilities.

FOUR

"Long Before the Weeping"

Re-Turning La Llorona

Past is present, remember. Men carved me,
wrote my story, and Eve's, Malinche's, Guadalupe's,
Llorona's, snakes everywhere, even in our mouths.

— PAT MORA, "COATLICUE'S RULES"

THE READINGS OF the artifacts analyzed in the previous chapters show how Chican@s are working within or redrawing the boundaries of La Llorona stories to generate cultural criticism. Identifying revisions of the lore that feature the legendary figure as a symbol of resistance brings to light the ways in which La Llorona can serve as an agent of change for other women. Artifacts that retain the tale's salient features, such as its structure and primary narrative elements, reveal that there is power for her community in her wandering and wailing. However, the combination of the narrative, its structure, and its entrenchment in the cultural imagination curtails her subversive potential for she remains initially defined, as her name suggests, by her weeping and later by the infanticide in traditional narratives. If, as Luis D. León proposes, "La Llorona is a possession of group memory, a product of a place and a historical experience," then one radical method for imbuing her story with new meaning would involve returning her to or before the historical moment, whether actual or narrative, that gave rise to her legend (20). This paradoxical endeavor involves taking her back to a time before the defining moment in her life so that we may consider or recuperate who or what she was before becoming the Llorona we know. Some may argue that if we imagine La Llorona, for instance, without her definitive weeping or eliminate her act of infanticide, then she ceases to be the woman of legend and is rendered unrecognizable. But re-turning La Llorona, and our attention, to the past allows us to see the cultural forces that have shaped and continue to shape contemporary representations of the legend, thus drawing attention to our ongoing need of her and her story.

For Chican@s, La Llorona is one of the stories that we tell, and that tells us, about suffering, punishment, and resistance. We are not defined exclusively by these experiences, but her story helps us to understand how cultural/social forces or a single act can shape a person's or figure's entire identity. In *The Truth About Stories: A Native Narrative* (2003), Thomas King maintains that identity is derived from stories: "The truth about stories is that that's all we are" (2). La Llorona lore is one place from which many of us draw an understanding of our own cultural identities, so these stories can also serve as the place where we reimagine her in order to reimagine ourselves in the face of an ever-changing cultural, social, and political landscape.

Reading for re-turnings or recuperations involves identifying those ways in which Chican@s turn La Llorona to the past to reclaim those characteristics or traits that were left behind, abandoned, or written over by Natives, mestizos, and non-Natives in an attempt to subdue female power. Two distinct kinds of radical recuperations emerge in the artifacts discussed here. Cultural producers emphasize, for example, La Llorona's behavior as a woman outside of the narrative and chronological scope of conventional or revised representations as in Xavier Garza's mixed-media artwork *La Llorona* (2001) and his "tabloid page" from *El Chisme Daily News* (2001), Cordelia Candelaria's poems "La Llorona at Sixteen" (1993) and "La Llorona: Portrait by the River" (1993), Yxta Maya Murray's short story "La Llorona" (1996), and short stories from Alma Luz Villanueva's collection *Weeping Woman: La Llorona and Other Stories* (1994). In addition, artists such as Juana Alicia Montoya, José Ramirez, and Santa Barraza, as well as novelist Ana Castillo in *So Far From God* (1993), deify her by re-turning her to a place among the goddesses of the Mexica pantheon. Both are strategies of resistance, but they primarily serve to recuperate La Llorona, via counternarratives and images, from the tragedy that initial readers of the sixth sign or portent made her defining characteristic.

As mentioned in Chapter 1, many of the folk stories about La Llorona begin with some variation of the sentence, "There was a woman." The line is important for a number of reasons: it establishes the authority of the storyteller; provides temporality, separating past from present; and assigns the events recounted to an individual female. Yet most of all, it stresses that before becoming La Llorona, the predatory ghost at the center of the tale was a flesh and blood human being—a fact often lost, forgotten, or ignored in favor of other details. Placing emphasis on La Llorona's unthinkable actions and the suffering that ensues helps to create physical and emotional distance between the storyteller and the events she/he is recounting. The open space created by this distance is then filled with cultural and moral commentary about La Llorona's behavior. The emphasis, therefore, is not on her humanity, but her ostensible lack of it in the defining moment of her life.

In the first set of artifacts discussed in this chapter, artists and writers close this gap between La Llorona and her folk community by showing us the woman she once was, or giving her a voice with which to speak and an actual name that is not metaphoric. These artifacts encourage cultural readers to reconsider critically how our views of La Llorona might change if we focus on unseen or previously undiscussed elements of her life.

Artist Xavier Garza disrupts conventional interpretations of the lore through the introduction and inclusion of a recovered image of La Llorona that depicts a time before she became set in the cultural imagination. Born and raised in the Rio Grande Valley, Garza grew up hearing stories about La Llorona and her propensity for snatching children who wandered far from home: "My grandmother, I remember, gave me many a warning of how I shouldn't go near the river that ran close to her house because she herself had seen La Llorona lurking about just a week earlier. My grandmother's warning, however, had more to do with her fears over my safety than with any real spectral apparition. Still, La Llorona came to be a major part of my childhood" (pers. comm. 2005). Garza translated his grandmother's protective gesture and her tales into a number of projects incorporating La Llorona's story and/or her image, including a master's thesis in art, two short stories, a work of "tabloid art," and a set of Lotería cards used as cover art for one of his books, as well as the two pieces discussed below. In 2006 he also served as curator for a Llorona group show at Gallista Gallery in San Antonio, Texas. Though Garza admits that he sees La Llorona as "a complex woman that has been used as a symbol of the oppression of women by a machismo dominated culture," cultural readers can identify the way in which he offers his own cultural and social critique of the lore by presenting multiple, often contradictory, representations of La Llorona in a single work (pers. comm. 2005).

Through the form of the piece and the tension created by juxtaposing narrative, visual images, milagritos, and childhood mementos, the artist creates a discursive space from which to interrogate the lore (figure 4.1). Garza's art box "recalls the *nichos* (niches, recesses) of Mexican colonial art in which resided a venerated saint [. . .]" (Keller et al., 141). The folk religion associated with the form is one way that Garza incorporates the divine element from traditional

FIGURE 4.1. *La Llorona* (2001, mixed media, 13" × 8" × 5"), by Xavier
Garza © 2002. Used by permission of the artist.

versions of the lore. Garza's use of the nicho encourages religious interpretations of the objects included in the work. For example, bronzed sets of baby
shoes adorn the inside and the top of the box. Audiences may readily translate
the zapatitos inside the box as reflecting the belief that children are a blessing,
and those outside of it, in relationship to the lore, as symbolizing the children's
ascendance to heaven. However, Garza invites the same critical consideration of
religion and its role in the shaping of the lore as he does regarding La Llorona.

While familiar angelitos appear in and outside of the nicho, Garza substitutes the image of a saint with a cuento about and images of La Llorona before and after the infanticide. By locating La Llorona in a space usually occupied by a saint or some other holy figure, Garza challenges his audience to think about La Llorona as a secularly sacred being whose position in the cultural imagination often goes unchallenged.

Garza also recontextualizes the iconographic image of a Madonna and child within the framework of the art box and the lore. A dozing infant lies cradled in the arm of a woman who is tenderly suckling the baby (figure 4.2). Above the scene, we see the words LA LLORONA spelled in all capital letters, which at once represents the title of the piece and the authority of the legend. The dissonance created by pairing an image that traditionally calls to mind the Virgin Mary with the name La Llorona leaves audiences unsure as to the identity of the woman in the picture. Garza addresses the incongruence between the title and image by inserting the following question between the written and visual texts: "Who is She?" For those familiar with conventional versions of the legend, the question appears to be a rhetorical one. In regard to the picture, though, the answer is unclear because even for audiences familiar with La Llorona's story, the image of a nurturing mother is not one directly attached to the legend. The question invites audiences to reflect critically on our understanding of the lore and La Llorona's position in it, but it does not help us initially decipher the image in relationship to its surroundings or determine if it constitutes a re-turning.

The answer to both the question about the woman's identity and how the image is a recuperation lies in the written narrative included in the piece. Garza offers audiences a traditional version of the legend with one noticeable addition: the protagonist, a "beautiful woman born to poverty and tragedy" named Christina, kills her children by drugging them, placing them in a rock-filled sack, and then throwing them into a river. Christina's desire to marry a wealthy older man in order to escape her life-long poverty motivates her deed.[1] Instead of a story about an unnamed woman, the events are attached to a person who had a specific identity and desire to escape poverty before becoming La Llorona. Some might argue that this is not a significant enough detail to constitute a major re-turning of the figure, but the assignation of a name, other than Maria, which evokes the Virgin Mary, gives La Llorona an identity independent of the legend. The inclusion of this detail foregrounds her humanity, illustrating that her behavior is the result of a specific circumstance, poverty, while at the same time demonstrating that her actions are a singular response to her particular situation.

Nowhere in the narrative does Garza give cultural readers any indication that

FIGURE 4.2. *La Llorona* (2001, central image, interior), by Xavier Garza © 2002.
Used by permission of the artist.

the image on the back wall of the interior is Christina. Yet based on her physical
beauty and the positioning of the text beneath the image, we can conclude that
the image recovers a moment in Christina's life before she became La Llorona.
Because scenes such as these are erased by narratives like the one Garza includes,
he admits to purposely providing a counterimage: "Rather than portraying her as
an evil woman stealing a helpless child, I chose to portray her in a more maternal
role as she cuddles the child, allowing it to suck her finger as if it were a pacifier"
(pers. comm. 2005). By making this secular Madonna and child image the focal
point of the box, Garza fills in vast narrative gaps in conventional versions of

the legend, therefore subverting its more oppressive ideological messages. The introduction of this image invites us to reflect on poverty as an oppressive force at work on women like Christina to understand the way in which economic deprivation might make them consider infanticide as an option. Less visible are the interior scenes on the left and right panels, which feature a crone-like La Llorona attempting to snatch children playing in the river and wandering with a wailing infant. Blue and yellow curving lines call to mind the movement of water, pushing the audience's line of sight out from the central image toward these inside panels that visually narrate scenes of La Llorona in the afterlife. Spatially, the artist marginalizes the conventional images. The locating of scenes, text, objects, and icons around the central image implies a direct causal relationship between the woman and events that surround her. But if we consider the direction of the movement, as conveyed by the swirling lines, as moving toward, rather than away from, the central image, then the nurturing, loving aspects of the woman are what lie buried beneath conventional renderings. Garza asks audiences to think about how the image, or scenes like it, can disrupt the flow of conventional interpretations of the lore.

The discursive space is not confined to the interior of the piece but overflows, like water, pulling readers outside of the nicho. In terms of our understanding of the lore and the way in which we imagine La Llorona, Garza literally asks us to think outside of the box. The central image is duplicated in color on the outside right panel (figure 4.3). An affixed set of disembodied eyes protrudes from the box and hovers in the night sky above the mother and child. The eyes compel us to see and contemplate the image before us: a child cradled safely in its mother's arms. Their position in the sky serves as a means of incorporating divine judgment, while the eyes, with God-like authority, watch us as we look upon and judge Christina against her future actions.

Each exterior panel offers a different side of La Llorona as presented in conventional versions of her story. A ghost woman howling and flying through the night appears on the right panel, and on the back, a woman weeping and wandering is framed against a starry sky. To these images, Garza adds a loving mother. The open side of the box, where a fourth image of La Llorona might appear, becomes the place where audiences are encouraged to devise their own understanding of La Llorona based on traditional interpretations as well as the recuperated scene that Garza provides. The artist reminds us through the bronze baby shoes, representative of the future, and the ornamental jewels that line the box, which suggest value, that we should not minimize the future worth of La Llorona's story or ongoing critical conversations about her.

In a framed mock-up of a newspaper called *El Chisme Daily News,* Garza once again brings together multiple interpretations of the legend to create a discursive

FIGURE 4.3. *La Llorona* (2001, right and back panels, exterior), by Xavier
Garza © 2002. Used by permission of the artist.

space from which to address a question that is also the title of the piece: *Is La
Llorona Stalking Our Children?* (figure 4.4). The "newspaper" is devoted to stories
about and images of La Llorona. The Madonna and child image from the nicho
serves as the central image of this piece as well. The drawing is surrounded by
competing conventional visual renderings of the lore that position La Llorona
as a bogey-woman. Articles featured in the work include a revised version of the
tale ("La Llorona, Fact or Fiction?"), revealing that the children and Christina
drowned while attempting to flee her ex-lover, who wanted to take the children

FIGURE 4.4. "Is La Llorona Stalking Your Children?" From *El Chisme Daily News* (2001, framed mock-up), by Xavier Garza © 2002. Used by permission of the artist.

because his new wife was barren; an exposé ("Missing Children") on the unexplained disappearance of children in the barrio; a piece ("La Llorona: Was She Framed for her Children's Murders?") about a law professor seeking to clear La Llorona's name and file charges against the "real" culprit—the husband; and finally, a celebrity news story about La Llorona's appearance in a milk commercial ("La Llorona Makes Television Commercial").[2] The last element acknowledges and engages the cultural artifact without directly critiquing it. Drawing from a variety of sources and disciplines (folklore, law, and popular culture), Garza illustrates the complex and changing relationships Chican@s have with La Llorona.

Garza's investment in a visual recuperation of La Llorona mirrors Cordelia Candelaria's poetic efforts in "La Llorona at Sixteen" and "La Llorona: Portrait by the River," which complete her triptych initiated with "Go 'Way From My Window, La Llorona," discussed in Chapter 3.[3] These poems bookend the events recounted in conventional narratives, thus allowing readers to trace the Weeping Woman's evolution from a hopeful young girl of sixteen to an aged, world-weary woman. The poet hints that the events recounted are relatively recent, yet she does not revise La Llorona's story. Instead, Candelaria re-turns the reader toward conventionally muted aspects of La Llorona's existence prior to and after the deaths of the children. La Llorona emerges from this context not simply as a figure of tragic despair, but as a real person who once possessed the innocence and optimism of youth "long before the weeping" ("Sixteen," 26).

The picture Candelaria develops of La Llorona as a teenager reveals that La Llorona's life was not defined by a single heartbreak. In traditional renderings, we learn of La Llorona's status within her own community only after the tragic events take place. Candelaria, however, returns La Llorona to an incident that happened "At Sixteen," when she was still young. Cultural audiences familiar with the tale often know very little about the girl who grew up to become a legend, so many may find that the inclusion of this additional information intensifies the horror of the future infanticide as well as the reasons behind it. The opening line of the poem begins with the word "Sing." Readers are asked to sing lines of a child-like rhyme:

> [Sing:
> I'm forever blowing bubbles
> blowing bubbles in the air
> they fly so high
> nearly reach the sky
> they fade and   ] (1–6)[4]

The lines closely resemble lyrics from a popular song written in 1919 called "I'm Forever Blowing Bubbles," the melody for which sounds eerily like music that accompanies a carousel, an amusement park ride that travels 'round and 'round, never changing its course. Cultural readers familiar with the song will notice that although the lyrics approximate the song, they do not replicate them.[5] The instruction for the audience to sing serves to unite our voices with that of the girl featured in the poem, making us a part of the same community, one that ultimately fails her. As we sing about an untroubled existence, a young woman finds herself in the midst of a definitive tragedy.

Candelaria deliberately mixes images of innocence and carefree youth with the girl's emergent womanhood and its attendant obligations. La Llorona's age in the poem is significant because one year has passed since her quinceañera, or fifteenth birthday, traditionally a time when young women of Mexican ancestry are formally presented to the community as adults who can begin to date. We sing along to a tune that the girl perhaps favored and see that before becoming La Llorona, nothing in particular marked this happy young woman for future tragedy. By including moments of joy in the life of the young woman who will become the legendary lady of sorrow, Candelaria heightens the tragedy.

Despite the song's lighthearted tone, the featured lines are about watching creations float away in the air, an image that foreshadows the girl's fate, for the act is repeated *forever*. This constant repetition, like the carousel that forever spins around, alludes to her future of eternal weeping and wandering. The song ends abruptly as a third-person speaker intervenes to narrate the girl's story:

> and when she realized she did not have it
> she fell apart inside
>
> no, no, she cried
> frantic (7–10)

Though the nature of the loss remains ambiguous, knowledge of the lore and the previous scenario help cultural readers to determine exactly what the girl "did not have" (7). Her age also becomes a factor in this determination because it corresponds to a time in a young woman's life when she begins to menstruate. Therefore, the "it" she did not have is her period. Candelaria lays bare the girl's emotional turmoil, and we see her panic build.

The young woman has lost her innocence and control over the direction of her life—losses reinforced by the third-person narration. We listen as she tries to convince herself that she is not pregnant, "yes, yes, of course it s here" (11).

The line reflects her hope that each new day might bring a sign of blood, a point underscored by the fact that the period, as punctuation, is noticeably absent from the poem. Even in her frantic state, she remains optimistic, a characteristic that will serve her well in the future as she searches for her lost children:

> she crooked a smile to fettle up
> her scrambled heart
> ever alert it might turn up
> somewhere
>
> she looked and looked
> and didn t tell (12–17)

However, as the speaker tells us, the young woman is surprised to learn "she *could* not have It" (19). Here again, the "It" is ambiguous, but most likely refers to the understanding that intercourse can result in pregnancy, and for most women, the interruption of one's monthly cycle. This realization causes the collapse of the young girl's youthful aspirations. "It" could also be agency or the power to terminate the pregnancy. She responds by screaming at all the mothers, the women who came before her who did not prepare her for this experience or this particular kind of obligation:

> ¡ay, qué sorpresa!⁶
>
> and when she realized she *could* not have *It*
> gritó a todas madres
> a scream so piercing
> its blade popped each fragile sphere
>
> adrift in   air (18–23)

The young woman's shriek penetrating the "fragile" bubbles alludes to the penetration that results in the loss of virginity and frequently pregnancy. In this scene, Candelaria captures and comments on the silence that often surrounds Mexican Americans and Chicanas, particularly about their own bodies. La Llorona's scream becomes an accusation, one that implicates all women who do not teach girls about their bodies. By extension, however, the scream is a cultural recrimination of women that make discussions of these kinds taboo.

The young woman, in an attempt to retain her optimism, does not believe that what is lost remains unrecoverable. In other words, she believes that this event will not become the defining moment in her life, so she continues "looking / searching / long before the weeping" (24–26). Her instinct is, in fact, correct, for the pregnancy will not define her in the same way that the infanticide will. Readers are left to believe that at sixteen the young woman does not find what she is searching for, foreshadowing her inability to locate her lost children after the infanticide. We learn, therefore, that La Llorona's complaint and quest began before the murder of her children, for as a young woman she had the audacity to believe she could have "It"—a life filled with hope and dreams of her own making. Finally, Candelaria suggests that La Llorona's infanticide is the direct result of a community failing her.

Candelaria provides readers with her most sympathetic drawing of La Llorona in "Portrait by the River," the final installment of her poetic trilogy. In the same way that the poet gives us a glimpse of La Llorona's early life, she also recovers brief moments of peace in La Llorona's life well after the tragedy has taken place. Instead of seeing La Llorona wailing in the night, we see her bathing by the river as she rests wearily on the shore, seeking renewal from the very waters that initiated her suffering. She sits quietly by "The soft curves of el rio's current" (4). The scene is set at dusk, and the narrator tells us "La luz es todo: light is crucial" (1). When the light fades and the sun sinks below the horizon, La Llorona will once again begin to live out her fate and pierce the silence with her howl. But in these moments before sunset, the narrator reveals a different side of La Llorona as she "bends to rinse tired feet" (8). She performs a ritual bathing with waters that "Paint her flesh an instant shine / Bright as tears. Or hope" (9–10). Here, the river is both the site of La Llorona's anguish and her place of comfort. Similarly, she herself symbolizes both suffering and hope. These seemingly contradictory features commingle in the fading light of "a retreating sun" (3).

The speaker sympathetically recounts La Llorona's endless years of wandering from Tehuantepec to Culiacán, in all types of weather, repeating nightly her "lavando   llorando / andando" (16–17).[7] La Llorona, sluggish from an eternity of sleepless nights, moves "her weary flesh from shore / To shore" in the hope of recovering her children (20–21). Each night La Llorona's suffering is born anew, sending "persistent footsteps 'round every shore" (11). Returning to the final moments of light, as La Llorona rubs tired feet with "Bony hands" and smoothes back "stray wisps of hair, / Loose threads of gray on a tight weave of black," we see that she still retains the dark hair of her youth and realize that in the course of eternal punishment, her suffering has only just begun (21, 23–24). The narrator imparts a final image of La Llorona: "Each haunted glance / She sinks into river's reflection" (27–28). She haunts and is haunted by the river where her children died. As she leans over the water, she sees her babies, "Shivering cold and wet" (30), stretch out their hands to her from beneath the surface, but she cannot reach them. This initiates her nightly torment, creating what the narrator describes as "la hambre eterna" (31).[8] La Llorona's eternal hunger is created by her children, who are beyond her reach. Each night she must relive their deaths and face her inability to save them. As we are haunted by La Llorona, so is she haunted by her children.

From this series of portraits, Candelaria captures La Llorona as a human being who presumably faltered on her journey to recoup what was lost in her youth. By speaking to the silence in the lore about La Llorona's humanity, Candelaria also speaks to the way that silence is a strategy of dominance as well as a symptom of being dominated. Other cultural producers who feature La Llorona as the subject of their work frequently deny her a place as a speaking subject because she is defined almost exclusively by her wail. Candelaria, however, gives La Llorona a voice, which she then loses along with her innocence, neither of which can be recovered in the poems.

Yxta Maya Murray's "La Llorona: A Story," told in the first person, represents one of the few instances, along with Anita Endrezze's and Pat Mora's poems discussed in previous chapters, in which a cultural producer gives or returns La Llorona's voice: the one taken from her after the conquest, the loss of which limits her ability to serve as a symbol of resistance for her people. With it, La Llorona recounts her own version of events narrated in the lore. Her interpretation, however, does not resolve the legend's central issue; in fact, her story further complicates our understanding of the infanticide and the reasons behind it. Instead of highlighting La Llorona's humanity, we see that she has been turned into a "monster." Therefore, those expecting the speaking Llorona in Murray's story to offer excuses for her actions will find no satisfaction. She begins her story with a shocking scenario about cannibalism as a contrast to, and seemingly an attempt to minimize, the horror of her chosen method of infanticide: "I could have cooked them up and eaten them with some fine dark wine, a few dry crackers" (24). La Llorona provokes the reader's outrage when she makes clear that her actions were a premeditated response to win back her husband's attention. Later we learn that the depths of her despair and rage were such that if she had had the courage, she would have preferred to devour her children. La Llorona believes that had she consumed them, and her husband as well, she could have kept her family intact. Even after having suffered the consequences of her own decision, the intensity of her conviction is such that we realize this *was* a woman capable of and willing to do anything for her family. La Llorona does not use her voice to endear herself to the reader. Rather, she uses it to speak of domestic problems that went unspoken far too long in her home and community.

Murray inverts the familiar model of a storyteller recounting a Llorona tale by having the subject tell her own story directly. La Llorona recalls a time when she was still human by comparing herself to the reader: "I was once like you are" (24). The second-person address engages an ambiguous "you," though it soon becomes clear that La Llorona means "human." Her observation also alerts the reader to the fact that she has undergone a transformation from her previous state. Her former existence is revealed to have been that of a dutiful wife. In the past, she attended to the needs of her family, a responsibility that defined her life completely; prior to the infanticide, she had no name, which represents another kind of silencing or effacing. Her lack of identity and immersion in wifely duties contributed to her view that her family was *her* possession, an idea most often attributed to the man in traditional versions of the lore. La Llorona staunchly maintains that "A husband is forever, he belongs to you, as do his children. They cannot leave no matter how hard they try, it will turn them into beasts, it will make you into a monster" (24). Murray shows readers through La Llorona's subsequent actions that situations involving abandonment, neglect, and/or infidelity can physically transform everyone involved.

La Llorona acknowledges her own contribution to the now legendary outcome of her story. Prior to her husband's emotional and later physical abandonment, La Llorona performed her expected roles as a wife and mother without question. Only in hindsight does she understand the limitations placed on women. She asks, "What is a woman?" Her answer, based on first-hand experience, reveals that being a woman means "waiting" and "praying to God" (24). In other words, passivity is not only expected of women socially and culturally, but is also their defining characteristic. Biding her time until her husband returned was something she, like so many other women, was expected to do. While most traditional versions of the tale cite the infanticide as evidence of La Llorona's madness, La Llorona says that the constant waiting, of placing everyone's needs before their own, is what makes women mad: "To think of the things that will happen to you, that you will let others do to you, it is madness" (24). La Llorona is not alone in her frustrations, yet we see no cohesive community of women that might have helped make this waiting bearable. The decision to kill her children symbolizes her effort to end her isolation and disrupt the silence that defines it. The infanticide becomes a revolutionary act meant to overthrow male dominance in her own home.

Murray distinguishes her Llorona by making her a shape shifter and a suspected bruja, the latter accomplished through the narrator's identification with

Medea. The allusions to Medea (to whom the narrative refers as "a woman like me"), and references to her sewing of the deadly garment that would immolate the princess Jason married, are meant to associate La Llorona with power—not through the infanticide, but through the dark arts, specifically witchcraft.[9] The townspeople see La Llorona's ability to shape shift as evidence of her brujería and avoid her, which in turn compounds her isolation. Their fixation on La Llorona diverts their attention from the truth about the epidemic of emotional abuse and neglect in their town. Llorona's despair, loneliness, and anger about her husband's abandonment, in addition to the thought of her sons growing up to be like him, serve as catalysts for her shape shifting.[10] In the form of a mongoose, she steals into other people's houses, where she learns that her suffering is not singular. She sees "how other men take their lovers in different houses, the noise of their sex filling the late sky, sweeter than the simple duty of home" (25). The wives of these men lie at home like she did before she acquired her ability to transform. La Llorona sees an invisible community of women who are completely unaware of the existence of others like them and, because of their passivity, refuse to respond to their husbands' betrayals. La Llorona cannot see this hidden community of suffering women as a source of power because she views them as contributing to women's suffering, theirs and others', as she once did.

La Llorona's shape-shifting ability pales in comparison to the power she exerts over the lives of her children. The knowledge she gains in her altered state reinforces her resolve to make her husband suffer, which she can best accomplish in her human form, and moves her to act quickly. However, in the process of killing their children, holding them beneath the surface of the river while shrieking and howling in the wind, she too slips into the water, following her children into death. Upon learning of the fate of his family, the husband cries out in despair. His grief, which echoes La Llorona's, emasculates him, for she notes: "he cried and screamed just as a woman would, a woman with a heart in her" (26). Admitting only a "small" victory in inducing his suffering, she carries her sorrow with her into the afterlife. "Dressed in green plants," she haunts people with songs meant to induce suffering in those who are caught in or perpetuate cycles of abandonment or abuse (26).

The re-turning in this story is the most ambiguous example discussed in this chapter. On the surface, the narrative appears antifeminist and antirevisionist. In allowing La Llorona to narrate her own story, we see how she firmly believes that she was releasing her family from madness. We also listen as she tries to convince us of the "joy" she has found following her death and the deaths of the children. Yet this view is undermined when occasional memories of her former life eclipse her "joy," and when we see how little in the community has changed, for her legend has traveled only a "short distance" (27). Her act of agency changes nothing and leaves her weeping along the shore. A conservative interpretation of the re-turning, then, tells us that the story exists in its original or traditional form for a reason, and that allowing La Llorona to share her version of events does not dissipate any part of the tragedy, though like Candelaria's "At Sixteen" it does implicate others' roles in it.

Nevertheless, La Llorona's transformation after the infanticide offers readers another possibility for reading the narrative as a re-turning, one that recontextualizes her actions within the narrative by positioning her as a "goddess," a word that appears in the second line of the story. This recontextualization emphasizes La Llorona's status outside of traditional renderings of the lore and deifies her. After the tragedy La Llorona confines herself to the banks of the river, where she is dressed in green plants and has green gills. She describes her hair as "wild wet ropes around [her] breasts" that wrap around her hips and coil snake-like around her legs (26–27). Murray's Llorona, who clearly resembles the Greek goddess Medusa, also has characteristics of Coatlicue, particularly the way in which her hair forms a skirt of snakes. Yet it is through her association with the color green and her residence in and by the river that calls to mind Chalchiuhtlicue, the Mexica water goddess (figure 4.5). Patroness of birth and baptisms, Chalchiuhtlicue is described in the Florentine Codex as having "a green-stone necklace; [. . .] Her shift, her skirt were painted like water waves. She bore a shield ornamented with a water lily. [. . .] She wore foam sandals" (Sahagún, I:22). Given the necessity of water for human survival, the Mexica carefully tended to the needs of the goddess to ensure her continued presence in their lives and to acknowledge her power: "Hence she was esteemed, feared, held in awe; hence she caused terror. She drowned one, plunged one in water, submerged one; she caused the water to foam, to billow over one; she caused the water to swirl over one. Thereby she carried one into the depths" (21). In conceiving of Murray's Llorona in this way, cultural readers gain an additional understanding of her aquatic home and the power she derives from it. When we view her as a Chalchiuhtlicue figure, we can read her "offering" of her children as an attempt to secure their well-being through a cleansing and ritual rebirth that only water can provide.[11]

Reading Murray's short story as a recuperation is a subversive act because one could interpret La Llorona's narrative as the ramblings of a madwoman. While not necessarily insane, she is angry at the community's complicity and silence, which lead to the alienation of women and children. It is through the figure of Chalchiuhtlicue that cultural readers can see La Llorona's decision to commit infanticide as a response to larger cultural and social problems. Identifying the association between Chalchiuhtlicue and La Llorona in this instance requires

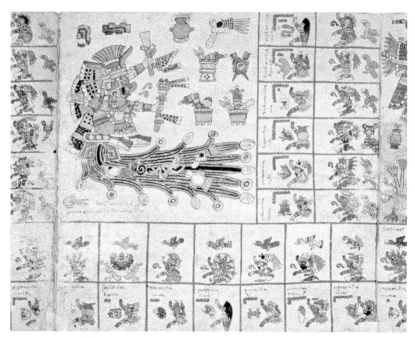

FIGURE 4.5. *Chalchiuhtlicue,* Codex Borbonicus, page 5. Note the people entangled in her skirt. Used by permission of ADEVA, GRAZ/AUSTRIA.

extensive excavation on the part of the cultural reader, but the identification is aided by certain features of the narrative. Although the above reading is dependent upon knowing specific details about figures from Mexica mythology, not all of the elements that facilitate re-turnings or recuperations are obscure. In Alma Luz Villanueva's collection *Weeping Woman: La Llorona and Other Stories,* the author foregrounds the correlation between two main characters and their antecedents in the Mexica pantheon. This relationship allows cultural readers to see the many ways in which Chalchiuhtlicue and Coyolxauhqui, the moon goddess discussed in Chapter 3, serve as metaphors for the lives of contemporary Chicanas in the urban landscape.

Villanueva directly connects her protagonist, also named Luna, to Coyolxauhqui, who symbolizes women and children lost as a result of cultural and social violence (figure 4.6). This strategy is reminiscent of Moraga's reimagining of Coyolxauhqui's human counterpart in the character Luna, though Villanueva emphasizes the other symbolic possibilities associated with the image of the moon goddess. Like Coyolxauhqui's dismembered corpse, Luna's life, and the lives of the other women and children found in the collection, is literally in pieces. Villanueva individualizes their suffering, which allows each to experience her/his own grief, no matter how horrific. As the central figure whose stories frame the collection, Luna operates as an allegorical figure that represents the imagined reality of reuniting those fragments into a symbolic whole. The author's conceptualizing of her protagonist as a contemporary Coyolxauhqui prepares the reader for the recuperation of La Llorona as Chalchiuhtlicue, the same goddess of rivers, lakes, and oceans called to mind in Murray's story.

The relationship between Luna and La Llorona parallels the one between the two goddesses and the entities associated with them: the moon and the ocean. One affects the "movement" of the other. In her guise as Luna, Coyolxauhqui directs La Llorona/Chalchiuhtlicue toward her symbolic "children" who need a rebirth or renewal in their lives.[12] La Llorona, whose actual identity as a goddess is known by only two characters, serves as a protective force to women and children who have gathered like shells on her shores. She watches over the ma-

FIGURE 4.6. Coyolxauhqui Stone, Museo del Templo Mayor, Mexico City. Used by permission of Fabrice Chassat.

jority of the female characters who experience or participate in some aspect of oppression, such as racism, classism, sexual assault, or other forms of violence. La Llorona/Chalchiuhtlicue can intervene in the lives of suffering women in limited ways, for only the women are capable of deciding the outcomes of their lives and of those around them. In making these decisions, they are literally reborn or baptized into a new phase of life. The appearance of a shell or shells in the stories becomes representative, even in La Llorona's/Chalchiuhtlicue's absence, of her watchful and protective influence in the lives of many of the characters who, like Luna, are lost. Through this representation, Villanueva, like Trina Lopez in her short film *La Llorona,* paints the woman of the water as a guardian who attends to those in need, illustrating that they are never alone in their pain or grief. While we see La Llorona's influence on a number of characters, she is most intimately connected to Luna.

After being sexually assaulted as a child, Luna receives her shell, an indication that she is under the guardianship of La Llorona. Before the attack, Luna learned about La Llorona from her grandmother, Isidra. However, Isidra's Llorona is not a helpless or tragic victim; she is, instead, a caring mother with the powers of a goddess. This markedly revised rendering of female triumph becomes the means by which Luna can save herself from the tragedies in her own life. Villanueva begins with Luna's introduction to the legend at age seven and concludes by presenting readers with four different portraits of Luna at middle age, at which time La Llorona asks to see the condition of the shell she once gave as a gift. In each instance, Luna inadvertently re-turns La Llorona/Chalchiuhtlicue to the site where they originally met, and the goddess helps Luna to rediscover that part of herself that is lost.

Luna is able to extricate herself from La Llorona's inevitable fate, proscribed in traditional versions of the lore, with the help of Isidra. We learn that since her arrival in the United States Isidra has not heard La Llorona's weeping because, she believes, there are too many gringos and not enough room for La Llorona. This absence of a source of cultural and historical identity makes even more meaningful Isidra's passing on of the tale to Luna. Isidra offers her granddaughter a story about the legendary figure that is, on the surface, a conflation of biblical lore and the conquest narrative: "When the great flood came, and the terrible men from the great ocean came, she turned her children into fish" (2). This rendering of the tale positions La Llorona as a pre-conquest goddess with the power to transform her daughters in order to save them from the Spanish invaders and establishes a direct link between La Llorona and Jade Skirt. According to the Mexicas, Chalchiuhtlicue presided over the world during the Fourth Sun until the earth was flooded with water and all of the humans turned into fish.

La Llorona, then, is not the abandoned victim of the traditional narrative but a figure of power with the means, according to Isidra, to return her children to their natural form by scooping her black shawl into the river and fishing them out. The Llorona whom Isidra constructs for Luna is one who "saved her daughters from the terrible men [of the Spanish invasion]" who killed children, although she could not save her sons, who perished in the battle against the evil marauders (3). Isidra casts La Llorona as the savior of her children, and the male invaders as their murderers. In addition, by relating that La Llorona protected her *female* children, Isidra teaches Luna that a daughter's life is valuable and worth saving. Although constructed as a sympathetic figure, the Llorona of Isidra's tale still poses a threat, for if she is unable to scoop up her children, she "kills as many people as she can. Mostly men, but one never knows" (3). In spite of this more sinister aspect, Isidra tells Luna that she does not blame the goddess for her actions because she has many reasons to be angry and every reason to weep. As a mature woman who has seen the deaths of her husband and children, Isidra is acquainted with La Llorona's suffering and sympathizes with her retaliatory actions. The grandmother makes such a compelling case for the goddess that Luna thinks she likes the legendary figure "A little bit" (4). Isidra's version of the story offers Luna a model for resistance that is accomplished by re-turning Luna to a mytho-historic past from which she can draw power.

To further subvert the tragedy of the traditional narrative, Luna is first inscribed into it, which occurs when an assailant sexually assaults her in a public park. A young man posing as a police officer assaults and threatens to kill her. Although he is not the oppressive lover of the traditional tale, in Villanueva's contemporary rendering he personifies the patriarchy's attempt to silence and oppress women. Because Luna cannot bring herself to scream, La Llorona is shown giving voice to the child's pain and suffering by weeping in the distance. La Llorona appears powerless here, but her presence at the site of violence provides Luna with the strength to survive it. As a consequence of her silence, Luna, like La Llorona, is interrogated for her role in the event; her mother does not believe that anything serious has happened to her. Isidra, on the other hand, believes Luna, who has not stopped trembling since the attack. She takes her away that night to meet La Llorona by the ocean, for she knows that to face La Llorona is to confront one's pain. When Luna sees La Llorona, who is "tall and strong," her trembling stops (7). In taking her granddaughter to see the goddess, Isidra shows Luna that women can overcome their suffering and that La Llorona can help others avoid becoming lost in their grief. With the help of Isidra's empowering view of La Llorona, Luna moves past, with varying degrees of success, her traumatic experience.

Readers revisit Luna in the concluding stories of the collection, when Villa-nueva presents four different portraits of Luna's life at middle age. In these sec-tions, the author recuperates other symbolic possibilities for La Llorona by pre-senting her as a guardian or muse who provides Luna with the means to come to terms with her troubled past and transcend the traditional La Llorona narrative into which she was cast years earlier in the park. The beach setting brings the collection full circle as Luna returns to the site where she first saw La Llorona and was given the means to write herself out of her own tragic narrative. She explains to the Weeping Woman the choices she has made since that time, and we see the positive presence La Llorona has been in Luna's life, even in the most desperate of situations. La Llorona, unlike God in some conventional versions, does not sit in moralistic judgment of Luna's confession. Instead, she helps Luna, now an archetypal suffering woman with four different narratives and identities, to recover what she has lost.

Villanueva's dark foray into the tragedy of women's and children's lives con-cludes with four images of hope, and they are all connected to the healing pres-ence of La Llorona. As a child, Luna learns about a Weeping Woman of the water who has the powers of a beneficent goddess who is not victimized by men, and who not only survives but also overcomes adversity. It is this image of the goddess with the power to save her children that becomes a source of strength for Luna. Although she temporarily loses sight of this power, La Llorona/ Chalchiuhtlicue revisits her at age fifty to help her recover her confidence, find forgiveness, recon-cile her seemingly contradictory identities, and show the importance of handing down stories of female power. In recasting La Llorona as a protective rather than threatening figure, Villanueva restores her power to heal and watch over her symbolic children who are disappearing in the urban landscape. Looking at the Coyolxauhqui stone, we can imagine a unified or whole female form through a process of reassembly. La Llorona/Chalchiuhtlicue serves as a force that helps Luna and the reader reconcile their different parts to see that the power and force associated with water is such that it can alter destinies or carve out new ones, even those written in stone.

Re-turning a Her-story of Power

Another kind of radical recuperation involves identifying La Llorona's Meso-american antecedents in order to associate her with divinity and reinstate a sense of awesome female power into the story. Cherríe Moraga, for example, includes Coatlicue, Coyolxauhqui, and the Cihuateteo in a larger conversation about the systematic and cultural progression of patriarchy as it works to diminish women's power and their historical and cultural connections to figures of power. These goddesses, along with Cihuacoatl (Snake Woman) and, in more recent cultural productions, Chalchiuhtlicue (Jade Skirt), also represent figures analogous to La Llorona.[13] As such, reading for recuperations or re-turnings entails either identifying the ways in which cultural producers position La Llorona as a direct descendent of the Mexica goddesses or reimagine her as an actual goddess.[14] Therefore, this strategy requires knowledge not only of the deities but also of the iconography associated with each.

When looked at historically and within the context of the Mexica worldview, however, the use of these figures as antecedents for La Llorona presents certain problems. For example, some of the goddesses are associated with a hunger for blood, particularly Cihuacoatl, whose priests complained at the palace of the emperor every eight days that the goddess was "starving" (Brundage, 170). Human sacrifice characterized the ritualistic theatre of daily Mexica existence, yet sacrifice and the shedding of blood in religious ceremonies are not exclusive to any one religion or set of spiritual practices. Ana Castillo asserts in *Massacre of the Dreamers* (1994), which takes its title from Motecuçoma's response to his magicians' unsatisfactory interpretation of the portents, that "the mythology that has affected civilization in the last four to five thousand years was created out of the imaginations of men" (106). In the interest of power, these men also decided how to interpret and apply these mythologies, which they then used, according to Castillo, to launch a "direct attack against woman as creatrix" (106). An excellent example illustrating this kind of manipulation of a female goddess again involves Cihuacoatl's priests, who "at unscheduled times" were known to surreptitiously hide a bundled sacrificial knife in the marketplace:

> There it would be left in the custody of some unsuspecting female vendor, who was asked to tend it until it was called for. It was, of course, not called for. Eventually, before the day was over, the bundle would be unwrapped and the grisly secret would come out: the goddess had been among the people and had left her thirsty offspring as a sign that the lords were not feeding her properly. Thus was pressure constantly exerted upon the state to seek further wars so that Snake Woman need not lack sustenance. (Brundage, 170)

Reimagining La Llorona and re-turning her to her antecedents, then, within the context of the male-created and -controlled pantheon becomes a subversive act that challenges Native, and later Christian, religious practices controlled by men. Those unfamiliar with the critical conversations taking place among the

Chican@ intelligentsia about the disempowerment of the female goddess may feel alienated from this reading strategy. Yet these cultural productions represent direct efforts to re-turn La Llorona to and for her community by conceiving of her as derived from powerful forebears whose history belongs to all of us.

Villanueva gives La Llorona the powers of a goddess, but she never identifies one specifically. Only in the history that Isidra recounts and in her physical description does she become identifiable as Chalchiuhtlicue. Juana Alicia Montoya, a painter of Russian and Tejana ancestry, places an unmistakable image of Jade Skirt side by side with La Llorona in her mural *La Llorona's Sacred Waters* (2004), located on the corner of Twenty-fourth and York Streets in the Mission District of San Francisco.[15] Juana Alicia relies primarily on shades of blue and red, the colors of water and blood, both necessary for life. Chalchiuhtlicue, depicted with a tear rolling from her left eye, presides over the mural. The property most associated with the goddess, water, is used to unite women in Mexico, India, and Chile in their opposition to governmental and industrial policies and/or practices that exploit women and the poor. In one portion of the mural, set in Ciudad Juárez, Mexico, women protest the ineffectiveness—or, as some believe, unwillingness—of the local police and Mexican government in investigating the brutal murders of hundreds of young women, many of whom worked in the factories along the border.[16] On the opposite end of the mural, women in the Indian states of Gujarat, Maharashtra, and Madhya Pradesh stand chest deep in water to demonstrate against the damning of the river in the Narmada Valley, which floods their ancestral homelands and makes their residences uninhabitable. Between the scenes set in India and Mexico, we see women in Cochabamba, Bolivia, face off against police to protest the exorbitant increase in the price of water set by the Bechtel Corporation, the construction and engineering conglomerate contracted by Bolivia to oversee water distribution. These women across the globe are connected through their resistance as well as loss. Juana Alicia highlights the strength these women exhibit in the struggle for control of a natural resource, something polluted and held captive by men and corporations but given freely to those who attend to and respect the power of Chalchiuhtlicue.

Amidst these scenes from around the globe, La Llorona, with a tear falling from her right eye, appears in the mural kneeling right of center. The goddess and La Llorona are connected not simply through the symmetry of their tears, but also through the image of a water lily, the flower often featured on a shield carried by the goddess.[17] La Llorona's right hand reaches out across or toward the water. On her wrist she wears a bracelet etched with water lilies. It is through this image of the aquatic plant that Juana Alicia recovers an ambiguous relationship between the goddess and the Weeping Woman of legend. Cultural readers may conclude that La Llorona is under the goddess' protection or that she is a human manifestation of the deity. In either case, La Llorona is not portrayed as an entity that causes suffering. Instead she suffers along with women around the globe and reaches out to the restorative and nurturing powers of water. While the mural, as Leticia Hernandez observes, "falls within a tradition of rewriting the Mexican mythology of women ongoing since the 70's by Chicana artists and writers [. . .]," Juana Alicia demonstrates the imagistic power of recuperating Indigenous female icons. Displaced by the conquest, both Chalchiuhtlicue and La Llorona represent the effects of colonization or, in this case, globalization, on Indigenous communities.

All of the images and scenes found in the mural flow from Chalchiuhtlicue, an effect meant to demonstrate that she is a source of sustenance and that the boundaries or circumstances that separate the lives of the individuals featured in the mural are arbitrary. In the goddess' cascading skirt of water, we see people drawing nourishment from the life-giving source. The fishermen and the woman gathering water represent the people who were most devoted to the goddess: "those who gained their livelihoods from water, those who brought water in boats, those who owned boats, those who lived on the water, the boatmakers, those who served water in the market place" (Sahagún, I:22). Yet historically Chalchiuhtlicue was revered by all, and the people "paid honor to the waters, [for] they remembered that because of her we live. She is our sustenance. And thence come all things that are necessary" (22). Juana Alicia's mural suggests that La Llorona now weeps for this forgotten connection.

La Llorona is the second largest image in the mural. Calling to mind the radiant heavenly aura emanating from the Virgen, Juana Alicia creates the same effect by positioning La Llorona, on an earth-bound plane, in front of a prickly pear cactus. Through this reimagined and repositioned La Llorona, Juana Alicia offers women a potent Mexican symbol of female resistance whose own story can accommodate those new forces at work that separate us from our children. She is a massive figure with large hands, breasts, arms, and legs, all of which are meant to communicate strength and power. Nothing in the mural, however, suggests that La Llorona poses a threat to those around her, in particular the child encircled in her loving embrace. Her left arm wraps around the child's waist with her hand positioned in front of him, holding him back from the water. Juana Alicia depicts the legendary figure reaching out with her right hand to the water, but the water is polluted, so it can no longer nourish or restore. La Llorona gently restrains the boy to keep him from getting too close to the poisoned river. As imagined by Juana Alicia, La Llorona weeps for the destruction and pollution of the environment by factories along the Mexico/US border—and for our failure to protect this life-sustaining element.

The mural identifies the maquiladores, positioned over the boy's shoulder, as the main source of pollution, both environmental and social, along the border. Smoke belches from the factory stacks, forming blood-red crescents in the sky, and waste runoff pours out of the factory into the river. In addition to this output, the factories also generate violence and death. Inadequate pay, housing, and transportation, along with the economic disenfranchisement of Mexican males, make the young women who leave their native communities to work in the factories vulnerable to other kinds of pollution: exploitation, sexual assault, and murder. Between the factories and La Llorona are mothers, clad mostly in black, wandering along the shore of the Rio Bravo and crying out for justice for their murdered daughters. Juana Alicia depicts this area as a wasteland where rolled razor wire lines the top of the border fence, and Blackhawk helicopters and owls, as competing symbols of death, fly overhead. In contrast to the image of Chalchiuhtlicue, water as represented in the border scene offers neither life nor livelihood.

Because women are not alone in their struggle against globalization and injustice, Juana Alicia does not exclude men entirely from the mural. La Llorona protects a male child, and the artist positions men, young and old, in the scenes set in India and Chile. But the artist purposely assigns males secondary roles in order to celebrate the heroism of women. While these minor images position men as allies in social change, the fact remains that infanticide by mothers is far more rare than the deaths of children by male-dominated endeavors such as war, pollution, and corporate negligence. In this sense, the traditional tale obscures primarily male responsibility for the murder of children, represented by the most prominent male in the mural. Appearing to the left of Chalchiuhtlicue, he is offered as the source of the oppressive forces at work on women and children, namely Christianity, industrial globalization, and corporate greed. Juana Alicia recasts the biblical tale of David and Goliath as a metaphor for a contemporary battle that took place in Bolivia between the impoverished natives and the multinational conglomerate Bechtel. The bottoms of the man's boots are stamped with a logo bearing a likeness to the company's emblem, thus coding the man as the embodiment of the corporation. The image captures the David-like victory of the Boliviana over the corporate giant, who is shown falling backward as a result of a few well-thrown stones.

The rewriting of the biblical narrative is not the only reference to Christianity. A chalice, an object often associated with Christ (known in the Bible as "the living water"), falls from the man's left hand, symbolizing the release of his controlling grip over the life-giving water and, by extension, over people's lives. By infusing the scene with allusions to and symbols of Christianity, Juana Alicia positions men and God in opposition to women and Chalchiuhtlicue, for the men act as gods in their control and taking of, rather than giving, the resource. Whereas Juana Alicia has water flowing from Chalchiuhtlicue as a natural extension of her body, it erupts from the man's chest wounds, draining him of the water he has held hostage. The image symbolizes the way in which men/corporations covet and seek to control natural resources for profit. In the man's body, the water, stripped of its creative energy, is transmuted into a wholly destructive force, like corporate greed. The effects are depicted in the mural through scenes that call to mind the biblical flood and the flooded villages in the Narmada Valley in India where the river is "DAMNED," the land is "DOOMED," and the people are "DROWNED," as one protestor's sign indicates. The man's position, on his back, in contrast to the standing Chalchiuhtlicue, visually reinstates the authority of the goddess and positions her as a creative force opposed to the man's destructive power.

While death and destruction are tied to each of the scenes featured in the mural, Juana Alicia does not include them directly, choosing instead to emphasize how communities of women have mobilized to effect change with various outcomes around the world. For example, as a result of the protest in Cochabamba, the Bolivian government cancelled its contract with Bechtel, which in retaliation filed a $25 million lawsuit. In the face of mounting criticism from the international community, along with protests in San Francisco, Bechtel dropped the lawsuit in January 2006.[18] While the victory in Bolivia is unquestionable, the women in Mexico and India still await justice. These women, who share in a global struggle over water, are united under the mural's two central figures. Juana Alicia demonstrates that La Llorona and Chalchiuhtlicue can serve as potent symbols of power not only for Mexicanas and Chicanas, but also for women around the globe.[19]

La Llorona's AlterNative Antecedents: Toward a New Past

Thus far, I have focused exclusively on Chalchiuhtlicue as an antecedent for La Llorona, but because Chican@ cultural producers are turning to other goddesses in the Mexica pantheon to tease out new, and in some cases re-turn old, meanings to La Llorona, cultural readers should look to these goddesses as well. Some artists are even choosing to conflate deities to bring to the surface their overlapping or shared characteristics. Painter, muralist, teacher, children's book author, and Los Angeles native José Ramírez infuses in his painting *Ciocoatl/Chalchiuhtli* (1999; oil on canvas) the physical attributes of both goddesses. Neither is named as a precursor to La Llorona or directly connected to La Llorona.[20] Instead this relationship is implied through the selection of the piece as the cover art for Luis D. León's book *La Llorona's Children: Religion, Life, and Death in the U.S.-Mexican Borderlands* (2004), in which the author uses La Llorona as a "guiding metaphor" for his "recovery of borderlands prophecy and memory" (21, 16). As a paratextual element, the cover art offers an Indigenous starting point for León's discussion about the evolution of contemporary Mexican American religious belief and practices.[21]

Ramírez fuses Chalchiuhtlicue with a much older, and some would argue more powerful, deity, Cihuacoatl (Snake Woman), an alternate aspect of Coatlicue, who, as Burr Cartwright Brundage indicates, "has some claim to be considered the most feared and effective of all the goddesses" (168). Her reputation derives from her physical countenance and the fact that "more victims were offered to her than to any other goddess" (170).[22] According to Native accounts, "as she appeared before men, she was covered with chalk, like a court lady. She wore ear plugs, obsidian ear plugs. She appeared in white, garbed in white, standing white, pure white" (Sahagún, I:11). The pronounced emphasis on her white appearance, along with her tendency to walk by night "weeping, wailing," establishes a correlation between Cihuacoatl and La Llorona (I:11). Cihuacoatl's appetite for human victims furthers this connection, calling attention to the predatory nature of both the goddess and La Llorona. As a goddess of significant power, whose roar was an omen of war, "[Cihuacoatl] was referred to as a horror and a devourer: she brought nothing but misery and toil and death" (Brundage, 168). While the goddess maintains most of her prominent features in the guise of La Llorona, she is stripped of her ability to rouse her people with her roar.

The dominant theme of the painting, independent of the book's title, is death. Ramírez complicates this view through the title of the work, which suggests life, rebirth, and renewal, as associated with Cihuacoatl and Chalchiuhtlicue. A young, shapely Native woman reaches out with arms stretched wide as if to offer an embrace. The lower half of her body forms a point, calling to mind a knife. These physical attributes align the figure primarily with Cihuacoatl, who possessed the "ability to change herself into a serpent or into a lovely young woman who could entice young men who, after intercourse with her, withered away and died" and who carried on her back a sacrificial obsidian blade "swaddled as if it were her child" (169). But Chalchiuhtlicue, like many gods of the Mexicas, also required a human sacrifice, and each year a young woman was offered to honor the goddess.[23] Radiating out from the image are churning lines reminiscent of

water or fire, both elements of purification and renewal. Thus as a Chalchiuhtlicue figure, the woman is offering both death and life.

The positioning of the book's title between the goddess' outstretched arms
transforms the Ciocoatl/Chalchiuhtli in the painting into La Llorona, who, in ac-
cordance with both conventional versions of the lore and known characteristics
of the goddesses, is either reaching out for her children or trying to seduce men.
The addition of the book's title thus creates a visual palimpsest revealing the one
way in which La Llorona's story is written over much older stories about female
power and sacrifice. Assembling Cihuacoatl, Chalchiuhtlicue, and La Llorona
into one visual space complicates the history of La Llorona and our reading of
her in the present.

Artist Santa Barraza, a native of Kingsville, Texas, re-turns our attention to
an additional figure in the pantheon so that we might consider the parallels between Chicomecoatl, the corn goddess, and La Llorona. The artist features the
legendary figure in several works, including the retablo *Apparition of La Llorona*
(1994; oil and enamel on metal, 11″ × 16″), *La Llorona I* (1995; charcoal drawing
on paper, 48″ × 97″), *La Llorona II/The Weeping Woman* (1995; oil on canvas, 49″
× 87″), and *Teotl* (1995; charcoal drawing on canvas, 112″ × 74″). Each piece is
discussed in detail in *Santa Barraza, Artist of the Borderlands* (2001), edited by
María Herrera-Sobek.[24] Barraza, who shares her own insights on her work in an
autobiography included in the collection, believes La Llorona's legend emerged
from the myth of the Cihuateteo, feared women "associated with bodies of water,
the transformative element of the journey of death, and crossroads" (Herrera-
Sobek, *Santa,* 30). Unlike Moraga, the artist depicts, in individual works, Coatlicue and Coyolxauhqui, along with the Cihuateteo, as being intimately connected to La Llorona. In all of these representations, as Herrera-Sobek notes,
"La Llorona is reconceptualized and reinterpreted as a figure denoting life and
renewal" (xix). Barraza offers an overall more empowering view of La Llorona
by associating her with the goddesses.

The choice to align La Llorona and Chicomecoatl therefore seems obvious,
for the latter held power over the people through her ability to provide a renewed
source of sustenance and nourishment necessary for life.[25] Presented in codex
format, *Diosa del Maíz y la Llorona* (1993; acrylic on canvas, 43½″ × 39¾″) features Chicomecoatl with an arm stretched out toward the sun in a pose reminiscent of a plant leaning toward the light to draw nourishment (figure 4.7). Her
other hand points down, directing the sunlight toward the earth, toward her
roots. The form is important, for pre-Columbian codices represented "one of
the first formats for extensive methodical thinking and written communication
in the Americas" (Barraza, 47).[26] In using the codex format to encourage con-

FIGURE 4.7. *Diosa del Maíz y la Llorona* (acrylic on canvas, 43½″ × 39¾″),
by Santa Barraza © 1996. Used by permission of the artist.

temporary critical reflections on La Llorona, Barraza re-turns a pre-Hispanic
heritage to Chican@s and offers "the world at large a window into a sacred space
that at times has been forgotten or repressed, to the detriment of all concerned"
(Herrera-Sobek, *Santa*, xix). The combined form and subject of the piece ask us
to reflect critically on La Llorona's past and our own.

As noted by art historian Constance Cortez, Barraza often employs the technique of merging "pre-Columbian and colonial pasts with contemporary realities," as in this work (36). If we interpret the sun in the upper left-hand corner of
the canvas as a compass rose, also featured as the first in a row of symbols at the
bottom of the piece, then Chicomecoatl is facing west, toward the setting sun. At
her back, in the east, La Llorona stands in a maguey plant. The image represents
the coming of a new age. In the west, the sun sets on the Mexicas and rises over
the Spaniards, who will transform goddesses like Chicomecoatl into weeping
women; however, La Llorona's position in the ancient maguey complicates this
reading, for though she represents change, she also represents the permanence

of the land and its Native people.[27] Brundage offers Mecitli, believed to mean "Maguey Grandmother," as one source of the tribal name Mexica.[28] Some argue that Mecitli "was simply another name for Huitzilopochtli," but if the tribal name is derived from that of a goddess, then a sacred woman is both the source and at the very center of tribal identity (135). La Llorona, then, is not standing in but emerging from the maguey, positioning her simultaneously as a visible representation of the goddess and the Mexicas. Therefore, as long as magueys survive, so do the Mexicas and La Llorona.

The artifacts analyzed above encourage cultural readers to prefigure La Llorona's transformation from Native goddess and/or woman into her now legendary state as depicted in the lore. But the final artifact discussed in this chapter challenges the original reading of the portent documented in the codices. In the darkly comedic novel *So Far From God*, Ana Castillo re-turns cultural readers to "the sixth sign" to suggest that its originator was a *goddess* wailing, weeping, shouting, or merely speaking, depending on the source and translation, about the future of her children.[29] The narrator directly cites several corresponding figures in Mexica mythology that may have given rise to La Llorona's legend but privileges Cihuacoatl. The goddess' post-conquest disenfranchised state exposes the effects of the ongoing project involving the erosion of female power, a project that began when the "male-dominated Azteca-Mexica culture drove the powerful female deities underground by giving them monstrous attributes and by substituting male deities in their place [. . .]" (Anzaldúa, *Borderlands*, 27). The Catholicism of the Spanish, particularly during the colonial era, facilitated the continuation of this legacy, which is still at work on the novel's matriarch, Sofi, and her four "fated" daughters. Though many women in the novel are fated, they are not helpless. According to Theresa Delgadillo, the novel "counters a pervasive stereotype of Chicanas as passive individuals victimized by oppression or subordinated by a patriarchal church by presenting a cast of female characters who resist domination every day of their lives—though some days more successfully than others" (888).[30] This resistance manifests in the re-turning of La Llorona to recover alterNative sources for the legendary figure.[31] So while cultural readers may not have to sift through the entire pantheon of gods in search of antecedents for La Llorona, Castillo's work presents readers with a different set of problems that involve reconsidering the cultural and social implications of this re-turn, which directly challenges the authority of the Catholic Church and the use and form of the conventional folktale.

Castillo imagines the implications of interpreting the original sign simultaneously as Cihuacoatl's lament and a call to action. Such an interpretation reveals that women have the power to transmute grief into a galvanizing force for change. Re-turning La Llorona to a place among her Mexica predecessors restores her power and, in some cases, extricates her from the colonial narrative, but it does not necessarily make her immune to the effects of patriarchal authority as seen in the novel. Nevertheless, Castillo clearly positions women as revolutionary agents with the power to answer Cihuacoatl's call and shape a new future.[32]

The five female protagonists—Sofi; her youngest daughter, La Loca; and her three older daughters, whose names call to mind the Christian virtues as identified by the apostle Paul in 1 Corinthians 13:13, Esperanza (Hope), Fe (Faith), and Caridad (Charity)—suffer for or are redeemed by their individual personal and professional desires, which often run counter to the male-dominated, heterosexist world in which they live. La Llorona emerges as a key figure in the lives of these women, especially for Sofi and Esperanza. As she exists in conventional versions of the tale, La Llorona represents, on numerous levels, what Sofi and her daughters are struggling against. Sofi's decision to reject the patriarchal allegory embedded in La Llorona's story and her refusal to pass on any version of La Llorona's story to her daughters allows them to discover the legendary figure on their own and live beyond the gender constraints present in conventional versions of the folktale. After recuperating La Llorona's more empowering aspects, ones derived from Mexica goddesses, Sofi rejects, revises, and finally embraces La Llorona.

On the surface, Sofi's decision to withhold La Llorona lore from her daughters is empowering, allowing them to imagine possibilities other than depending on men for economic and emotional security. For example, the life of Sofi's eldest daughter, Esperanza, in many ways parallels that of La Llorona. When her college beau, Rubén, leaves her to marry a wealthy Anglo woman and starts a family with her in the suburbs, Esperanza does not fall into despair. Although La Llorona's abandonment by her lover for a woman of higher station leads to her incessant mourning, Esperanza's capacity for happiness does not die after Rubén leaves. Instead, she places all of her energy into advancing her broadcasting career. Yet when Rubén's wife leaves him for another man, he returns to Esperanza, prompting her to give up a job opportunity as an anchorwoman to rekindle the disempowering romance. B. J. Manríquez observes that "[b]ecause she harbors an attraction for machos, she continues to allow her renegade boyfriend to use her for sex and spending money" (42). Nevertheless, Esperanza eventually severs the relationship to accept an offer in Washington, D.C., as a media correspondent. We also learn that while in college she was an organizer who fought for the Chicano Studies program, rallied students, and advocated the causes of La Raza. It is there that she learned about the legend, and we see that she is free to decide its meaning on her own. Even though she is a modern woman attempting to build a professional name for herself, Esperanza identifies with La Llorona's struggles, but she relies on a feminist reconfiguration of the tale that casts La Llorona as a loving mother.

By relying on her own interpretation of the legend, Esperanza, even in death, is able to speak through La Llorona to comfort her family, a move that becomes necessary after she is kidnapped, tortured, and killed while reporting on the first Gulf War. Moreover, Esperanza is the first to re-turn and imagine La Llorona as a loving mother goddess, a decision that lays the groundwork for Sofi to do the same. Believing that the woman of legend will relay news of her death to her family with great sympathy and offer them comfort, Esperanza asks La Llorona to contact her youngest sister, La Loca. Esperanza effectively uses the elements of the lore, such as the river and time of day that La Llorona is known to appear, to communicate with her family. Additionally, she not only revises La Llorona's role by entrusting this figure of scorn with a most delicate task, but she also imagines La Llorona as a caring entity who, as a result of her own suffering, can comfort the living. The narrator reinforces this redefinition of La Llorona when recounting Esperanza's ghostly reflections: "Who better but La Llorona could the spirit of Esperanza have found, come to think of it, if not a woman who had been given a bad rap by every generation of her people since the beginning of time and yet, to Esperanza's spirit-mind, La Llorona in the beginning (before men got in the way of it all) may have been nothing short of a loving mother goddess" (162–163). In Esperanza's view, men stripped the goddesses of their power but allowed them to retain their defining characteristics, while at the same time translating these goddesses' power over life and death into the infanticide found in most modern versions of the Llorona legend. Esperanza carries with her, even in death, a revisionist perspective of La Llorona that re-turns her former power "before men got in the way of it all" (163).

In order for La Llorona to facilitate healing for Esperanza's grieving family, Sofi must confront her own negative views of La Llorona's construction within the patriarchal allegory to receive Esperanza's (Hope's) message. Sofi must re-visit the story she heard as a child from her father and come to terms with La Llorona's legacy and its meaning in her life in order to reunite with the spirit of her murdered child. In her youth, Sofi not only rejected her father's version of the folktale, but also asserted her agency by denying the very existence of a Weeping Woman. She refused to believe her father's scary bedtime stories, for she could not understand why La Llorona's punishment was meted out before Judgment Day. Dismissing the truth of the tale, the young Sofi discerns correctly that parents use the story as a scare tactic to control their daughters, "a kind of 'boogy-woman,' to scare children into behaving themselves, into not straying too far from their mothers' watchful eyes" (160). Sofi's rejection of the legend gave her the freedom to do adventurous things as a child without fear, such as swim in the river alone. Later she marries the man she loves, without the consent of her father or the sanction of the Church. Sofi's refusal to internalize the prescribed roles for women, as presented in sources like the folktale, permits her to live beyond conventional social and cultural strictures. For her, anything, including a life alone, is possible.

Sofi's rejection of La Llorona's story as a patriarchal allegory about the dangers of defying male authority is what allows her to think critically about La Llorona and the legend's origins. While Sofi is aware of what La Llorona meant to people like her father, she calls upon an Indigenous mytho-historic past to make meaning of La Llorona in the present. Like Esperanza, Sofi comes to believe that La Llorona could have been a goddess:

> Matlaciuatl, the goddess of the Mexica who was said to prey upon men like a vampire! Or she might have been Ciuapipiltin, the goddess in flowing robes who stole babies from their cradles and left in their place an obsidian blade, or Cihuacoatl, the patron of women who died in childbirth, who all wailed and wept and moaned in the night air. (161)[33]

Sofi looks beyond the male-generated stories about the Weeping Woman to conceive of La Llorona in a way that speaks to her and her daughters, and she later uses this knowledge to re-view her own life. Like the women in her family, the goddesses Sofi recalls are active, even in their grief. Though Sofi gains a new understanding about La Llorona by a re-turning, she has yet to see the way in which the unfolding of her own life has contributed to this new, empowering view.

Sofi's re-turning is replicated on a narrative level when we see that her own life closely resembles that of La Llorona's. After Sofi's husband leaves, she is known as "la Abandonada," the abandoned woman. She even measures her life directly against La Llorona's and in doing so reveals the inadequacy of the comparison: "Sofi had not left her children, much less drowned them to run off with nobody. [. . .] And all her life, there had always been at least one woman around like her, left alone, abandoned, divorced, or widowed, to raise her children, and none of them had ever tried to kill their babies" (161). Sofi's own life illustrates that women do not necessarily collapse after the men in their lives leave, as she raises and supports her children alone while running the family business.

The elements of Sofi's life appear to mirror those of La Llorona's, especially as she begins to lose her daughters one by one, but Sofi retains the strength she spent a lifetime building. After La Loca relates La Llorona's message that Esperanza has been tortured to death, Sofi *does* collapse in grief, though not like a distraught Llorona; rather, she and her mournful daughters are described as "Cihuacoatls," women of power: "all three women began to wail and moan like Cihuacoatls, holding each other and grieving over the loss of Sofi's oldest child" (162). Significantly, after receiving La Llorona's message, Sofi remembers that Domingo did not in fact make the decision to leave her; she had ordered him to leave, an important detail that everyone, including Sofi, had forgotten for twenty years. With this realization, Sofi responds to Cihuacoatl's call for action by again sending away her husband, who has recently returned only to lose the family home and business as a result of his gambling debts. She also establishes an organization called M.O.M.A.S (Mothers of Martyrs and Saints) that places women in the center of contemporary Catholicism. This recovery of her mythic memory facilitates Sofi's healing and gives her the strength to continue moving forward with her life, even after the deaths of all four daughters. In other words, as Manríquez attests, "[. . .] Sofi survives because she is able to work through and with the customs and cultures she inherited. Without turning her back on her culture, she modifies it" (47). The outcome of the novel proves liberating for both Sofi and Cihuacoatl/La Llorona. Sofi translates her grief into cultural and political action, illustrating Delgadillo's point about the larger objectives of a novel that "asks us to see cultural resistance alongside political resistance, and to recognize women as agents of social change" (889). By uniting other mothers who share experiences similar to her own, Sofi creates a critical mass of women who, indeed, initiate change in the Catholic Church. On the other hand, La Llorona's power is re-membered in the figure of Cihuacoatl, knowledge that Sofi carries with her and uses to shape a new Fe/Faith and future where Esperanza/Hope and Caridad/Charity can endure.

By imagining La Llorona outside of the tragedy that defines her, or by narratively and visually connecting La Llorona to an Indigenous past, the cultural artifacts turn us toward an important part of our history. Echoing Thomas King's idea, Anaya reminds us "we have a long history and many stories to tell. The stories from our tradition have much to tell us about the knowledge we need in our journey" ("La Llorona," 55). So while La Llorona provides one method of telling us where we have been, she can also tell us where we are going. Whether we imagine her wailing, shouting, or roaring, what is most important is that we continue to imagine and hear her, for as the next chapter highlights, she is moving beyond the boundaries of her cultural community. As she makes this potentially perilous border crossing, critical reading strategies rooted in Chican@ storytelling traditions can help us not only to evaluate but also to engage in meaningful dialogue with non-native cultural productions so that together we can safeguard her future and our own.

FIVE

La Llorona Lore as Intercultural Dialogue

Dialogue has never existed between the First and Third worlds. We must not confuse dialogue with neo-colonialism, paternalism, vampirism, or appropriation.

—GUILLERMO GÓMEZ-PEÑA

THE CRITICAL STRATEGIES offered in the previous chapters are useful also for reading La Llorona artifacts generated by non-Chican@s. Critical interpretive strategies of La Llorona lore provide us with a means of reclaiming the power of interpretation, the power to reconstruct our own images, and the power to determine meaning, even if we are not the ones responsible for creating those images. The objective of this chapter is to analyze what happens to La Llorona when people who are not Latin@ or of Mexican ancestry produce artifacts that represent her story and image.[1] When encountering artifacts that represent La Llorona, cultural readers should ask the following of both the image and/or the artist: How is La Llorona being used? How is she being represented? What are our reactions to these representations?

We must be mindful of the way in which those outside of La Llorona's native or parent culture appropriate or represent her and/or her story to their benefit and our detriment, in spite of the fact that "cultural activists of color will continue to be lambasted for attempting to control access to images and ideas through notions of cultural property" (Fusco, 76). The possibility of self-representation for native artists certainly exists, but these productions, especially ones that include La Llorona as contesting or critiquing sources of oppression, are often ignored or in direct competition with representations generated by those outside of the parent culture. For instance, based on availability and distribution, mainstream readers are more likely to encounter La Llorona in the novel *Summerland* (2002) by Michael Chabon due to the author's international reputation and the massive promotional campaign funded by Hyperion Books, a division of Miramax, than in Monica Palacios' short story "La Llorona Loca: The Other Side," which appears in *Chicana Lesbians: The Girls Our Mothers Warned Us About* (1991) from Third Woman Press, a small publisher with limited promotion resources. While overshadowing other cultural productions, Chabon and Miramax profit simultaneously from the production and circulation of a book that promotes La Llorona—and by association, her native community—as both a monster and helpless victim.

I want to state explicitly that I am not insisting that only Mexican@s and Chican@s or Latin@s should engage in cultural transmission of the lore. Ideally, cultural producers of La Llorona artifacts, native and non-native alike, should privilege, whenever possible, sources from inside La Llorona's native community and augment their representations with an acknowledgment of how La Llorona functions, as well as what she can represent, within that community. For example, photographer and artist Douglas Kent Hall's multimedia piece *La Llorona* (2004), which is part of his "Border" series, includes a photo, barbed wire, and other found objects. In an interview about the work, Hall explains that "The images are more spontaneous than they are thought-out ideas of what I might say or how I might use an image for a meaning. They are really what the border has to say about itself" (pers. comm. 2005). Instead of speaking for La Llorona or the border, he tries to allow both to speak for themselves. Artist Rob Jefferson also features the legend as the subject of his woodcut print *La Llorona* (2003). The image is layered in such a way that the woman at the center of the work could be read as a Llorona whose fate is being overseen by a ghostly, weeping woman in white (figure 5.1). Through the litter of bottles, tires, and discarded shoes, Jefferson casts pollution and poverty as the forces at work on the woman who is "in a world of discarded items" where "nothing holds value" (pers. comm. 2005).[2] Jefferson admits to constructing his version of La Llorona from "an amalgam of many versions of the story" gathered by sifting through Greater Mexican cultural elements found on the Internet.

More than simply drawing from material sources on La Llorona, Angela Alston, in her short film *The Weeping Woman: Tales of La Llorona* (1993), balances her own creative vision with recountings by four Tejanas whose voices are actually included in the production (figure 5.2). The filmmaker replicates the lore along with her own visual interpretations, a brief history of the legend, and

FIGURE 5.1. *La Llorona* (2003, woodcut print, 30″ × 22″), by Rob Jefferson © 2003.
Used by permission of Clay Street Press, Inc.

academic commentary on folktales.[3] She does not limit herself to strict interpretations of the oral narratives recounted in the film. Instead, she "weaves together
impressionistic visual images drawn from the story and the evocative Texas landscape" and intersperses black-and-white images with the sporadic use of color
"to produce a dream-like effect."[4] Her creative vision is reflected in the stylization
of the film, which combines the visual characteristics of film noir, French New
Wave films, and Hollywood horror from the Golden Age of cinema. Alston's
privileging of the Tejana voices foregrounds La Llorona's folk community and
allows them to define their own complex relationships to the lore through the

FIGURE 5.2. Still of Renée Nuñez as La Llorona in *The Weeping Woman: Tales of La Llorona* © 1993. Used by permission of Angela Alston, director.

narratives they tell. The result is a highly captivating film that ends too quickly and leaves the viewer wanting more.

Hall, Jefferson, and Alston offer compelling depictions of La Llorona and/or her legend. All of these artists, despite their ethnicity, approach the subject matter with respect, not by representing La Llorona or the legend positively, but rather by drawing from the geographic and cultural communities that gave rise to and sustain the legend. They also highlight forces at work on La Llorona's cultural community, such as militarized borders and poverty. Non-native artists who represent La Llorona must work to convey her complexity and the various levels on which she can operate to dispel any assumption on the part of the reader that non-native renderings are authoritative. Fulfilling this obligation can contribute to a substantive intercultural dialogue about La Llorona that can promote a broader understanding of the long history of contact and conflict between Chican@s and other communities in the United States.

For many years, Joe Hayes, a long-time storyteller in the American Southwest, has devoted himself to the promotion of intercultural dialogue through his bilingual stories and repertoire of tales from "Hispanic," American Indian, and Anglo cultures. However, in the most recent edition of his most famous book, *La Llorona, The Weeping Woman: An Hispanic Legend Told in Spanish and English*

(2004), the storyteller has taken on an authoritative stance critiquing those who seek to alter or politicize the folklore.[5] Hayes began publishing his stories in 1982 in order to share them with a larger audience and has since become a regular feature in schools and community centers across the Southwest. When telling stories, Hayes identifies the cultural origins of each tale and is careful to say that his version is "inspired by" some other or "represents one of many," as he does throughout *Here Comes the Storyteller*. Through Hayes' efforts, children are encouraged to recover and impart their own versions of tales from their respective cultural communities.

Hayes first learned about La Llorona as a boy after his family moved from Pennsylvania to southern Arizona. He learned Spanish from his Chicano friends, who also introduced him to a rich storytelling tradition that included La Llorona. Although uncertain if he "believed" the story about the ghost woman who wandered in the arroyos crying for her lost children, he did recognize that the story "had a lot of truth in it."[6] When he began his storytelling career, Hayes included the story of La Llorona "because he knew almost everyone loved the story of the weeping ghost as much as he and his friends did."[7] Hayes' own Llorona story is a conventional one about a woman named María. Although he gives her a specific identity, it does not alter her fate within the framework of the tale.[8]

Hayes' book about La Llorona is important for the sheer number of copies sold (more than 70,000), its accessibility, and its appeal to various audiences. What is most notable about the work is that Hayes carefully situates La Llorona—for young readers, in particular—in a specific cultural context and identifies her as part of a Mexican or, as Hayes identifies it, Hispanic storytelling tradition. Although he affirms the importance of the tale, his assessment is not without its problems:

> Storytelling isn't practiced so much today, and many of the old tales
> have been forgotten. But one old story continues to work its spell upon
> the people—the story of La Llorona (lah yoh-RROH-nah). It is told
> throughout the Southwest, and all over Mexico as well. No other story is
> better known or dearer to Hispanic Americans. LA LLORONA is truly
> the classic folk story of Hispanic America. (1987, 6)

Hayes does not identify for young readers which particular tales have been forgotten, nor offers any direct evidence of the actual diminishment in the telling of stories. His tone is nostalgic, as he confines storytelling traditions to the past. He goes on to emphasize the way in which storytelling "was" a means for the "old ones" to transmit cultural knowledge and how this tradition lives on in the telling of Llorona stories: "This is a story that the old ones have been telling to children for hundreds of years. It is a sad tale, but it lives strong in the memories of the people, and there are many who swear that it is true" (9). While Hayes distances himself from this circle of believers, thus creating a space for doubting the veracity of the tale, he is careful to emphasize the truths embedded in it, rather than the truth of the tale itself, thus demonstrating for readers that cultural outsiders can find truths in stories that are not their own. He concludes the book by identifying La Llorona's story as an ongoing cultural tradition, instilling in audiences that her story is one that people are choosing to pass on: "the old ones still tell it to the children, just as they heard it themselves when they were young. And in the same way the children who hear it today will some day tell it to their own children and grandchildren" (30). La Llorona's story, in Hayes' determination, represents the last of its kind that is directly tied to tradition.

Hayes has proven elsewhere that he has a heightened sense of awareness about his problematic position as a teller of American Indian and other native stories, saying, "I think it's wrong for people who don't belong to a culture to present themselves as spokespersons or interpreters of that culture" (*Here Comes the Storyteller,* 66). It is curious, then, that on the final page of the hardback edition of *La Llorona,* under the heading "Note to Readers and Storytellers," Hayes delves into La Llorona's complicated cultural history and offers readers different ways of thinking about types of Llorona tales: "In the oral tradition, references to La Llorona fall into three categories: 1) vague warnings that she might be wandering about; 2) legendary tales that explain the origin of the crying ghost; and 3) anecdotes of encounters with her" (32). Such information is useful for initiating in young readers a process of critical thinking about the lore (the focus of my next chapter), but for someone who does not want to be an interpreter for another culture, he mediates and even criticizes cultural constructions of La Llorona that "deviate" from convention.

Hayes is inexplicably invested in distinguishing La Llorona's story as folklore rather than legend. For example, Hayes cites the tendency of recent writers to relate La Llorona to Malinche, a move on their part to "put a political spin on the narrative," implying that a story that fails to include this association is somehow *not* political (32).[9] He does say that if this association were "true," then her story would be a legend. If veracity defines legends, then "un-truth" is the marker of folktales, or so Hayes would have us believe. Cihuacoatl is also cited as a possible inspiration or model for other writers' Lloronas, and Hayes mentions the "[d]ocumented references to the crying woman [that] date from 1550 in Mexico," but he does not cite the portent of the woman crying in the streets of Tenochtitlan prior to Cortés' arrival in 1519 (32). Continuing in this comparative vein while privileging European antecedents, Hayes states that a "comparison, if not a connection, with the Greek myth of Jason and Medea is *obvious*" (32; emphasis added). Most troubling is that he purports to "give the tale a more *logical* structure than it had in the renditions [he] heard in [his] youth" (32; emphasis added). His suggestion is that folk storytelling styles or methods are somehow "illogical." In the past, Hayes has focused primarily on stories and storytelling. His move toward a more authoritative position is best understood as a result of his being perceived as an authority.[10] Hayes' views reflect an investment in maintaining a conservatism in regard to Llorona lore, one in which the story may take on different configurations yet ultimately remains the same.

The previous chapters have illustrated that La Llorona has a power that extends beyond her own community but always begins there. While clear differences exist between the representations of La Llorona generated by her folk community and those outside of it, I am not attempting to ghettoize or "barrioize" La Llorona. To do so would ignore that her story is evidence of the violent mixing of Indigenous, Spanish (including African and Jewish), and other European traditions. La Llorona's story often reflects how each of these groups has contributed to the shaping of her legend through various means. Readers should keep in mind that naturalization in Greater Mexico is not determined solely by nationality or blood but also by residency, proximity, and, most notably, by a willingness to commit to and privilege a Mexican@ or Chican@ worldview over an Anglo one.

The works examined in this chapter are distinguished by the ways in which they "use" the lore. I am interested especially in producers who make some effort to transmit information about La Llorona's legend by drawing from sources in her cultural community, the means by which they do so, and the possible influence this information has on the perception of Greater Mexicans in the respective interpretative communities of both cultural outsiders and insiders. I am also invested in providing a culturally informed means for Chican@s to interpret artifacts produced by cultural outsiders, and in identifying those cultural productions by non-natives that lend themselves to intercultural dialogue. La Llorona may seem an unusual cultural emissary, but bridging different cultural communities has always *been* one of her roles.

Like many people not born into the Anglo numerical and ideological majority, I am familiar with at least two basic worldviews—Chican@ and Eurowestern.[11] My home and community education were Mexican American, but my institutional education was almost exclusively Anglo. My understanding of La Llorona is also born of these two influences: I first learned about her from my uncles but became reacquainted with her in college, where I was usually the only Chicana in a classroom of Anglos. Therefore, I am equally comfortable offering cultural insider and cultural outsider readings. The history of our own mestizaje tells us that much can be learned and lost in the merging of two different worldviews. In my own analysis of La Llorona as depicted in works by cultural outsiders, Eurowestern and Chican@ cultural readings of these artifacts appear side by side in order to suggest how different audiences might interpret La Llorona and her wailing.

As established in previous chapters, La Llorona folklore can initiate wider discussions about gender, class, ethnicity, and other topics. This ability is neither limited exclusively to representations generated by Chican@s nor to representations by non-natives. In other words, even racist or culturally biased depictions of La Llorona can generate important critical discussions. I have considered elsewhere non-native cultural productions such as Paula G. Paul's *The Wail of La Llorona* (1977), Mel Odom's *Bruja* (2000), Tony Hillerman's *The Wailing Wind* (2002), Michael Chabon's *Summerland* (2002), and the pilot episode of the television program *Supernatural* (2005) — all of which reinforce Anglo mythologies about domination. Therefore, I focus here on two different works of art, one by Dan K. Enger and the other by Diana Bryer, that feature La Llorona as the subject. I also consider the image featured on the packaging for La Llorona brand coffee, a film by David Lynch, and a novelette by Don L. Daglow. These works contribute to or extend the dialogue about La Llorona in culturally sensitive ways and inspire through their representations of La Llorona folklore cross-cultural dialogue about issues such as Indigenous identity, colonial history, the oppression of women, and cultural appropriation.[12]

Cultural reading strategies that account for the ways that La Llorona is being reimagined and re-turned can aid us in determining how non-natives are using La Llorona and in formulating our responses to these productions. Doing so provides one way to initiate further conversation about this important cultural figure so that we can decide what she represents to Chican@s and mainstream communities at large. Revisions of the lore by non-natives are noticeably absent from this discussion, in part because they are dependent upon an audience's prior knowledge. Therefore, what we may perceive as "changes" to familiar elements or basic framework of the cuento may simply reflect a lack of familiarity with the subject. As in the previous chapters, I have grouped the artifacts discussed here on the basis of their level of engagement with the lore. The analysis that follows is not meant to be exhaustive, though at times I offer multiple interpretations of complex productions based on the use of different reading strategies in order to tease out their various levels of meaning.

Cross-Cultural Hauntings

Mexican Americans and Chican@s are the primary, but not only, audience for works done by native artists that represent La Llorona. Chican@ artists like Carmen Lomas Garza and Oscar Lozoya, whose work is discussed in Chapter 1, include elements found in traditional renderings but make no overt attempt to critique the legend. Cultural readers conversant in the legend assemble the visual elements (such as a woman depicted wandering, wailing, and/or weeping, a body of water, and children) included in a production and conclude that the piece is about La Llorona or a version of her story. While non-native representations parallel Chican@ productions in terms of themes such as loss, vulnerability, and death, an artist's or audience's lack of cultural or historical knowledge about La Llorona means that the representation will likely be read as having a different message than the one attached to the legend.

When cultural outsiders, including those who draw from native sources, render La Llorona's narrative or image for non-native consumers, there can be little expectation that their core audience will be conversant in the legend. Therefore, the decision to include context in the form of a basic outline of the lore or through the identification of its primary features can influence how audiences read a work representing La Llorona. The inclusion of this information, while potentially useful, is nevertheless problematic because it allows cultural outsiders to assign meaning to La Llorona that is often based on cultural interpretations informed by Eurowestern symbols and figures. This information can contribute to cross-cultural dialogue about analogous, even archetypal female figures, but can also rob La Llorona of her culture or, worse, portray her cultural community as primitive, violent, exotic, or quaint, ultimately reinforcing dominative ideologies about people of Mexican descent. Consumers may even conclude that La Llorona is simply a generic figure not grounded in any particular cultural or storytelling community. Therefore, the inclusion of a context does not guarantee a substantive contribution to the cultural dialogue about and surrounding La Llorona, while its exclusion does not negate the possibility.

Woodblock printmaker Dan K. Enger chooses to represent La Llorona without providing a cultural context for his audience to use as an interpretive frame.[13] He includes a work entitled *La Llorona* (2001; ink on paper, 9″ × 12″) in his "Wild West" series on the "Nuevo Mexico Macabre" that is based "on the history, legend and folklore" of Taos, a region he describes as "remote."[14] Enger confines La Llorona to the past, a point that may give consumers the impression that she is exclusively a historical phenomenon. He does not comment overtly on La

Llorona or direct the audience's attention toward a specific interpretation of the work. Audiences remain unaware how Enger learned about the legend (from a book), how the legend captivated him (literally haunting him during a stay in an isolated cabin in the mountains above Mora Valley), or how he drew from sources around him (native loved ones and family) to create his replication of the lore (pers. comm. 2005). Even though audiences do not learn about La Llorona or Enger, he gives them a richly textured rendition of her. Enger codes his widely disseminated image of La Llorona—found in encyclopedias and on Web sites, T-shirts and posters—with symbols that lend themselves to discussions of power, Indigenous identity, colonial history, and poverty.

In the absence of an interpretive directive, audiences unfamiliar with La Llorona lore may seize upon certain visual elements—such as skeletons, a full moon, wind, or victims—and assemble them in the context of the horror genre, for example, in order to make meaning of the image, a technique employed by Anglo viewers of the Llorona milk ad.[15] Featured prominently in Enger's print is a skeleton holding a lantern in the darkness, and a girl and boy, accompanied by their dog, holding hands in the light of a full moon (figure 5.3). The scene calls to mind the Grimm Brothers' tale of Hansel and Gretel, who are abandoned and left to the mercy of an evil witch. Wind whips through the scene, blowing the dead woman's hair and tearing apart the round seed heads of dandelions. Enger codes the image with seemingly conflicting messages about power: the girl and boy, presumably siblings, are given visual authority through their positioning above the female ghoul, but her position in the foreground gives her visual prominence. Other than the fact that the print bears her name, Enger gives audiences no information about who or what a "Llorona" might be. Yet based solely on the inclusion of the above-mentioned generic elements, audiences can discern that the relationship between the entities in the print is clearly antagonistic: a "monster" wants to hurt the children, whose only defenses are each other and the dog.

Within the interpretive framework of the horror genre, but not exclusive to it, the woman signifies malevolence and death in contrast to the children, who represent virtue and life. Enger conveys the malice of the figure through her visage, whereas the innocence of the children is established through their age and their location in a cloud of dandelion seeds, which perhaps were dispersed after the children "wished" upon the cotton-like clusters. In the print, light emanates from two visible sources: the lantern held by the gruesome figure and the light of the moon, which is reflected light from the sun. The shadows of the children are thrown forward toward the woman, allowing her to touch them, thus indicating that they are within her grasp. A third source of light, also reflected by the moon, is the metaphoric light of the children's life force. Enger's use of light and dark

FIGURE 5.3. *La Llorona* (2001, woodblock print, 9″ × 12″), from "The Wild West" series on the "Nuevo Mexico Macabre," by Dan K. Enger © 2006. Used by permission of the artist.

parallels the contrast between life and death, as represented, respectively, by the children and La Llorona. The female figure, drawn by the light of the children's lives, attempts to lure them from the safety of the hilltop to the river with a light that is meant to convey safety but clearly represents death.

Other elements unrelated to horror that are present but might be overlooked, even in a close reading, communicate the class of the children and hint at an additional source of their vulnerability beyond age and innocence. The ragged state of the children's clothes suggests that they are poor. Their poverty may explain why they are on their own; perhaps they are unsupervised because their parents are at work. Given the rural setting, the parents may be laborers who cannot afford child care. Another possibility is that the children are lost. Possibly having wished upon the dandelion heads to find their way home, they may misinterpret the light in the darkness as their salvation. In the absence of adults, the girl, whose height suggests she is older, assumes the maternal role of protector. Positioned slightly in front of her brother, the girl is an obstacle, along with the river, between the dead woman and the boy. The woman is an archetypal female predator, posing an imminent threat, although it is left to the audience to determine the outcome. If read through the lens of the Grimm Brothers' tale, readers could conclude that the sister's bravery will allow the children to escape, especially if, Gretel-like, she is able to dispatch the witch. However, if read through the lens of La Llorona lore, the outcome of the scene remains far more ambiguous, and the outlook for the children is ominous.

When read independently of the legend, those unacquainted with La Llorona may be left puzzled about the significance of additional details, such as the woman's clothing, the Christian symbols, and the specific reason the woman poses a threat to the children. For cultural readers, however, this lack of context gives us greater freedom to interpret the image through the lens of the folklore without first having to navigate Eurowestern interpretations. Drawing from sources other than horror conventions or visual signifiers of class, cultural readers may readily identify that the print is not simply a representation of the legend, but also one that depicts a nationalist version. Enger imparts a traditional narrative that emphasizes La Llorona as a subject of God's punishment and alludes to the devastating effects of Christianity on Native communities. Several details in the print contribute to this interpretation. The rough-hewn robe La Llorona wears is reminiscent of a tilma woven from agave, usually worn by Mexican Indians. Enger also ornaments La Llorona with crucifixes and a cameo broach of Christ, who, like the woman, is also depicted as a skeleton. These symbols, respectively, hint at an unknown sacrifice and indicate that for La Llorona, Christ represents ever-lasting suffering instead of life. She, in turn, will provide the children with the same fate that Christ offered her: death. Arguably, they will most certainly be exempt from La Llorona's particular brand of suffering in the afterlife.

The broach and its style speak to class, history, and gender oppression. Cameos are usually antiques or heirlooms of the wealthy. Thus, the implication is that the pin, along with Christianity, was a legacy handed down to or imposed on the figure. These features of the print situate Indigenous beliefs in opposition to Christianity. Also, through the lens of the lore, one can logically construe that the broach was a gift from the woman's lover. Therefore, the phallic pin used to affix the ornament on the garment writes a legacy of violence and penetration across the body of the dead female figure and points to an unseen male as the source of these violations. Finally, the broach contrasts with the tilma, evoking the meeting of two cultures (indio and Spanish/criollo) and two classes (poor and rich), details that would be overlooked by those unfamiliar with the variations of the legend.

The complex print also lends itself to a radical cultural reading, revealing that the image can be understood as a recuperation of the lore rather than a simple replication. The analysis hinges on the relationship between the skeletal figure, the children, and the moon. If we see the female figure as Coatlicue, and the moon as her daughter, Coyolxauhqui, who was destroyed by her sibling Huitzilopochtli, then the children, as reflected by the moon, symbolize an opportunity for a reunion between Coatlicue and her own lost child. Knowledge of specific myths from the Mexica pantheon allows readers to see the piece as hopeful rather than despairing. Ultimately, the lack of context for Enger's work is liberating for the cultural reader, but limiting for the cultural outsider.

In contrast to Enger, New Mexican artist Diana Bryer makes an effort to offer a substantive context for her 1987 painting *La Llorona* (oil on linen, 36″ × 40″), which depicts a woman sloshing through a river while carrying a doll (figure 5.4). Her interpretation of the legend was the first visual image of La Llorona that I encountered. I was given a card featuring the image after successfully defending my dissertation on La Llorona and have kept it with me ever since. The Chicano professor who gave me the card knew very little about Bryer, except that she was a painter who included Mexican, American Indian, Hispano, and Jewish themes in her colorful works. I eventually contacted Bryer via e-mail, and she kindly shared with me the history of her wide interest in "anything 'of the people.'"[16] Bryer's decision to make La Llorona the subject of the painting was inspired by her interest in the story and the fact that, at the time (1977), she could find "no images of her." Yet Bryer has more than an affinity for La Llorona.

Bryer's interest in La Llorona began not long after her arrival in New Mexico in 1977. After relocating from Los Angeles, she "immediately felt a bonding in general with the Hispanic people [. . .] in Northern New Mexico," who "felt like family." As a result of this connection, Bryer, who identifies as "Eastern European Jewish," feels that she "must have Spanish blood in [her] ancestry," although she is unable to confirm this belief. She first heard about La Llorona from a local teacher and recounts the story as follows: "He told me the most common legend about how she had two children who didn't mind her, so she took them to the river and drowned them and God punished her and made her wear chains and walk forever looking for her lost children, and she cries as she walks, so don't go

FIGURE 5.4. *La Llorona* (1987, oil on linen, 36″ × 40″), by Diana Bryer © 1987. Used by permission of the artist.

near the waters because La Llorona might take you [the children] thinking you are her children."[17] The storyteller emphasized the importance of discipline and what can happen to children who do not obey their parents.

With her interest piqued, Bryer began reading "everything [she] could on La Llorona." She even interviewed friends and neighbors. During this process she heard a version of the story that resonated for her personally. For the most part, it is a traditional version of the story with one major revision:

> La Llorona was a woman in love with a married man. She had two children by him. She begged him to leave his wife and marry her. Her lover

was very rich and powerful and his wife of high class. He decided to hire two church officials to get her children and drown them. When La Llorona found out what had happened she went hysterical. The police took her and put her in a dungeon and either she hung herself or they burned her at the stake. Her ghost wanders the waterways looking for her lost children.

Making the Church and its agents exclusively responsible for the deaths of La Llorona's children constitutes a major revision of the lore, but notably, the outcome is the same. Although devoid of cultural context, this rendition is substantive and poignant, focusing on the class difference between La Llorona and her lover, and including allusions to Church corruption, torture, and witchery.

Rather than translate these narratives literally or combine their distinct characteristics in one piece, Bryer streamlines the story in her visual translation, focusing solely on the woman, her weeping and wandering, and the river. She adds her own interpretative touch by including the doll, which for cultural readers may present the one problem area of the piece. The red-haired, fair-skinned doll, a visual surrogate for La Llorona's own lost child or children, calls to mind a white rather than brown child, which is not to say that there are not red-haired, fair-skinned people of Mexican ancestry. The image, however, is one of uncomplicated visible whiteness. When read subversively, the doll represents the historical displacement of Mexican and Chican@ families by Anglo settlers and their children. This geographic displacement pushes her children further out of her reach, but also positions La Llorona as a threat to all children, not simply brown ones.

Without an accompanying explanatory narrative, audiences might conclude that the woman depicted in the painting is delusional, suffers from a psychological disorder, or has Alzheimer's. In other words, the source of her pain is pathological rather than maternal, cultural, social, or political. Other than the title, there are few clues to decode the image. A woman weeps, but the artist does not indicate why. Cultural readers acquainted with the legend, however, can judge the subject of the painting against its title, which begs for a particular kind of consideration. The deceptively simplistic painting can be read as capturing the moment after La Llorona has drowned her own children. Or we may be seeing La Llorona after she has lured a child down to the river and drowned him or her. In either case, she is left with only a lifeless doll. Other possibilities include her having found the doll and mistaking it for her child, or that she carries it as a reminder.

In an attempt to inform her audience, Bryer, unlike Enger, directs them toward a specific interpretation. The following narrative, which appeared on Bryer's Web site, is included on the back of art cards featuring her rendition of La Llorona. Bryer identifies La Llorona as a feature of "Hispanic" culture, but speculates that the legend may have its origins in the classical world:

> La Llorona (Weeping Woman) is a legend who haunts the country streams of all Hispanic lands. The legend may have originated in the ancient Greek Medea who murdered her children. La Llorona is said to have drowned her little ones and is doomed to search for eternity, calling and crying along rivers, ditches and arroyos. So mothers here warn their children never to go near the running waters at night.

The pseudo-anthropological overview accentuates major features of the legend, including the infanticide, and locates it in a cultural community. In spite of her own cultural heritage, Bryer privileges an Asian woman as represented in Greek drama over Lilith, the analogous figure from Jewish lore, who is said to fly through the night, preying upon newborns.[18] While Bryer includes portions of the original narrative that inspired her interest, she ultimately offers La Llorona as a Western creation. Bryer tempers her assertion by using the word "may," yet does not direct the audience to a source that offers Medea as a direct anteced- ent to La Llorona.[19] She does not establish a link between Hispanic and Greek cultures and therefore reinforces Eurowestern assumptions that all tragedy has Greek origins.

An End to Silencio

A cultural history or overview is not the only means of providing audiences unfamiliar with the legend direction for interpreting representations of La Llorona. For instance, David Lynch, in his film *Mulholland Drive* (2001), in- cludes La Llorona in a pivotal scene at a critical point in the movie.[20] Though she is on screen for less than five minutes, the course of the narrative is drastically altered after her appearance. Audiences unfamiliar with the legend may discern this change, but they will not understand the cultural mechanism used to bring about the transformation. Cultural readers, particularly those reading the rep- resentation of La Llorona in the film through the lens of resistance, will likely comprehend the hidden message that La Llorona imparts to the main Chicana character, though they will have to work diligently to achieve this level of under- standing, for Lynch's film is difficult and confusing regardless of one's cultural background.

Reading for resistance reveals that La Llorona's actions in the context of the story are a direct response to economic, gender, and social oppression. To audience members unfamiliar with the tale, Lynch introduces a Greater Mexican female archetype beyond the virgin/whore binary that also speaks to audience members with specific cultural knowledge of her. While Lynch's film does not prevent additional Chican@ filmmakers from making movies that focus exclusively on La Llorona or rely on her as a primary metaphor in a narrative, his access to resources does give him a clear advantage over native artists in terms of creating and circulating her image. Notably, to date, the DVD productions *Haunted From Within* by José L. Cruz, *The Wailer* (2006) by Andres Navía, and the 2006 Llorona trilogy (*The River: Legend of La Llorona, Revenge of La Llorona,* and *Curse of La Llorona*) by Terrance Williams, along with Bernadine Santistevan's film *The Cry* (mentioned in Chapter 1), are the only feature-length films about La Llorona by Mexican American or Chican@ filmmakers.[21] Lynch's film, though, is not about La Llorona. Still, he manages to convey La Llorona's complexity, teasing out the layers of meaning found in her story. Moreover, he illustrates the disastrous consequences that befall a white woman who attempts to manipulate a Chicana, who in this case is under La Llorona's protection, to suit her own needs, desires, and obsessions.

Lynch arguably "assimilates" La Llorona into his film, but more accurately stated, he makes visible, within the landscape of his film and its geographic setting, a resident of the land who serves as a metonym for La Llorona's folk community. By drawing her as a protector and figure of resistance, he allows her to stand on her own, fully realized, a symbol of untapped Greater Mexican female power capable of articulating pain, loss, and the desire for redemption. She calls to us, sings to us, and asks us to listen so that we might ease her suffering and our own.

To present clearly the analysis that follows, I divide the film into two distinct parts and narratives. The first part, with its vivid colors and drawn-out fantastical moments, visually depicts the dream of Betty Elm (played by Naomi Watts), who arrives in Hollywood with the hope of becoming a famous motion picture actress. Upon arriving at her Aunt Ruth's apartment, Betty discovers a light-skinned Chicana, who is the victim of a car crash, living in Ruth's home. This, too, is a part of the dream. Although the Chicana has no memory of her identity, she adopts the name "Rita" after seeing a movie poster in the apartment of the 1946 film *Gilda*, which starred Rita Hayworth. Like Hayworth, who was born Margarita Carmen Cansino, the daughter of a Spanish-born father and a European American mother, Rita (played by Laura Elena Harring, born Laura Martinez Harring in Sinaloa, Mexico, D.F.) "selects" a name that masks her ethnicity. Together, Betty and Rita attempt to uncover Rita's "true" identity and in the process become lovers. In the second part of the film, best described as its "cinematic reality," Camilla Rhodes (also played by Laura Elena Harring) is a successful Hollywood actor who has an affair with Diane Selwyn (also played by Naomi Watts), an aspiring actor. The power dynamic in the first part is inverted in the second part with Camilla wielding both professional and sexual authority over Diane. Camilla's decision to terminate the affair leaves Diane distraught to the point that she desires revenge for her heartache.

La Llorona serves as a guardian of the gateway between these two narratives where power, seduction, love, and loss intersect to leave someone "llorando." Her cry rouses dreamers from sleep, as it does Rita. While dreaming, Rita speaks as though in a trance: "Silencio. Silencio. Silencio. No hay banda. No hay bata. No hay orquestra. Silencio. . . . Silencio. No hay banda. No. No." Her rather cryptic mutterings suggest that while she is lost in silence, Rita has the capacity to break that silence, but she must first awaken from her dream state, psychologically and physically. The power of articulation, the ability to speak for oneself, is embedded in Rita's subconscious, though the fact that the voice reaches her in the vulnerable state of sleep suggests that someone else controls her waking "story." Also, in the place about which Rita dreams, there is no band or orchestra; it is a location devoid of music and life. Clearly, Rita would like to resist the invitation to wander in the night, as indicated by her refusal, "No. No." After Betty awakens Rita from her dream, telling her that everything is "okay," Rita responds, "No it's not okay. Go with me somewhere." Only Rita knows where they must travel, for La Llorona calls to Rita alone. Rita then guides Betty, a cultural outsider who does not hear La Llorona's wailing, into the darkness.

The journey toward Club Silencio begins with a cab ride over a river, a traditional location used in La Llorona stories to indicate her territory and one used to separate Anglos from Chican@s in Los Angeles. The river crossing reveals that the club is situated on culturally specific terrain, one inhabited by La Llorona de Los Angeles. Once inside the club, Betty, dressed in red and black, and Rita, wearing black clothes and a blonde wig that calls to mind Hayworth's own dyed tresses, descend into a theater holding hands. Lynch uses the red and black colors in this scene to identify binaries and archetypes, such as seduction and death, respectively. While her black apparel suggests Rita's doomed fate, Betty's future is undetermined, for the colors she wears signify both seduction and death. Once seated, the two witness a performance, or a simulation of a performance, emceed by a man who states: "No hay banda. There is no band. [. . .] This is all a tape recording. No hay banda, and yet we hear a band. [. . .] It's all recorded. No hay banda. It is all a tape. [. . .] It is an illusion. Listen!" Rita begins to understand the source of her spoken dream and learns that disembodied sound and illusion permeate Club Silencio.

As if in violent recognition of her outsider status in this environment, Betty starts to convulse in her chair after the emcee's command to listen and finally calms down when the announcer Cookie, a Chicano, introduces La Llorona de Los Angeles, Rebekah del Rio, who steps out between a parted curtain.[22] Lynch literally unveils La Llorona, placing her center stage and forcing viewers' eyes on her. Underscoring Betty's connection to La Llorona, del Rio too is dressed in red and black with a painted tear beneath her right eye. La Llorona's wrenching ballad disrupts the stillness of the club, revealing both Rita's past and her future; her voice is a powerful means of breaking the symbolic and literal "silencio." As La Llorona sings "Llorando," a Spanish-language version of Roy Orbison's "Crying," both Rita and Betty start to weep, overcome by the pain in del Rio's voice. In the middle of her performance La Llorona swoons, but her song continues, suggesting that a woman's voice is not exclusively her own or that the song is more powerful than any one singer. As film critic Anthony Lane notes, although La Llorona mimes to a tape recording, the "mimicry of passion [is] enough to fell her" (89). When women attempt to write or speak outside of the boundaries of dominating discourses, this articulation, even mimicking the act, has profound consequences. According to Trinh T. Minh-ha, "In trying to tell something, a woman is told, shredding herself into opaque words while her voice dissolves on the walls of silence" (79). Rita understands that La Llorona is trying to send a powerful message about identity, control, and power. Instead of allowing La Llorona's words to dissolve on the walls of Silencio, Rita internalizes them, and her expression changes visibly as Cookie and the emcee drag the unconscious del Rio off stage. Betty, who continues to weep, reaches over and discovers a blue box in her purse, where she may have been hiding it all along. After handing over her discovery, Betty disappears from the first part of the film before viewers have time to puzzle out the fact that she and La Llorona are wearing the same colors. Rita eventually takes possession of the box to which she literally and symbolically holds the key. She opens the mysterious blue box with her key and takes us into the darkness of self, other, and sexual containment. The box functions as a portal, transporting viewers from one narrative to another. With La Llorona's work partially done, Rita must continue the search for her identity alone. In this way, she is a contemporary Llorona, lost to her self as the result of some forgotten or suppressed violence.

As we move into the second part of the film, we see Rita, now as Camilla Rhodes, write herself out of containment. Instead of continuing her lesbian relationship with Betty, now Diane, Camilla ends the affair by telling Diane that she is leaving her for a man. In this way, Camilla will not assume the role of La Llorona, the one abandoned for another lover of a higher station. She refuses the mantle of weeping and wandering for lost love. Instead, Camilla abandons her lover to perform heterosexuality with not just any man, but the first man — Adam. Keenly aware of the kind of power and protection this relationship can offer, Camilla knowingly pairs herself with Adam, who in previous scenes has been in contact with God, a cowboy in Lynch's imagination. The appearance of God- and Adam-like figures speaks to the omnipresence and omnipotence of the patriarchy that dictates women's lives. It may seem that Camilla has sacrificed one way of life for heteronormative behavior, but she simply attaches herself to the ultimate representative of the patriarchy while maintaining and pursuing other lesbian affairs. In other words, she willfully and successfully manipulates the patriarchal order to suit her needs. As Camilla passionately kisses her new female lover in front of her ex-lover and while Adam's back is turned, Diane is faced with the realization that *she* is the abandoned one.

At this moment, cultural readers gain insight into one possible connection between the two narratives. As the one left behind, Diane, who hails from Deep River, Ontario, is cast in the role of La Llorona. This fact is underscored by her association with a river as conveyed by the geographic place name, Deep River. Also Diane is associated with the colors red and black, the same colors La Llorona wears at Silencio. If this in fact is the case, we can interpret the first narrative as Diane's attempt to reinvent herself as Betty and to erase Camilla's strength and power. In her dream, Diane rewrites Camilla as Rita, a lost woman without self or memory who becomes wholly dependent on Diane. Moreover, Diane in her dream has reinvented herself as Betty to guide, protect, and possibly save Camilla. Despite Diane's efforts, she is a Llorona who remains lost, physically and morally, even going so far has to have Camilla murdered rather than be without her. So while the patriarchy may not be able to control Camilla, Diane unwittingly becomes an agent of that order in an attempt to do what it cannot.

However, Camilla's power reaches beyond death and, like La Llorona, she returns to haunt Diane. Rather than allow herself to be tortured by her actions, Diane fantasizes about Camilla to save her from the death Diane orchestrated and to keep Camilla as a lover forever. What we see, then, in the first part of the film is the fantasy Diane has *after* Camilla has been murdered. Through her dream, Diane imagines she can alter Camilla's fate and the outcome of the re-lationship by shifting the balance of power in her favor, without realizing that Camilla, even in death, still maintains control over Diane's life. In an effort to dictate this game of seduction, Diane naively attempts to position Rita as La

Llorona, believing perhaps that she is only a woman who weeps about lost love and nothing more. Diane assumes the role of an oppressor by relegating Rita to a position inferior to her own. As if to confirm that she has "successfully" written Rita into this role, Rita wears mostly red and black throughout Diane's fantasy, the colors that will later link Betty and La Llorona de Los Angeles. Diane as Betty directs every aspect of Rita's life and does not allow Rita to articulate her pain or horror. Indeed, as La Llorona's performance implies, Rita, like del Rio in the scene previously discussed, is not allowed to voice her own pain and suffering. She is simply performing the role of the doomed woman that Diane assigns her. When the two discover the dead body of "Diane Selwyn" in the first narrative, Rita's initial inclination is to scream, but as she opens her mouth to do so, Betty forces her hand over Rita's mouth to maintain silencio. In spite of the fact that Betty's reaction is apropos to narrative concerns about the duo avoiding detection for breaking into "Diane's" home, Betty's behavior reveals an additional level of meaning: Diane gets to witness Camilla's despair over seeing the dead body, Diane's body, while Betty contains Rita's grief, greedily keeping it only for herself.

When Diane writes the scene at Silencio with La Llorona into the Betty/Rita narrative, she does so to acknowledge literally and symbolically that women suffer. Diane, as Betty, empathizes so greatly with La Llorona's "llorando" that she openly weeps as the song virtually pours from del Rio's mouth. What Diane does not acknowledge is that in her construction of female anguish, it is the Chicana who suffers and swoons to give pleasure, even in pain, to the cultural consumers in the club. Furthermore, she does not realize that she cannot control La Llorona. By including La Llorona in her fantasy, she unwittingly provides Rita and Camilla a means of escape. Diane, in her attempt to re-create Rita in her dreams, has given herself over to seduction, unaware that, as Jean Baudrillard explains, it "seizes hold of all pleasures, affects and representations, and gets a hold of dreams themselves in order to reroute them from their primary course, turning them into a sharper, more subtle game, whose stakes have neither an end nor an origin, and concerns neither drives nor desires" (124). Diane's fantasy or game has been rerouted from one where she is seemingly in control to one in which she is completely powerless; La Llorona's appearance and song ensure this fact. Simply put, Diane is meddling with a force she does not fully understand, because not only is La Llorona a weeping woman who suffers, she is a woman who, in some versions of the lore, exacts revenge. Rita, who initially shares the same reaction as Betty to La Llorona de Los Angeles' performance, ultimately changes her view when del Rio faints from the sheer intensity of the song she mimes. A momentary look of recognition and even anger washes over Rita to reflect a kind of cultural knowing, one that makes her fully aware that she *must* not be the one left crying.

Even if Diane does control the first narrative, she can neither dictate nor contain Camilla's ethnicity and cultural roots, which come to the fore when Camilla sleeps and asks for Silencio. Nor can she disengage the cultural connection between La Llorona and Camilla. Even in the assigned guise of Rita, Camilla seeks to silence Diane's narrative, and La Llorona makes this possible by calling to Rita and warning her, by giving her back her self, her identity as Camilla, as represented by the box, and ultimately saving her, for a time. Diane loses control of the narrative and herself in the end. Not even in dreams will Camilla allow herself to be oppressed, for La Llorona is her ally there as well as in the waking world. Overwrought, Diane succumbs to guilt and takes her own life. In this scene, the room fills with smoke, and a representation of the dark primal self slowly fades in and is then replaced by the image of a blonde Rita and Betty superimposed over the skyline of the city. This suggests that Diane's eternal punishment, her hell, is to remember Camilla as Rita moments before Diane lost her forever. The final scene of the film takes us back to Club Silencio, where a regally dressed, blue-haired woman of obvious prominence sits in a theatre box and utters the word "silencio." Her gilded dress and box seat imply that "silence is golden" in women. Lynch seems keenly aware of the ways in which the patriarchy silences women, but he also illustrates how women participate in silencing each other. Only La Llorona's voice endures to shatter both kinds of silencio.

Steeped in Legend

As I explain in the introduction, non-natives can represent La Llorona, and those who do are willing to acknowledge, critique, and even relinquish various forms of privilege in order to foreground the worldview of La Llorona's cultural community. The producers of La Llorona brand coffee and writer Don L. Daglow, in the creation of their Lloronas, can be seen as recuperating and returning, respectively, specific cultural and historical contexts that not only foreground aspects of La Llorona's parent culture but also open lines of dialogue between cultural communities about Indigenous mythology.

Reading for re-turnings or recuperations is difficult because both require more than cursory knowledge of the legend. They are also the most political in the sense that they are often anti-colonial, for example, and the most elite, in that they require access to certain obscure and privileged histories. As illustrated in Chapter 4, cultural readers must also be conversant in the pantheon of the Mexica, pre-colonial and colonial Mexican history, and the intricacies of Chicano nationalism, for example, in order to decipher depictions of La Llorona that include neglected features of most replications (for example, her childhood or individual identity), cultural antecedents (like Mexica deities), or alternate contexts that gave rise to the legend. Cultural readings for recuperation reveal the way in which our Weeping Woman, under the name La Llorona, is uniquely our own, born from specific cultural, historical, psychological, and political circumstances.

Reading for recuperations in non-native productions may seem futile, for it requires looking for something that in all likelihood will not be there unless the producers have unwittingly coded their images with symbols and images suggestive of recuperation. Non-native productions of La Llorona that can be read as recuperations often yield as much information about the producer as they do about their representations. Cultural readers will note that the non-native producers in this section appear to display more than a passing knowledge of Mexican and Chican@ history, icons, attitudes, and values. In addition, Eurowestern and even Anglo thought is subordinated to a Chican@ worldview. Though Eurowestern icons are written over Greater Mexican ones in the Llorona artifacts discussed in this section, the latter bleed through, creating a cultural palimpsest representative of the syncretism of and conflict between cultures without obscuring their violent histories. Unfortunately, this category has few examples because the images contained here are the most radical ones, often opposing stereotypes and Eurowestern hegemony. As cultural palimpsests, the artifacts in this category reveal the way La Llorona was written over older, differently named versions of herself.

One such instance of a newer representation obscuring but not completely hiding an older one is found in the Coffee Shop of Horrors, a name derived from the musical *The Little Shop of Horrors*. The shop offers for sale through its web site a host of products, including T-shirts and toys, but as its name suggests, it specializes in "really scary coffee." With four notable exceptions, many of the coffees carry names intended to evoke the haunted and horrific; for example, "Burial Ground," "Witches [*sic*] Brew," "Skull Island," and "Sundown Blend." Most have place names in the titles: "Kenya," "Ethiopia," "Puerto Rico," and "Peru," to name a few. The four exceptions to the above designations include "Zombie Dirt," "Reanimator," "Montezuma's Revenge," and "La Llorona." On its Web site the coffee shop furnishes no explanation for the use of Greater Mexican historical and cultural figures, respectively, in its product names. In the absence of this information, consumers unacquainted with the individual significance of certain cultural icons—for example, La Llorona—might simply read the images

FIGURE 5.5. *La Llorona,* by Gary Pullin. Used by permission of
Brice Vorderbrug, owner of Coffee Shop of Horrors.

within the context of the horror genre and interpret the figure as a forest bogey,
one with a striking resemblance to the Virgin Mary (figure 5.5).[23]

At first glance, the image on the bag appears merely to represent the legendary
figure. The front of the packaging includes the name of the coffee shop displayed
prominently above the product name "LA LLORONA." Featured directly below
is a foregrounded image of a woman weeping at the edge of a forest. Tears stream
from the woman's closed eyes toward a skull necklace affixed beneath her chin.
Below the image, the lines of text read: "Medium Roast" and "ORGANIC MEX-
ICO." Yet by reading the image through the lens of the lore as a recuperation,
the image and the words, together, reveal an interesting rendering of the legend

that is not immediately recognizable without cultural knowledge. An informed reading of the iconography uncovers the possibility that embedded in La Llorona's story are those of the Virgen and one of her Indigenous antecedents, Cihuacoatl. Those familiar with Mexican Catholic icons will note that the woman, with hands clasped in prayer and head tilted slightly to the right, bears a striking resemblance to the Virgen de Guadalupe. The figure is also garbed in the Virgen's recognizable cloak, though it lacks the stars that dot the cloth in familiar renderings. Whereas the stars emphasize the Virgen's place in Heaven, the absence of these important symbols locates this figure on an earthly plane. In this case, a mist-filled forest of scraggly trees supplants the Virgen's radiant corona.

Two additional details distinguish the woman from the Virgen: tears and a necklace with a skull pendant. The former provides a visual translation of her name, while the latter associates her with death. But the piece of skeletal jewelry, for the cultural reader, evokes Cihuacoatl, the serpent-clad goddess of the Mexicas, whose accessories include a skull necklace. The woman, reminiscent of Cihuacoatl, represents a "dark double" of the Virgen. The image suggests either the syncretism of Christianity and Indigenous spirituality found in Mexican Catholicism or the opposition of the two religious beliefs. When considered solely on the basis of visual clues, La Llorona is presented as simply another potent earth mother, though from the Central Valley of Mexico, whose image is used to sell a "pre-modern" product of an exotic Mexico. In spite of being marketed to a mainstream audience, the product is coded in such a way that, if looked at as a recuperation, it can contribute to cultural dialogue about La Llorona.

The words that accompany the image help to enhance this view. An "organic" coffee product means that no chemicals or pesticides were used to cultivate the trees from which the beans are gathered. But "organic" can also refer to a natural or coexisting relationship between elements, in this instance, between La Llorona and Mexico, the final word included in the text intended to identify where the coffee beans are grown. The image and language, when taken together by the cultural reader, indicate that La Llorona, as a resident of the borderland, has a natural relationship to Mexico, the land and its people. The two not only coexist but also depend on each other for their lives and livelihood.

The example may seem frivolous to some, but in light of the fact that when conducting a Google Image search, the Coffee Shop of Horrors' rendering of La Llorona was once one of the first to appear, we cannot ignore its potential significance for those using the Internet to gather information about her. While reading the image through the lens of the lore yields the above interpretation of the image and the product, I am not convinced that La Llorona brand coffee is meant to contribute in any real or significant way to cultural knowledge about her, but for the cultural reader, it does. Artist Gary Pullin creates a complex image of La Llorona by cobbling together Greater Mexican images—a weeping woman, a Virgen, a Día de los Muertos or "Aztec" skull—to paradoxically create an image that closely resembles La Llorona's actual history.[24] The interplay of the words and image are lost, most likely, on mainstream consumers of the product, who believe that they are simply purchasing a coffee promoted through the retailing of various cultural "horror" figures. On the other hand, based on some consumers' reactions to La Llorona being used to promote milk consumption, I doubt cultural readers would be anxious to consume a La Llorona brand of anything. Because she is associated with death, even if Chican@s do not "believe" in La Llorona, a product bearing her name and, by extension, the consumption of it would be linked by those within her parent culture with loss of life.

Whereas the above image lends itself to the recovery of one of La Llorona's Mexica antecedents, Don L. Daglow conjures up another cultural forerunner of La Llorona. In his "novelette" *The Blessing of La Llorona* (1982), La Llorona is the spiritual double of a priestess, aptly named Nahualla. The character Nahualla's name is derived from *nahual* or *nahualli,* an idea rooted in Native Mexican spiritual practices and beliefs. A nahual is a double, be it an animal or some other aspect of nature, of a god, shaman, or even a common man, according to Mexica belief.[25] Through the character of Nahualla, Daglow introduces readers to a little-known Mexica concept of "doubling." Furthermore, Daglow has La Llorona articulate through her double why and how she serves her community.

The Blessing of La Llorona takes its title from how the community sees her, and the plot centers on the way cultural outsiders meddle with forces they do not understand. The protagonist, Steve Sorteaux, is an anthropology student who is interested in "the La Llorona myth in one barrio (Mexican neighborhood) of Southern California" (33). The original object of the study that would comprise his thesis was "to compare the telling of the ghost story, 'La Llorona' (pronounced yor-o-na, 'The Crying Woman') in three different environments: the major cities of Northern Mexico, rural villages of the same region, and the barrios of the Southwestern United States" (33). Daglow characterizes Steve as unaware of the existing research on both sides of the border on the subject of La Llorona, which even then was extensive.

Steve positions himself as a cultural expert who will teach the uninformed, as indicated by the inclusion of the phonetic pronunciation of her name, about his "discovery." He begins the "mundane process of interviewing others who believed they had seen or heard La Llorona" in order to achieve his foremost goal of distinguishing himself from his peers by conducting research worthy of publication (40). Like many of his anthropological contemporaries, Steve never considers how his research experience might change him.[26] In the end, Steve is forced to confront his own ignorance and includes his professional and cultural revelation as a part of his finished thesis. Steve imparts the story in hindsight, having reached the following conclusion: "I didn't know when to stop sticking my nose in other people's cultures, in things I thought with all my wonderful training I understood. Things I didn't really understand at all" (33). Daglow structures his story by offering this confession in the introduction for readers to use as a critical lens, along with the lessons attached to the lore, to interrogate the position Steve claims as a cultural authority and to warn those who might follow a similar path.

In a move uncharacteristic of many non-native cultural productions that feature La Llorona and her parent culture (such as Michael Chabon's *Summerland* or Tony Hillerman's *The Wailing Wind*), Daglow gives the members of La Llorona's native community, both children and adults, speaking subject positions that afford them the authority to impart cultural knowledge and underscore Steve's location as a cultural outsider. Children make up his initial pool of interview subjects and are the primary sources of the novice anthropologist's initial information about La Llorona. Lisa Lopez, a former classmate of Steve's and a grade school teacher in Cucamonga, arranges for Steve to interview her students. When Steve, who is skeptical about La Llorona's actual existence, attempts to coax more information about La Llorona from an interview subject by assuring her that "telling a story can't hurt" her, the girl replies: "'That's what *you* think!'" (35). She then looks at Steve like he is "an idiot," an assessment based on her perception that he lacks understanding about La Llorona and is ignorant about the power of storytelling (36).

Lisa Lopez, Daglow's cultural mediator, is an actual member of La Llorona's parent culture who challenges Steve's authority. Lisa's charge that Steve does not "care about the people or their culture, only about whether [he] got a job" calls attention to the way in which some anthropologists raid cultures purely out of self-interest (44). She criticizes Steve's inability to thoroughly understand the implications of the project he has undertaken when uttering the following: "'for all of your studies and your degree, you don't know more than the most superficial aspects of Mexican culture, let alone all the permutations of the Chicanos in the United States. You're studying the Llorona in a vacuum'" (46). By pointing out that academic training alone is not enough to understand the complexities of cultural communities, Lisa wounds Steve's pride and inadvertently motivates him to prove her wrong.

Daglow also problematizes Lisa's role as a cultural mediator. She serves as both an informal field researcher and later as Steve's Malinche-like translator, which directly underscores further the anthropologist's own language deficiency, but she has conflicted sentiments about continuing in these roles. Her knowledge that people like Steve have the power to circulate primitive or demeaning ideas about Chican@s while ignoring the consequences of their actions causes her uncertainty and leads her to impart to Steve the following lesson on cultural ethics:

> "There are a hell of a lot of gavachos—whites—running around spouting lots of high-sounding phrases about helping the poor people in the barrio or recognizing the importance of Chicano culture and how the dumb Mexicans deserve everyone's pity. After a while they move on to greener pastures, and everything's still the same. All the Mexican culture most people want they can eat at the Taco Bell or see at the bullfights in Tijuana. When it comes to the real beliefs, the values of the people, they start asking, 'why don't those Mexicans want to be like everybody else?'" (45–46)

Instead of Lisa playing the role of the compliant cultural dupe, she excoriates Steve for being a cultural tourist and accuses him of "trying to exploit the Chicanos of Cucamonga in order to further [his] own career [. . .]" (44). Steve resents her accusation but cannot deny its truth.

In spite of her feelings, Lisa ultimately agrees to help him, but only if he redirects his focus toward La Llorona's social function in her community. While some cultural readers may be disappointed in her decision, it reveals her desire to have the Chican@ community portrayed as more than a source of social or economic problems, for as Lisa states:

> "[A]t least this seems to be some project that doesn't show all Chicanos as vicious gang members or job-stealing wetbacks. I liked how you were looking at the social function of the story, how the community used it to promote moral values for the family, even in the worst situations. That's where you finally began to stumble across real Mexican and Chicano culture, the ways people try to keep the old values in a new country that doesn't respect them. But you *did* respect them, and even though you sometimes make me mad as hell with your goddamn academic condescension, that's why I'll still help you." (46)

Because she was not privy to his demeaning response to the written narrative, Lisa believes that Steve has conducted his research respectfully. This conviction informs her decision to continue to offer him assistance with his project, but before proceeding, she feels compelled to articulate the cultural, social, and political consequences of Steve's research, all of which he has failed to consider. As a result, she emerges as Steve's Chican@ cultural conscience.

Although she eventually abandons Steve to his foolish desire to find empirical, first-hand evidence of La Llorona's existence, Lisa for a time navigates the cultural terrain for Steve and ushers him deeper into La Llorona's territory, specifically when she introduces him to others in the community who have definitive knowledge of La Llorona's existence. Steve's singular devotion to gaining professional recognition at any cost makes him vulnerable to La Llorona; however, he fails to register the nuances in the stories he has collected.

Acting on information gathered from the community but against his informants' warnings that La Llorona is "'not somebody you want to go wandering around in the dark looking for,'" he parks on the Arrow Highway Bridge, over the wash where La Llorona is said to wander (39). Here he finally gets the first glimpse of his object of study. He sees an old woman standing in the middle of the bridge moments before a Cadillac traveling at break-neck speed crashes into Steve's car, rips off its roof, and plunges off the bridge, landing in a fiery explosion that kills the driver, a known drug dealer in the neighborhood. More importantly, he distinctly hears the sound of her weeping. The event, which lands him in the hospital with a broken arm, does not end his search. As a result of actually seeing a woman weeping, Steve entertains three possible explanations for La Llorona's existence: (1) She is "a senile old lady who wanders around here at night crying, [who] becomes associated with the story through [. . .] coincidental resemblance"; (2) a woman "may have consciously taken up the role, representing La Llorona to the community as a sort of spiritual vigilante"; or (3) a "noncorporeal creature [. . .] stalks the wash stealing the souls of those sinners unfortunate enough to meet her" (47–48). He remains reluctant to admit that she exists physically, so the third theory becomes feasible, for Steve sees it dovetailing with his idea that La Llorona is a physical projection of her community's fears, but not a ghost.

Despite his near-death experience, it is not enough to deter Steve from his quest to find a larger [read: scientific] explanation for La Llorona. After Steve recovers from the crash, he resolves to have a face-to-face encounter with the woman whom the community mistakes, in Steve's opinion, for La Llorona. He goes back to the wash and positions himself behind a dumpster to wait for her. Eventually an old woman appears dressed in white, shuffling along and dabbing her eye with a tissue. Steve, who only moments before believed that his whole search was "crazy," quickly abandons his position of safety to hurriedly snap a

photograph of the woman. Emboldened by the rationalization that "deadly monsters don't carry Kleenex," Steve approaches her. Lisa's accusations about Steve
only knowing the superficial aspects of Chican@ culture prove true. Because he
does not speak Spanish, he misinterprets the question the old woman utters as
she draws near, "'¿*Tienes tú un alma para mí, señor?*'" (49). Believing that she is
asking for alms, he tries to give her the few coins he has in his pocket. She rejects
his offer and tells him: "'*Ya debes regresar a tu propia gente*'" (50). Her final words
are an apt criticism for a monolingual anthropologist studying a Greater Mexican
legend: "'*Me puedes ver, pero jamás me puedes entender!*'" (52).[27] The result of this
encounter leads him to believe that he has solved the mystery of La Llorona: that
she is simply a pitiful old woman. He does not entertain the possibility that he
has had an encounter with, and perhaps narrowly escaped, death.

He does, however, begin to rethink his assumption that the woman is harm-
less. Although unconvinced that he has had an encounter with The Llorona, the
coins that she returns burn his hand, creating an injury that no Western medicine
can cure. He then reluctantly concedes that the old woman may have had some
supernatural power. The sore begins to fester and ooze, causing Steve nonstop
pain. In her final act as cultural mediator and navigator, Lisa takes Steve to a
curandero, who inquires about the cause of the injury in order to formulate the
best remedy. After Steve describes the event, the curandero clarifies for Steve that
the woman he met was actually La Llorona.

Although he tends to Steve's wound, the curandero explains that only La
Llorona or a bruja has the power to cure him. Against his better judgment, and
perhaps because he knows her true identity, the curandero directs them to the
bruja Nahualla de Miclante, whose name should give cultural readers pause.
In exchange for a cure, Nahualla makes Steve promise that he will never again
go looking for La Llorona. But when he discovers that the indisputable photo-
graphic evidence taken on the night of his personal encounter with La Llorona
lacks a certain subject, namely La Llorona, he defies Lisa's advice and breaks his
promise to Nahualla. He returns to the wash to obtain the visual proof he thinks
he needs.

Though Daglow does not include detailed information about the nahualli,
choosing instead to offer his own interpretation, a brief overview of the concept reveals that Daglow does recuperate an Indigenous identity for La Llorona
through Nahualla, who is revealed as La Llorona's "source."[28] According to Burr
Cartwright Brundage, in his work *The Fifth Sun: Aztec Gods, Aztec World* (1979),
"[t]he concept of the *nahualli* is peripheral to the Aztec's concept of his fate. In
addition to his soul a man could possess, as a part of the power of his personality,
a special affinity for an animal or some other aspect of nature. When considered

in this fashion a man was a *nahualli,* a transcorporate being" (182). Brundage goes on to explain that men and gods were capable of these kinds of transformations. To Mexicas, in particular, the nahualli carried two different and specific meanings: "In the first instance it meant a person [usually a shaman] who could magically transform himself into some other being or object, generally for nefarious purposes. He usually transformed himself into a beast such as a jaguar, a coyote, a dog, a snake, an eagle, or an owl" (182). The alternate concept of the nahualli had to do with dedicating a child shortly after birth to an animal that corresponds to his birth date. The lives and fates of the animal and person become intertwined, so much so that if harm befalls one, the other experiences the same effects. Additionally, "the two could exist simultaneously," which means that a man could take on the form of the animal and, theoretically, vice versa (183). In Daglow's story, Nahualla assumes the form of La Llorona, a fact revealed in Steve's final, fateful encounter with her.

When he meets La Llorona for the last time at the wash, Steve, who has grown confident from the belief that he has solved her mystery, confronts her with his conclusion that she is nothing more than a noncorporeal entity. In response to this accusation, La Llorona inquires: "'And this is what you would write in your book? That everyone may stand before the Llorona with no danger because she is like a reflection in the mirror, they see her but she is not there? You would write that her power is only in their minds? [. . .] And many people would read this book? [. . .] The things you say will be repeated many places, many times?'" (60). He once again misinterprets her questions, though posed in English, as a validation of his suppositions. His intent to publish his "discovery" elicits La Llorona's anger, for she is concerned about the cultural impact of his work, as evidenced when she asks: "'So then many people will stop to fear the Llorona, and she will not be able to punish the sinful'" (60). Instead of considering the ramifications of her inquiries, he worries that no one will believe his story. Before La Llorona reveals her actual identity, she expresses regret about his decision to circulate his conclusions and spells out her cultural purpose to Steve: "'That is sad [. . .] for that is the mission of the Llorona, to strike down those who betray the commandments by which the people of the community must live, to make an example for everyone'" (60). Her lament fails to register for Steve, who perceives her questioning as a weakness in her performance, the direct result of having been confronted with the "truth" about her existence.

Having given up hope of steering Steve away from his present course, La Llorona finally reveals her true identity as Nahualla, not out of defeat, but as prelude to his death. On the surface, Nahualla's capacity to bi-locate proves Steve's projection theory, especially when she concedes that his hypothesis was correct, in part, but Nahualla admits to having no "special power." She merely takes "the things the people of the town believe and use[s] them to change the way things are" (61). While Nahualla does acknowledge that La Llorona reflects the desires of the community, serving as a means of their wish fulfillment, this is only one of her many functions. As a projection of Nahualla, La Llorona serves as a kind of barrio vigilante, meting out justice and punishment as the *community* sees fit. She attempts to teach Steve something he and other cultural outsiders appear incapable of understanding: "'To outsiders La Llorona is a curse upon our people. To the families who have lived here for generations, who have raised their children here and seen them raise their children's children, she is a blessing who defends us against a . . . a world of many illusions'" (61). From Nahualla's perspective, the community that she serves sees La Llorona as a cultural guardian and as a gift. Finally, though capable of murder, Nahualla reveals that her capacity to do so while in the form of La Llorona is determined by the will of the community and should be used only as a last resort.

Acting on the community's desire to have their cultural beliefs left alone by those like Steve who would belittle or undermine them for their own purposes, Nahualla prepares to kill Steve. She regrets that he gave her, and the community, no other choice: "'We survive because our laws survive. The *nahualli* grow, we change, we move but we never die. As a priestess I must protect the people not only against the evil of temptation, but from those who would destroy our defenses against that evil. You are a kind man, and as a woman I am sorry" (62). After chaining Steve to a bridge and calling the water in the wash to rise, she terminates her projection as La Llorona, leaving Steve to confront his fate, which he manages to escape. His release then sets in motion a tragic series of events.

The confession offered in the introduction is the direct result of Steve's ignorance about the interdependent relationship between the nahualli and their projections, his guilt about causing and implicating two members of the cultural community in "unexplained" deaths, and his decision to abandon graduate school. He does achieve his goal of teaching the uninformed, but not as he imagined originally. Accompanying his thesis is a note to his director, in which Steve states: "[. . .] I've written down how it happened, with my thoughts and feelings intact, as a primary source for anyone who thinks that anthropology is a noble study and that detached observers can illuminate the life of man" (33). His work is a testament to the effects of a researcher neglecting his moral and cultural responsibilities. Daglow uses La Llorona specifically to criticize anthropological research that proceeds out of ignorance and without regard for the community that is represented through the work. Written in 1982, the story clearly anticipates the move toward a de-centered approach to cultural anthropology, one that problematizes openly the position of academic field researchers in relation to the communities in which they conduct their work. Daglow's story largely avoids the hazards that his anthropologist fails to navigate successfully. More importantly, it contributes to a cultural dialogue by offering the nahualli as an additional Indigenous antecedent for La Llorona.[29] The message of Daglow's work echoes David Lynch's own version of what happens when people who are unfamiliar with La Llorona underestimate her or try to undermine her purpose.

The above cultural producers are some of the people outside of La Llorona's parent culture who directly communicate her potency as a cultural symbol. Their works contribute to the vitality of the lore and to the ongoing dialogue concerning La Llorona's ability to continue to resonate in her cultural community. As this analysis reveals, the issues involved here are broader than positively representing La Llorona and the members of her parent culture. After all, the story *is* about a woman who murdered her children, in some cases butchered their bodies, and then threw them into a river. The folk of La Llorona's native culture possess culturally informed strategies for assigning meaning to, as well as decoding, the literal and symbolic significances of her actions. While La Llorona's behavior is in no way sanctioned, it is at least understood as a response to a culturally charged emotional event. Non-native artists must be mindful of why and how they are choosing to represent La Llorona, for stories are power. They are the means by which we make and shape the world around us. They are a reflection of what we value as a community.[30] Through their willingness to set aside a Eurocentric approach by privileging a Chican@, even Mexican, worldview in their own renderings of La Llorona, the artists included in this chapter demonstrate ways that outsiders can also show that La Llorona has much to teach us—all of us.

SIX

A New Generation of Cultural/Critical Readers

What incredible power lies in this woman of legend that we have dismissed
as a bogey woman of the river. We've used her to frighten children, when
we should be using her to raise them—the new children of a new era who
understand that each one carries the hope of the future.

—RUDOLFO ANAYA

FOR CLOSE TO five hundred years we have carried versions of La Llorona's stories with us across languages, time, and borders. At some point, Chican@s and Mexican@s may decide that La Llorona no longer has value, not even as entertainment. Leslie Marmon Silko (Laguna Pueblo, Mexican, Anglo) reminds us that if a story is "really important, if it really has a kind of substance that reaches to the heart of the community life and what's gone before and what's gone later, it will be remembered. And if it's not remembered, the people no longer wanted it, or it no longer had its place in the community" (Barnes, 88–89). Determining the place and future of stories is not exclusive to any one culture, group, or nation, but for marginalized people whose stories have been written over or displaced, the fate of certain stories can be tied to the future of the people. Still, questions remain as to whether and how Chican@s will pass the story of La Llorona on to the next generation. A survey of children's literature and other productions authored by natives and non-natives reveals that La Llorona is being used to teach children about cultural identity, storytelling, and cultural challenges. Through the use of La Llorona folklore, children are not only being prepared to read critically their own stories, but also to read other stories about their cultures.

In the face of a "post-ethnic" world, the illusion of solidarity has become, more than ever, a national project. Yet as a result of vigilante groups patrolling the US/Mexico border, immigration laws aimed at Mexicans, the termination of bilingual educational programs, the failure to establish a guest worker program, the resettlement of Aztlán, the political appointment of a Hispanic to a cabinet position, talk of building a Berlin-type wall along the southern border, and a host of other issues, Mexican@s and Chican@s remain one of the most highly visible majority minority groups. It is in this openly hostile, xenophobic environment marked by racist subterfuge that children of Mexican descent are negotiating their identities.

In my own experience, I have found that in both informal and formal settings, when asked about La Llorona, Chican@ students are reluctant to discuss her or often reply, "I don't know much about her, but what I heard was that she was some woman in Mexico who killed her kids. That's all I know." Many times, Anglos are the first ones to offer La Llorona stories, yet when I start to talk about her history, the legend, and the countless stories about her, "suddenly" the Chican@s and Mexican@s, even the stealth ones, remember, and begin to recount in great detail their own histories with La Llorona. Their suspicions of me as an academic, despite my status as a cultural insider, are set aside once they realize that my goal is not to use La Llorona against them to belittle, demean, or embarrass. In instances such as these, students assume a place of authority and are empowered through storytelling.

Many cultural producers actively use the folklore to empower and cultivate cultural pride in students of Mexican descent. While the more terrifying aspects of the tale remain characteristic of contemporary productions aimed at youngsters, these artists and storytellers choosing to transmit complex versions of the lore do so through the layering of visual and narrative replications in an effort to initiate for children broader discussions about culture, community, storytelling, and transformation. One such example is Carmen Lomas Garza's second bilingual book of family pictures, *In My Family/En Mi Familia* (1996). In the introduction, Garza explains to young readers that historically, Mexican@s and Chican@s were "punished for speaking Spanish" and made to feel "ashamed of our culture" (3). The book, which includes a vignette about La Llorona, is a catalog of select Garza paintings, each accompanied by a brief history and/or exposition of the piece. Garza's art, and the collection, is meant to heal old wounds, instill pride, and transmit lore and life to a new generation. Through written and visual replications of her family's version of La Llorona's story, Garza demonstrates how her own history with the legend, one handed down by her grandmother, fueled her imagination as a child. In her grandmother's version of the story, La Llorona kills her children to end their suffering from starvation. The murders are a merciful gesture on the part of the mother. Nevertheless, the story still inspired fear in Garza, who shares how her parents used La Llorona as a deterrent to keep her and her siblings out of the vacant lot across the street. On the facing page, in the painting *La Llorona* (1989), discussed in Chapter 1, children are gathered around the woman storyteller, and in the upper right-hand corner of the painting, La Llorona wanders. Like the woman storyteller at the center of the painting, Garza uses La Llorona as a means of educating children about familial and cultural history.

Garza's work and that of others are representative of the ways in which La Llorona can serve as a focal point for instructive learning about aspects of one's culture. Ethnically and culturally diverse theatre groups across the country that develop educational programming for children include La Llorona in productions or performances, using the legend as a means of promoting diversity and cross-cultural dialogue, as well as cultural pride and awareness. Great Leap, a Los Angeles–based multicultural performing arts organization rooted in the Asian American community, uses theatre, music, and dance in their production *A Slice of Rice, Frijoles, and Greens* (2003), which draws from Asian, Latino, African, and deaf American experiences. Paulina Sahagún incorporates a brief sketch on La Llorona as part of her segment included in the performance. Similarly, ChUSMA (slang for "the people"), also based in Los Angeles, includes a skit on La Llorona in its repertoire. Through a fusion of "'Neo-vaudvillian' [*sic*], early Mexican carpa, 60s teatro Chicano, multi-media, and performance art," ChUSMA's mission is to bring "comedy and consciousness into the new millennium" (ChUSMA). On the other side of the United States, Magical Rain Theatreworks in Durham, North Carolina, draws "upon methods from theater, art & learning theory" and mixes "theater, myths, and stories in [their] productions" (Magical Rain). "La Llorona Dolorosa" is part of a program that includes an original play about La Llorona followed by a "workshop in which the audience is encouraged to share similar ghost stories or urban legends or their own La Llorona stories" (Magical Rain). La Llorona's prominence in the Greater Mexican storytelling tradition makes her an interesting choice for a cultural ambassador to wider, culturally mixed audiences.

All of these productions transmit cultural knowledge and ensure the continuation of the lore for future generations through their interpretations and replications of the legend; however, a theatre group in Houston, in its 2003 production of *The Ghost of La Llorona* heightened the interplay and tension between different Llorona stories without giving authority to a single version. The production represents one of the most sophisticated dramatic offerings about La Llorona aimed at children. Since 1995, Express Children's Theatre (ECT) has staged *The*

Ghost of La Llorona, a one-act bilingual production written by Rodney Rincón with music by Joe Ramano (figures 6.1 and 6.2).[1] Storytelling and the contemporary relevance of folktales serve as the narrative backdrop for the action of the play. The executive director of ECT, Patricia A. Silver, offers the following outline of the action: "The family is camping, singing songs and telling folk tales. A storm approaches and the child wanders off. The ghost appears and tries to steal the child. It has very scary moments when the child is mesmerized and starts to go with the ghost into the water" (pers. comm. 2005). The production, with its spine-tingling action, is meant to foster discussions on the role of "legends, lessons and lore."[2] Children, then, are encouraged to explore their relationships to the stories in their own lives.

The 2003 production featured an intricate layering of La Llorona replications: visually, narratively, orally, and in the action of the play. Mary J. Tafoya's 2002 beadwork *La Llorona* (4" × 9", glass beads on Ultrasuede) serves as the inspiration for the stage backdrop (figure 6.3). Tafoya's piece is a replication of the legend, featuring La Llorona flying through the night sky above the river, her arms outstretched as if to grab any child who crosses her path.[3] An image similar to the artist's own is inverted horizontally on stage (seen behind the actors in figure 6.2), and represents a replication of Tafoya's replication of the legend. Against this visual representation, a drama that includes both La Llorona as a story and as a character unfolds. Through this production, audiences made up of cultural insiders and outsiders learn how multiple versions of the same story can coexist and even inform or contribute to the creation of new stories. Mexican American and Chican@ children, in particular, are encouraged to explore their own relationships to cultural stories and determine what role, if any, these stories can play in their lives.

The artifacts and productions discussed above replicate and disseminate conventional versions, for the most part, of the lore. While they promote and encourage children to tell their own stories, a vital endeavor, they do not demonstrate explicitly critical or comparative reading strategies that can help children engage, or even challenge, the world around them. Alfred Avila and Xavier Garza, in their story collections entitled *Mexican Ghost Tales of the Southwest* (1994) and *Creepy Creatures and Other Cucuys* (2004), respectively, published by Piñata Books, Arte Público's children's division, include conventional La Llorona stories and visual replications of scenes from the narratives. Alongside these, both authors include alternate versions of the legend. In "La Llorona of the Moon," Avila offers young readers a Llorona story that references an ambiguous Indigenous pantheon, one that La Llorona serves, while Garza, in "Another Version of La Llorona Story," cites the Texas Rangers as the original source of La Llorona's suffering. Avila's

FIGURE 6.1. (right) La Llorona, from the 1997 production of *The Ghost of La Llorona,* directed by Ed Muth. Used by permission of Patricia Silver, Express Children's Theatre.

FIGURE 6.2. La Llorona, from the 2003 production of *The Ghost of La Llorona,* directed by Trish Rigdon. Used by permission of Patricia Silver, Express Children's Theatre.

FIGURE 6.3. *La Llorona* (beadwork), by Mary J. Tafoya © 2004. Used by permission of the artist.

illustration merely replicates a scene from the story and does not demonstrate his alternate view of La Llorona. Garza, on the other hand, juxtaposes the image of his Llorona, named Christina, nurturing and tenderly suckling her child, with the written tale that details her depthless cruelty as evidenced by her drugging her children, placing them into a sack, and tossing them into the river to drown.[4] By including different versions in each collection, the authors encourage readers to compare them. Through this contrast, children are introduced to recuperation and revision as reading strategies. In these instances, La Llorona and her story are being used to teach children to become critical readers and writers from an early age. Along with Avila and Garza, cultural producers such as Gloria Anzaldúa and Rudolfo Anaya also encourage children to replicate, revise, recover, and reimagine their own versions of La Llorona's story.

Refashioning Cultural Truth

As a cultural activist whose work helped to empower people of color and women across the country, Anzaldúa turned her attention toward a new audience by writing her first children's book, *Friends from the Other Side/Amigos del otro lado* (1993), which focuses on people moving back and forth across the US/Mexico border. Anzaldúa followed up this work with *Prietita and the Ghost Woman/ Prietita y la Llorona* (1995), illustrated by Christina Gonzalez, in which she introduces young readers to both a traditional version of the lore, one that initially casts La Llorona as a threat, and a recuperated version that recovers her lost or hidden power. The story, written for ages four to six, focuses on four strong Chicanas and Mexicanas (Prietita's mother, Doña Lola, Prietita, and La Llorona) who join forces to save each other. Anzaldúa makes no direct reference to infanticide or a betrayal, although they are clearly demonstrated in La Llorona's isolation from her community (her figurative "children") as a result of Anglo ranchers fencing off of the land, making it inaccessible to Native and Mexican@ families who have lived there for generations. Young readers of the story are encouraged to explore such issues as coming of age, female power, community, colonization, folklore, and culture.

In the story, La Llorona represents both herself and the land to which she is tied. The owners of the King Ranch fence off the land and prevent people like Prietita, who needs the ruda plant to heal her mother, from gaining access to those remedios they need and have relied upon for their survival for centuries.[5] La Llorona cries because she is cut off from her people, but she takes the form of a deer, salamander, dove, jaguar, and lightning bugs to guide Prietita after she becomes lost on the ranch while searching for the ruda. When Prietita eventually hears the sound of a woman crying, instead of running away from the wailing, she runs toward it and discovers "a dark woman dressed in white [who] emerge[s] from the trees and float[s] above the water" (22). In Gonzalez's brilliantly hued illustrations, La Llorona looks like an older version of Prietita, indicating visually that in the process of looking for the plant that will cure her mother, Prietita comes across a future version of herself, one with the power to guide other young women.

Locating the ruda plant and learning about La Llorona on her own, in Doña Lola's view, serve as evidence of Prietita's transition into adulthood. A curandera, Doña Lola seems to be one of the few people who knows and understands La Llorona's true nature and purpose, as well as why people fear her. She confirms for Prietita and the reader that "'Perhaps [La Llorona] is not what others think she is'" (29). The search for the ruda plant becomes a symbolic search for Prietita's own strength and power to aid in healing. When she faces her fears and finds the ruda with La Llorona's help, her transition into adulthood is marked by the knowledge that what people believe about the Weeping Woman, including members of her own family, is not true. Prietita's discovery about La Llorona directly challenges the authority of her grandmother as well as Anglo colonial endeavors, as represented by the King Ranch.

Anzaldúa's version of La Llorona's story emphasizes the importance of women working together and relying on each other, and the book reinforces the idea that young women can have adventures and be strong. Not everyone familiar with La Llorona's story is receptive to shifting the narrative focus away from the terrifying outcome of the story and onto a positive one. An online reviewer in Cambridge, Massachusetts, complains on the Amazon.com Web page that Anzaldúa's "feminist version" of La Llorona's story is "boring" because "all of the suspense and horror" has been removed (phulana2). While the implication is that La Llorona's story has value only as thrilling entertainment, the cultural producers throughout this study have shown us that stories are one of the primary means by which we shape and understand the world around us. Using La Llorona to teach children that they can change the world is not only a worthwhile endeavor, but also a necessary one that can empower children, especially ones who look like or identify with Prietita.

Whereas Anzaldúa encourages children and, ideally, their parents to look beneath La Llorona's story for other meanings, Rudolfo Anaya uses La Llorona's story to initiate a discussion about storytelling, including revising and reimagining stories, for readers of different age groups. In his first children's book that includes La Llorona, *Maya's Children: The Story of La Llorona* (1997), written for ages five to nine, Anaya tells a Llorona story that does not include the infanticide. He explains that he wrote the story to achieve an objective other than scaring children: "Instead of using La Llorona as a character to frighten children—as she has been used by generations of parents—this story teaches youngsters about mortality. Through such motifs, I believe all myths or folktales can be adapted, especially for specific age-groups, to tell an interesting and valuable story" (3). The value of Anaya's story is that it encourages readers to reconsider La Llorona and the role she played in the loss of her children. Anaya also helps young readers to see the ways that we carry stories with us, explaining that while in Italy he heard La Llorona one day while traversing a forest and that her "cry urged [him] to tell her story to children everywhere" (3). The story Anaya was urged to tell diverges from conventional versions of the lore. Despite eliminating the horror of the infanticide, he replaces it with a kidnapping that produces the same result for the heroine: weeping and wandering.

Anaya shows his readers that before becoming the Llorona of legend, his protagonist's life was not defined by suffering. The story, which includes illustrations by New Mexican artist Maria Baca, is about an Indian woman who is given eternal life, a precious albeit lonely gift. To ease her solitude, Maya grows her children in clay bowls with the help of the animals and young men who offer her "seeds," but they are later stolen by Señor Tiempo (Mr. Time). In spite of the fact that Anaya reconfigures the dynamics of conventional Llorona stories to absolve her of the infanticide, the struggle for power between men and women remains central to the narrative.

Careful readers of the written and visual narratives will notice that they do not tell the same story. Baca's images—in particular, the last four illustrations in the book—tell a more nuanced story about La Llorona than Anaya's. Baca uses color and animals to communicate Maya's impending absolute isolation. When

Maya smashes the bowls from which the children were cultivated, she shatters the connection between her children and their eternal lives, as represented by the rejuvenative qualities that the fertile earth can provide. As Maya casts the broken pieces of pottery into the lake, Baca positions a heron in the corner of the scene with its mouth agape, foreshadowing Maya's doom. Baca's explosive use of reds, oranges, and blues, along with wild curving lines, captures both the swirling winds of the approaching "storm" and Maya's emotions, especially her panic about not being able to locate her children. The color or life begins to fade from the images after Señor Tiempo takes Maya's offspring. Baca then trades bright colors for muted shades of violet, indigo, and green in her depiction of Maya's mournful trek. Although animals are included in three of the final four illustrations, in the end Maya is alone, thus making her isolation and suffering absolute and completing her transformation into La Llorona. Thus while Anaya tells readers about Maya's despair, Baca shows it in Maya's face and posture.

Following *Maya's Children*, Anaya wrote a collection of stories aimed at readers ten and older called *My Land Sings: Stories from the Rio Grande* (1999), in which he provides aspiring raconteurs a model for contemporary storytelling, one that emphasizes the importance of updating stories for children. Consisting of five retold cuentos, including one about La Llorona, and five original stories, Anaya devotes considerable attention to a detailed discussion about storytellers and storytelling. Within this context, Anaya identifies La Llorona as having an important role in the Greater Mexican and Latin@ storytelling traditions: "Versions of the crying woman appear in hundreds of stories in New Mexico, Mexico, and throughout Latin America" (13). He goes on to say that "this tragic woman is the best-known character in the Latino oral tradition" (13). The author prefaces the collection by speaking to children and young adults about the social function of stories in his own community, emphasizing respect, knowledge, and wisdom:

> The stories I listened to as a child instilled in me a sense of belonging to a community and a knowledge of its values. Any event could become a story as the teller enhanced it with drama, and the beliefs of our people were woven into each tale. We may scoff at some beliefs and call them superstitions, but we must respect the body of knowledge each culture incorporates into its folk wisdom. (9)

In order to demonstrate the lasting impact of stories, Anaya offers his own history with La Llorona and uses the legend to emphasize the importance of oral narratives as sources for his own stories, telling readers: "I often use characters from the oral tradition, like la Llorona" (13). By giving his Llorona story, "Lupe and la Llorona," a place of prominence as the lead story in the collection, he suggests that contemporary Greater Mexican storytelling is derived from an oral tradition that includes, but is not limited to, stories about La Llorona.

For Anaya, La Llorona stories represent a means of continuing a storytelling tradition and contributing new stories to that tradition by updating or revising older cuentos. One method he offers for revision is synthesis, and he encourages children to explore this technique: "As a writer, I love to take traditional material and combine them into new stories. This is something you can try. Take a myth or a legend you like and write it in your own words. [. . .] We can enjoy both the traditional and the contemporary versions in different ways" (12). By offering his own methods for creating stories, Anaya models for his readers how to rework legends and create new ones on their own.

"Lupe and la Llorona" is the only story to include the woman of legend in the title; however, including the preface, there are actually four Llorona stories included in the collection: (1) the Llorona story Anaya heard as a child; (2) his re-counting of a childhood encounter with La Llorona; (3) the story about Lupe and La Llorona; and (4) the recounting of a Llorona story embedded in the narrative about Lupe. These different Llorona stories show young adult readers and writers the many ways that legends can be put to use in one's own creative endeavors, for legends can serve as a means of interrogating, challenging, writing, or even rewriting history.

The four stories also serve as a means for Anaya to show the evolution of a story from an oral to a written form. Like Garza and Avila, Anaya, in the preface, presents a conventional replication of the legend, one that includes the infan-ticide: "Long ago, in a fit of rage and jealousy, [La Llorona] had murdered her children. Now she searches for them eternally, crying as she wanders the dark river paths" (8–9). He emphasizes the physical effect of the fear La Llorona pro-duced in him and his friends: "As children, we believed she was real. Feeling her presence made our hair stand on end, and we bolted and raced for home" (9). His telling of the story serves to create a connection between the oral story and an actual encounter with La Llorona: "One evening I had stayed too late in town, playing basketball with my friends, even though my mother had told me to be home before dark. While crossing the river, I heard la Llorona's cry, a horrible mournful shriek. I saw her bright eyes in the dark, felt her fingers clawing at me. I ran! I ran as I had never run before!" (13). Anaya uses this encounter to explain the influence La Llorona has had on his writing over the years. The parallels between the author's experience and Lupe's might lead some to believe that the female protagonist's experiences are simply a masking of Anaya's own; however,

Lupe's Llorona proves different from the one Anaya knew growing up, and Lupe shows herself to be far more brave than the author as a boy.

In "Lupe and la Llorona," Anaya is not only passing along or introducing the legend of La Llorona to a new generation, but he is also attempting to show children how to revise it so that it reflects the challenges they currently face. For Lupe these difficulties include contending with burgeoning male power and authority, along with reconciling her gender performance with cultural and social expectations regarding conventional behavior for "young ladies." An encounter with La Llorona provides Lupe a means to confront these issues. Anaya therefore presents readers with a Llorona, similar to the one Prietita encounters, with the potential to be an ally for young women who challenge male authority.

Instead of using La Llorona's story as an allegory for mortality, in *My Land Sings* Anaya emphasizes the deadly effects of the strict division of social classes. Lupe recalls the most prominent La Llorona story she has heard:

> All her life, she had heard the different stories people told about la Llorona. Some said she was a young woman who long ago had lived in a neighboring village. She had fallen in love with a rich man's son and had a baby, but since she wasn't married to him, the young man's parents were going to take the baby away from her. The baby was all the poor girl had in the world, and she vowed not to let them take it. (21)

When the family sends for the sheriff to take custody of the baby, the young girl flees with her child. She throws herself in the river to elude the sheriff's deputies and their tracking dogs. The current of the river is so strong that the baby is torn from her arms and disappears beneath the water. The authorities eventually find the woman, but her baby has drowned. Although some of the villagers believe that she purposely drowned her child, "the young woman was overcome with grief. She walked along the edge of the river, looking for her baby. At night, the people of the village heard her crying and calling the child's name" (22). Acting like a rinche to the wealthy landowners in Texas who used the Rangers as their personal enforcers, the sheriff in the story Lupe recalls becomes an agent of the wealthy oppressors. The young woman in the narrative has broken no written law, though she has transgressed unwritten ones, including "straying" outside of one's class, a long-standing feature of many conventional Llorona tales.

Lupe also refuses to conform to her mother's expectations regarding her behavior. She is strong, adventurous, and independent, not to mention a great baseball player. Identified as a tomboy in the story, she does not allow gender conventions to restrict her behavior. In fact, Lupe's first physical encounter with

La Llorona is the result of a challenge issued by a male adversary meant as a direct assault on Lupe's authority derived from her superior skill as an athlete. Her accomplishments and self-assurance contribute to a one-sided rivalry with Carlos, a boy who perceives Lupe as a threat, in part because she led her baseball team to victory over his. In an attempt to diffuse Lupe's status, Carlos challenges her to venture to the river to "prove" her bravery by searching for La Llorona at the water's edge. The potential for harm is heightened by the fact that the "old people" tell the children not to play by the river because La Llorona might mistake them for her own lost child and take them away.

By consenting to look for La Llorona, Lupe defies both parental and community authority. Although she and Carlos flee from the figure they believe to be La Llorona, they both display the "courage" to go in search of her. Upon reflection, Lupe is uncertain whether or not she actually saw the Weeping Woman. She reasons that she might have fled from a shadow, misled in part by the sound of an "owl" or "cat" crying at the exact moment she spied the image. In attempting to preserve his image as a tough guy, Carlos does not admit to running away from the scene. Following the incident, Lupe becomes determined to learn the "truth" of La Llorona's existence.

Lupe's next encounter with La Llorona is also difficult to verify because it, too, occurs when she is alone. After bumping her head on a low-hanging branch while attempting to escape from a woman in a "long, tattered dress" with tangled hair, eyes red from crying, and sharp fingernails, she loses consciousness (28). When she awakens in a cave, La Llorona reveals her identity and makes the shocking announcement that she is the adoptive mother of the Greater Mexican bogeyman El Kookoóee, who was abandoned as a child. In the story, no explanation is given for El Kookoóee's monstrous appearance: a "huge head and red eyes," green skin, and enormous hands in which he holds a whip and sack for carting off children who misbehave (29). Readers, however, might conclude that his appearance is the reason for, or the result of, his abandonment. Here Anaya creates a direct relationship between two legendary figures, La Llorona and El Kookoóee, in one story. La Llorona tells Lupe that "good" children such as herself have nothing to fear from either the Weeping Woman or her "son." Finally, La Llorona wants Lupe to tell others the truth about their identities, as well as confirm their existence. At the exact moment the girl consents to become La Llorona's messenger, Lupe's father "saves" her. When she tells him about her encounter with La Llorona, he dismisses it as a dream or nightmare.

Ignoring her father's reaction, Lupe fulfills her promise to La Llorona and passes along the story of her encounter to Carlos and their friends, transmitting a new version of La Llorona's story to the next generation. Carlos immediately perceives her story as a challenge to his authority as a male and demands that they go to the river to find the cave where the alleged encounter took place. Lupe's father and some of the other men from the town follow Lupe, Carlos, and José, who has romantic feelings for Lupe. The patriarchs pretend to be La Llorona and El Koo-koóee and frighten Carlos, who runs away once again. Lupe proves her bravery to José by staying behind, and in doing so, she discovers the ruse. Inexplicably, Lupe suddenly becomes more interested in complying with her mother's wishes to attend the town fiesta and dancing with José than with adventures and legends. In the end, readers are never sure if the encounter is "real" or "imagined." Either way, though, the outcome is the same for Lupe: Anaya foreshadows the collapse of this tomboy into a "conventional" woman who will be expected to wear dresses and "dance with the boys who asked her" at the upcoming fiesta (27).

In light of her impending transition into womanhood, her search for La Llorona becomes the last adventure of her carefree youth. The suggestion is that girls can defy, to a limited extent, traditional and cultural expectations of gender performance, but once they become women, they must abandon these behaviors. *Finding* La Llorona can have additional consequences, as demonstrated in both Prietita's and Lupe's stories. Whereas Prietita gains access to a circle of female power, Lupe's encounter with La Llorona results in a symbolic death: the end of her life as a tomboy. Consequently, while Anaya may revise La Llorona's story and circumstances, he does little to change the existing power structure that denies young women a viable space to challenge these structures as adult women.

In casting Lupe as the protagonist of his story, Anaya attempts to show that girls can be at the center of great adventures. He admits that his decision was informed by the lack of heroines in the tales from his own culture, attributing this lack of representation to the gender of the storytellers: "In many legends and myths from our culture and from around the world, the main character is often a man or a boy. Perhaps this is because the storytellers are often men. Maybe I wasn't around when my mother told stories with her sisters and friends. When I wrote [the story], I tried to think and act like Lupe" (*My Land,* 15). Although Anaya's story serves as a corrective to the under-representation of women — young women, in particular — he also gives readers the impression that story-tellers are and have been predominately male. In fact, his decision to have the patriarchs play La Llorona and El Kookoóee reinforces the idea that men are the ones "behind" or "underneath" these stories. As such, young readers might believe that because men and boys are the ones who tell the stories, it is their responsibility to "write" young women into them

A pessimistic reading would tell us that Anaya's privileging of a male story-telling tradition encourages young women to believe that narrating their own experiences and those of other women is not a part of their cultural inheritance or that it should remain hidden or mystified. But Lupe *does* tell La Llorona's story. The problem is that the males in her community do not believe her. As such, throughout the story, Anaya does not discourage girls from seeing themselves as storytellers, but he does show them what they are up against when trying to tell or change traditional stories: the passage of time, patriarchal authority, and social conventions that require women to capitulate to the desires of men. In *My Land Sings,* Anaya shows readers that storytelling is a dynamic process, and that our stories can evolve as we grow, or rather, that our stories *should* grow as we grow.

Educators repeatedly turn to sources such as the ones discussed above to engage children in the classroom. La Llorona has been incorporated into lessons at various grade levels in California, Texas, Arizona, New Mexico, Colorado, Utah, Idaho, Florida, Nevada, New Hampshire, and Michigan, for example, by individual teachers and curriculum writers. In the fall of 2005, Miss Gretchen Eichberger's fourth-grade class in Onekama, Michigan, staged and produced a "spooky musical play for Halloween" about La Llorona, or as one fourth grader identifies her, "LaLaRona" (Onekama Consolidated Schools). Photos and student journals from the production, which dramatizes a conventional version of the tale that includes the infanticide, were posted on the Onekama Consolidated Schools' Web site. The dissemination of this information illustrates how La Llorona can be used as an effective and fun teaching tool that inspires creativity.

Whereas the fourth-grade class worked from a story outline to develop their production, a script is provided for the play *Cuentos,* cowritten by Carlos Morton and Angel Vigil, in Vigil's curriculum and educational instructional guide for grades four through eight, *Una Linda Raza: Cultural and Artistic Traditions of the Hispanic Southwest* (1998).[6] La Llorona is represented in the play through song, character, and narrative. Blending drama, humor, and satire, while drawing from teatro, folklore, and music (corridos, in particular), the bilingual play seeks to expand cultural awareness and address family, social, and community issues: "As the characters work their magic, the children learn the importance of family responsibility, the values of traditional culture, the wisdom of making good decisions and the strengths of their Hispanic heritage" (153). In the instruction guide, the play is included in the chapter on theatre, which begins with Spanish colonial folk drama and ends with what Vigil identifies as "Modern Hispanic theater," represented by *Cuentos* (145). Although Vigil does not offer teachers or students any strategies for interpreting the legend, he does illustrate the advantage of knowing one's cultural stories and figures.

The dramatic action of the play is similar to that found in Anzaldúa's *Prietita and the Ghost Woman*. Two grandchildren go in search of help and a cure for their ailing grandmother: "On their journey of discovery, [the siblings] confront folk figures from Hispanic culture: the Weeping Woman, Death, *duendes* and a *bruja*" (153). These urban children, who hail from Denver, appear to have lost touch with the land, as represented in the play by a "Valley Far Away," and the stories about other figures from Greater Mexican folklore such as duendes, mischievous gnome-like spirits. They learn about La Llorona from a bruja who transforms herself into the legendary figure. However, in the guise of La Llorona, the bruja does not threaten the children. Instead she provides them the means to protect themselves from La Muerte. The story of La Llorona offered in the play represents a conventional, nationalist version, through the pairing of a Spanish officer with an Indian maiden. Yet one interesting dimension Vigil and Morton do add is that when the Spaniard turns his affections toward another woman, this time she is a "Yankee woman" (162). The Spaniard who wants to marry the woman purchases her from the Comanches who held her captive and then makes his Indian lover a servant of his intended. As a result, La Llorona's brief appearance in the play does hint at the way in which miscegenation figures prominently into colonial endeavors.

As Vigil and Morton's play demonstrates, the legend has served as one means of transmitting the oral history of her parent culture, even when it is told for entertainment. Oppressive forces that gave rise to and shaped La Llorona's legend, such as colonialism, internecine warfare, patriarchy, and the dissolution of female power, are still in place. These hardly seem topics suitable for children, but keeping La Llorona from children indefinitely will not save them from confronting these issues in their own lives. Whereas in the past, La Llorona's stories were used primarily to frighten or entertain, they are now being used to empower and instill cultural pride as well as a sense of cultural history. Through formalized curriculum, virtual archives, community theatre, picture books, teen mysteries, art, and oral narratives, La Llorona's story is being passed on to future storytellers. By teaching children to challenge, revise, or reimagine conventional narratives like the ones about La Llorona, children discover the ways in which stories make, and can remake, the world around them.

Folklore as Critical Lens

IN TONI MORRISON's Pulitzer Prize–winning novel *Beloved* (1987), we are told that the narrative—made tangible through the lives of Sethe, Paul D., Baby Suggs, Denver, and Beloved, to name a few—is "not a story to pass on." Some readers may interpret the line to mean that no one should ever have to experience the events of the novel in this way and that "[r]emembering seemed unwise" (274). But I have always believed that this utterance is made by the collective voice of those who suffered, lived, and died on the torturous crossing of the Middle Passage, and that they are telling us that this is a story we cannot afford to ignore. In other words, we cannot neglect this story or fail to value it as potent and powerful "rememory," for although Beloved has slipped beneath the surface of the lives of everyone she has touched, she is not just the past: the traumatic history that she represents is always a powerful influence in the present.

The issues at stake in Morrison's novel are the same ones involved in determining whether or not La Llorona's legend is a story to pass on. In *Beloved,* storytelling becomes a strategy of survival, resistance, and a means of liberation. Sethe resembles the Llorona who performs the tender mercy killing of her children rather than allow them to suffer unimaginable cruelty.[1] However, though Sethe is Llorona-like, she is not La, or even a, Llorona. In fact, Beloved more closely

resembles La Llorona than Sethe, particularly through Beloved's emergence from
the river dressed in black and later her wandering by its shore: "Down by the
stream in back of 124 her footprints come and go, come and go" (275). Although
she disappears from the lives of the residents of 124, her story and what she represents remain. Ultimately, Morrison's novel impresses upon the reader not only
the value of cultural inheritance, but also the importance of figuring a response
to this legacy. La Llorona's story *is* one that we should pass on as both a critical
reading strategy and part of our cultural legacy.

Other Cultural Landscapes

The foregrounding of community storytelling traditions as sources of inquiry
represents one method of cultivating and privileging Chican@ critical thought
in the discussion of cultural productions that include La Llorona. One such example includes Gregory Nava's two-part episode "La Llorona" for the PBS series
American Family (2002–2004). The episode features three La Llorona stories
intertwined. Cisco, the youngest son of the Gonzalez familia, tells a traditional
story to his nephew, Pablito, and supplements it with pictures from a fictional
Internet Web site about La Llorona. By having a character tell a traditional version of the tale, Nava conveys the basic tenets of the Llorona legend to audiences
unfamiliar with the story. The secondary, but equally important, function is to
provide a narrative frame for the other stories in the episode about women who,
through drug addiction and deportation, have "lost" their children.[2] The structure of the episode encourages viewers to read the women featured in the other
story lines as Lloronas, although they are not directly identified as such. Through
this model, writer and director Gregory Nava shows audiences how to use La
Llorona lore as a critical reading strategy, while simultaneously preparing them
to conceptualize La Llorona in new or different ways.

The title of Nava's two-part episode, along with the formal Llorona story that
appears in it, points audiences in a specific direction for interpreting the events
and characters found in the episode. Alicia Gaspar de Alba, through her use of
lines from the Mexican folksong "La Llorona" as an epigraph, also encourages
readers to make connections between La Llorona and the lives of her protagonists
in the short story "Malinche's Rights" (1993) and mystery novel *Desert Blood:
The Juárez Murders* (2005). However, she is not as heavy-handed as Nava in
directing audiences toward a specific reading. The song serves as a lens through
which to view the two narratives, both of which include characters whose lives
are defined, in part, by pain, suffering, and death. "Malinche's Rights" focuses
on a woman coming to terms with her history as a victim of sexual abuse by her

father, who has recently died. The protagonist, though clearly not a Llorona or Malinche, finds a sisterhood with women who are united through their ability to survive, and even resist, abuse from men.

Desert Blood is a fictional mystery set against the backdrop of the real murders of young, poor, Mexican, and primarily Indigenous, women in Ciudad Juárez. The novel begins with four epigraphs that speak to the hundreds of mothers left weeping for their dead daughters, the effects of globalization, sexual violence against women, and the invisibility of the poor. While each serves as an interpretive strategy for understanding the multiple forces at work on the women in the novel, as well as in Juárez, the following lines from the folksong "La Llorona" appear first: "Hay muertos que no hacen ruido, Llorona / Y es más grande su penar . . . ."[3] Gaspar de Alba attempts to give voice to and seek justice for those women whose death cries went unheard, but the prominent positioning of the folksong also prepares the reader for the many Lloronas present in the novel. Ivon Villa, the protagonista, is positioned as a Llorona figure: first when the child she and her partner, Brigit, plan to adopt is cut from his mother's womb before he is born, and later, when her little sister, Irene, whom Ivon practically raised, disappears one night. The treacherous Ariel, who collaborates with men in their victimization of women, literally steals young women off the streets to deliver them to their deaths at the hands of snuff pornographers. La Llorona wanders in many forms throughout the story and her wails are heard, for example, in the shriek of the train that "sounded like a woman screaming" (144) and the sound of a mother's wail, "screaming . . . that ugly animal tone," upon learning of her daughter's disappearance (163). Despite, or perhaps because of, the desperate situation in Juárez, in the end Gaspar de Alba offers her readers hope by writing Ivon out of a Llorona narrative through her successful adoption of a boy whose mother is dying and through the rescue of her sister. Ultimately, Gaspar de Alba does not tell her readers what to think about her controversial story, but through the epigraphs the author does offer an interpretive framework for navigating a complex and compelling narrative.

Julie Taymor uses the La Llorona folksong in *Frida* (2002), her film about the Mexican painter and cultural icon, in a manner similar to that of Gaspar de Alba. Rather than a critical lens given to audiences at the outset, the song is sung to Frida after she discovers her husband, Diego Rivera, having sex with her sister. While in a bar, a mysterious man sings a traditional version of the Mexican folksong about La Llorona, one that emphasizes the pain of love but makes no mention of infanticide. Audiences familiar with the folksong or tale can begin to assemble moments in Frida's life into a Llorona story: the loss of her unborn child; Frida screaming in the hospital for the body of her son; the scene of the fetus floating in a glass jar; Frida submerged in water contemplating her inability to carry any children to term; her husband's chronic infidelity; and her crippling pain, the result of childhood disease and injury. Instead of succumbing to La Llorona's fate as recounted in conventional versions of the story, Frida redirects her pain and frustration into her art to create a lasting visual legacy.

Yet the application and usefulness of this critical approach extends beyond those productions that include La Llorona by name. It can be used also as a critical lens to read Mexican@ and Chican@ characters as Llorona figures, even when she does not directly appear in productions. Doing so can provide an indication of the place of and attitudes about Mexican@ and Chican@s. As I have illustrated elsewhere, the lore is useful for reading Allison Anders' *Mi Vida Loca* (1993), Gregory Nava's *Mi Familia* (1995), John Sayles' *Lone Star* (1996), and Andy Tennant's *Fools Rush In* (1997), films chosen because their principal narratives focus on Chicanas whose depiction is suggestive of primary elements of La Llorona lore.[4] An analysis like this one allows us to see beyond the "Sultry Señorita" or the "Spit Fire," classical Hollywood types for Latinas that have endured to this day, to view Chicana characters through a cultural construction of women informed by the story of La Llorona.

The strategy is also useful for reading characters like Ana Lucia Cortéz, played by Michelle Rodriguez, on the television series *Lost,* which focuses on the lives of plane crash survivors on a mysterious island. Viewers were introduced to Ana Lucia at the end of the first season in a scene of flirty banter with the soon-to-be island hero, an Anglo doctor named Jack. In a second season episode, "The Other 48 Days," Ana Lucia and a handful of others, including a "priest" named Mr. Eko, emerge as additional survivors on the island. The overall number of these survivors has been significantly depleted as a result of violent kidnappings from a mysterious band of Others who live on the island.[5] Ana Lucia is no longer flirty, but filled with a violent, unexplained rage bordering on paranoia.[6] Another character goes so far as to assess Ana as someone who is "already dead." Pieces begin to fall into place for Chican@ cultural readers when we learn that Ana failed to safeguard two children, who survived the crash, from the Others (see figure 7.1). Succumbing to her grief over the loss, Ana Lucia weeps for the first time in the river with a makeshift machete slung across her hips. The mingling of the biblical allusion to Christ's passion, the redemptive or rejuvenative power of water, the image of the soldadera, and the hand-made phallus hint at the complexity of Ana Lucia's character.[7]

Like the Llorona found in conventional replications, this Llorona's life has been defined by her suffering and transgressions. Viewers learn that Ana Lucia's "crime" is far greater than her failure to protect children from kidnappers. Flash-

FIGURE 7.1. Actress Michelle Rodriguez as Ana Lucia with the children from the *Lost* episode "The Other 48 Days."

backs in "Collision," a later episode, reveal that Ana is a police officer who was shot in the line of duty while pregnant. She is a woman of authority and power who carries a gun. Yet for all of her training and proficiency, she allows a fresh-faced Anglo suspect to convince her to momentarily lower her weapon during a raid, and he shoots her point blank. Authorities fail to apprehend the shooter, and Ana blames herself for the loss of her unborn child. Rather than weep and wander, this Llorona waits. Months later, when the assailant is brought into the police station and Ana is asked to verify his identity, she lies. After he is set free, Ana Lucia begins to hunt, not haunt, him. One night in an alley, she approaches the man, tells him that she was pregnant at the time he shot her, and then un-loads four rounds from her 9 mm into his body, finishing him off with three final bullets to his head. Yet the venganza of this Llorona does not bring her peace; it only exacerbates her suffering, leaving her searching for the children she has lost, not once, but twice. Reading Ana Lucia's character through the lens of the lore tells cultural readers that she is far more dangerous than anyone can imagine: her capacity for vengeance is the stuff of legends.[8]

The addition of Ana Lucia's character to *Lost* can be read as an attempt on the part of ABC to attract a Latin@ audience. For some time, television networks have been attempting to find a way to reach Latin@ viewers—not out of a sense of responsibility or desire for greater diversity of programming, but for profit.[9] In 2005, ABC made all of its regular prime-time programming "available in Span-ish through secondary audio program dubbing and closed caption subtitles" to tap into the billions of dollars attached to the "Latino" market (Rosenthal). An additional method of attracting Spanish-speaking audiences includes casting Latin@s in prominent roles on popular programs. The national and ethnic di-versity of the surviving passengers easily supports additional Latino characters (original cast member Jorge Garcia plays Hector "Hugo" Reyes, and characters played by Kiele Sanchez and Rodrigo Santoro were added and then killed off in the third season), especially one played by a well-known actor such as Rodri-guez. Finally, *Lost* writers have admitted to placing in episodes "Easter Eggs," a gaming technology term for hidden features or unannounced rewards in a game found only by the most loyal enthusiasts.[10] These *Lost* Easter Eggs have included references, both visual and spoken, to philosophers, graphic novels, literature, and myths, to name a few. Therefore, Ana's resemblance to La Llorona may very well be a deliberate attempt to entice Chican@ and Latin@ viewers into watching this very modern, very empowered, and very scary Llorona move through the landscape.

For audiences who know that no woman on television can have that much uncontested power for long, Ana Lucia's murder in "Two For The Road" near the end of the second season was no surprise. However, according to the moral uni-verse of the show, Ana Lucia should not have been killed immediately following her moment of redemption, which consisted of her refusal to murder an "Other," whom she held responsible for kidnapping her surrogate children. In spite of her death, she still has a real possibility of recovering her lost children, for the creators of *Lost* have proven that almost anything can happen on the island.[11]

The cultural status of Mexican@s and Chican@s can also be determined through the lens of the lore to illustrate Tey Diana Rebolledo's alternate posit-ing of the Weeping Woman in popular cultural productions as an iconic representation of Chican@s' marginality in Euroamerican mainstream culture and their lost state in contemporary society. If, as Rebolledo argues, contemporary Llorona figures are characterized by various degrees of lost-ness, then men can be seen as symbolic Lloronas who are isolated or alienated from their own community and/or the dominant culture. For instance, in the film *Mi Familia* (1995) by Gregory Nava, the characters of young María (Jennifer Lopez), Chucho (Esai Morales), Jimmy (Jimmy Smits), and Memo (Enrique Castillo) embody almost every characteristic of both traditional and contemporary Lloronas across genders. The males in Nava's film represent various degrees of Llorona-like lost-ness, suffering either from prejudice, violence, abandonment, or assimilation into a racist society. While the women suffer from these same dominating and debilitating forces, at times delivered on two separate fronts from both Anglo men and Chican@s or Mexican@s, the lore also helps account for ways that men act out violently as direct responses to infantalization and emasculation by dominating forces.

The strategy can also be used to read texts generated by both natives and non-natives that do not include Chican@ or Mexican@ characters. In these instances, cultural readers are not seeking to make non-native women, or even men, into Llorona figures. Rather a critical reader uses the lore to identify oppressive forces at work on these individuals that call to mind features of La Llorona stories. These characters are not Lloronas but do struggle under or against oppression. Used in this way, La Llorona lore helps clarify the dynamics of violence and oppression in terms of history and culture. For example, Grace Stewart, the protagonist of *The Others* (2001), directed by Alejandro Almenábar, resembles a Llorona, who, driven mad after her husband fails to return after World War I, kills her photosensitive children. Grace and her children haunt their former residence. Once the oppressive forces at work on her (Catholicism, war, isolation, motherhood, and disease, to name a few) are identified, points of comparison can be made between these characters and La Llorona or even Llorona figures; these comparisons allow readers to locate intersections between US/Mexican transnational concerns and those of other national economic, social, political, and even cultural communities.

Yet in our efforts to locate these intersections, we must use caution when using La Llorona lore as a critical tool to interpret the actions of individuals outside of La Llorona's cultural community in order to avoid generalizations that can erase cultural difference. For instance, George Aguilar casts Susan Smith as a contemporary Llorona in his multimedia installation "A Mere Extension of Herself, Susan Smith: A Modern Day Llorona" (2003), which includes still and video images of Smith throughout the search for her children and her subsequent arrest and trial.[12] The following lines of text set against the red and white stripes in the field of the American flag and presumably assigned to Smith by Aguilar also appeared in the piece:

> I SEE HER BEAUTY
> I HEAR HER CRIES
> I FEEL HER DESIRES
> YO SOY LA LLORONA
> LA LLORONA IS ME

Aguilar reads the infanticide of the case through the existing cultural framework of La Llorona lore to interpret and assign meaning to the Smith murders. The superficial similarities between La Llorona's story and Susan Smith's allow for the comparison (figure 7.2).[13] Also, the circumstances leading up to and surrounding the murder of her sons, Michael (three years old) and Alexander (two years old), reinforce the parallels between Smith and La Llorona: Smith, in love with the son of her employer, received from him a letter breaking off their relationship. In the letter, he cites his unwillingness to become part of a "ready made" family (Gibbs and Booth, 45). A closer comparison between the two reveals one key difference: Smith's privilege.

By conflating the two figures, Aguilar fails to interrogate the role that Smith's white privilege played in initially keeping her above suspicion. In the pursuit of happiness and financial well-being, Smith saw her children as an obstacle to her potential relationship with a man well above her working-class roots. Believing she could simultaneously eliminate her "problem" and gain sympathy from the object of her obsession, she parked her car near a lake, made sure Michael and Alex were strapped into the family's Mazda Protege, and released the handbrake, causing the car to roll into the lake with her children inside. As in conventional versions of the lore, Smith, like La Llorona, murders her children to "solve" a problem in her life. In a scene reminiscent of La Llorona standing before God and lying, Smith lies about having any knowledge of the whereabouts of her boys, a point the assistant solicitor, Keith Giese, made in his opening statement of the trial: "'For nine days in the fall of 1994, Susan Smith looked this country in the eye and lied'" (Wulf and Towle, "Elegy"). In her now legendary performance of grief, Smith blamed the disappearance of her children on the equally famous archetypal young black urban male criminal/thug, even going so far as to make an impassioned tearful plea to the nonexistent carjacker to return her children unharmed.[14] Even as a working-class white woman in the South, Smith was still able to capitalize on white anxiety and fear of black men to deflect blame from

FIGURE 7.2. *Drowning in Her Own Tears,* by Val and Bob Tillery © 1995. Used by permission of the artists. Smith's tears are a central feature of the image, which may explain why some readers transform her from a "weeping woman" to La Llorona.

herself. It is the latter point that best illustrates why Smith is *not* La Llorona. La Llorona never had Smith's power or white privilege. Arguably, had Smith been a bit more clever, she might have gotten away with the infanticide, for she had most of the necessary ingredients for her exoneration: (1) her own whiteness; (2) public sympathy; and (3) generalized white anxiety about the perceived threat of young black men.

Through comparisons like the one Aguilar makes between Smith and La Llorona, Latin@s can unintentionally reinforce negative stereotypes about Mexican@s and Chican@s. For instance, the association of Smith with La Llorona, and the violence of which she is capable, gives Anglo America a plausible "explanation" for how a seemingly innocuous white woman can commit such an atrocity.[15] While doing so places the focus on the individual act itself, where it belongs, in part, it also overshadows the ongoing mechanisms, such as racism, capitalism, classism, poverty, and gender oppression, that are equal contributors to tragedies such as these. Audiences may also overlook the fact that these types of atrocities are not exclusive to one cultural group.

The use of La Llorona lore as a critical reading strategy not only privileges a Chican@ worldview but also contributes to coalition building across cultures that accounts for individual, as well as intersecting, cultural concerns. Reading texts through and against the lore serves to privilege disenfranchised characters in these productions; highlights or exposes the forces at work on these characters that contribute to their marginalization; and allows readers to anticipate and interpret characters' responses to those dominative or dominating mechanisms and individuals within Indigenous and colonial contexts. Finally, the strategy encourages a specific consideration of both how these relationships are narrativized and the cultural sources (such as the Bible or TV) from which cultural producers draw for their creations.

The lore also allows us to see familiar or canonical texts in new ways. For example, at the conclusion of *Moby Dick* (1851) by Herman Melville, a ship named the *Rachel* rescues Ishmael, the narrator. The name of the wandering ship calls to mind the biblical mother Rachel who weeps for the lost children of Israel. This retrieval of Ishmael by a figurative Rachel is suggestive of a profound recovery, one with the power to ease Rachel's suffering and to provide a lost child with a home. Ishmael's survival and recovery by the *Rachel* affirms simultaneously the importance and superiority of Euroamerican men and Christianity through the sacrificing of Others, such as Queequeg, Tashtego, and Pip, for instance, who end up at the bottom of the ocean.

Folk collectors Edward Garcia Kraul and Judith Beatty note the similarities between the biblical Rachel and La Llorona, and begin their collection *Weeping Woman* by citing the following:

> "*A voice was heard in Ramah,*
> *Lamentation, weeping,*
>   *and great mourning,*
> *Rachel weeping for her children,*
> *Refusing to be comforted,*
>   *because they were no more.*" (Matthew 2:18)

Elements that align Rachel's narrative with that of La Llorona's include Rachel's weeping and the loss of "her" children. Furthering the similarity is Rachel's refusal to be comforted, which becomes her means of protest, her act of resistance. Rachel is not responsible for the deaths of the children; she does, however, symbolically bear witness to the slaughter of boys under the age of two in Bethlehem and its surrounding districts in Herod's effort to eliminate the King of the Jews.

The vision of Rachel's suffering was originally delivered to the prophet Jeremiah and is recounted first in the Old Testament, Jeremiah 31:15. When looked at carefully, and in context, the two figures are analogous only in their mourning, for Rachel is promised the return of her children. La Llorona is offered no such guarantee. Furthermore, when looking at the prophecy on the subject of Rachel in its entirety, readers learn that Rachel's weeping is not perpetual, for the Lord says: "Refrain your voice from weeping, / And your eyes from tears; / For your work shall be rewarded. [. . .] / And they shall come back" (Jeremiah 31:16). She is ordered to cease her mourning and to deny her grief. Rachel has no direct power to save her own children; God has already decided their fate.

Through the lens of the biblical prophecy recounted by Jeremiah, the *Rachel's* recovery of the lost children, or in the case of Ishmael, the lost child, represents the fulfillment of the Lord's promise that the children will return, while reinforcing the value of white children over those of red, black, or brown.[16] Unlike the story of La Llorona, the biblical narrative about Rachel neither accounts for the symbolic identity attached to that "recovered" child nor for the colonial legacy that has laid waste to tribes like the Pequots (whose members were murdered, captured, burned, drowned, and enslaved), the same legacy that contributes to La Llorona's fate and the shaping of her legend. The *Rachel's* recovery of Ishmael as the lone survivor of the *Pequod* becomes symbolic of the sole means of Native "survival" available in the novel. Natives are allowed to exist only in the stories of white men where the former remain captive creations that are repeatedly destroyed to affirm European superiority. Therefore, a reading of the novel through the lens of the lore, one that begins at the conclusion, reveals the way in which Melville "plots" conquest. A reading such as this one also reveals the extent to which Melville relies on Native issues, themes, and characters like Tashtego to shape his novel and the ways in which Native identity is transformed and "recovered" in the text.[17]

Whereas in the above example, La Llorona lore lends new insights into a canonical text from the American literary tradition, Ray Martín Abeyta in his painting *Ofelia y La Llorona* (2004) asks audiences directly to rethink one of Shakespeare's most beloved tragic heroines by reading Ophelia from *Hamlet* through the lens of the lore (figure 7.3). Calling to mind the famous painting

FIGURE 7.3. *Ofelia y La Llorona* (2004, oil on linen, 64" × 80"), by Ray Abeyta © 2005. Private collection. Used by permission of the artist.

Ophelia (1852) by the pre-Raphaelite artist John Everett Millais, Abeyta's Ofelia floats in the water with a bouquet of flowers clutched to her breast.[18] Reminiscent of the scene from Moraga's play where the Cihuateteos place La Llorona's veil on Medea, the outline of a watery veil appears around Ofelia's head. La Llorona, standing over Ofelia, gently cradles her head with one hand. In the other, La Llorona holds a rose delicately pinched between her fingers. Cherubs and water spirits hover above and beneath, respectively, the two women. The central image is framed by four smaller corner images. The upper right corner includes a drawing, rendered in the style of early botanical texts, of columbine flowers, which Ophelia gives to Claudius after her madness has taken hold. The flowers symbolize infidelity or betrayal (IV.iv). A portrait of Hamlet, dressed in a traje de charro and holding a red rose, appears in the bottom right corner. On the opposite side at the bottom, Polonius, dressed in a pin-striped suit, holds out a cigar. And in the top left, rendered in a consciously archaic style, is a scene of a man pouring poison into a king's ear, which mirrors the elder Hamlet's murder by Claudius. The three images featuring men, taken together with the columbines, reveal the direct cause of Ofelia's death: overwhelming betrayal. Abeyta implicates the patriarchy, specifically Ofelia's king/country, family, and lover, in her death.

Reading Ophelia's story through the lens of the lore reveals the thematic and narrative similarities between the two figures' stories. Water, sorrow, and death are associated with each, but in Abeyta's painting La Llorona helps deliver Ofelia from her suffering, an idea suggested by the rose La Llorona holds in her hand. Rather than taking the veil of a nun, as Hamlet, though speaking ironically, so advises, Ophelia is initiated into a completely different kind of convent, one headed by La Llorona. In her safeguarding of Ofelia, La Llorona serves, in the absence of Ophelia's mother in the play, as the young woman's symbolic mother, and Ofelia in turn becomes one of La Llorona's recovered children.[19]

To further the parallel between the two figures, Abeyta includes the theme of infanticide through Ofelia's clutching of her genitalia. The indication is that Ofelia has surrendered her virginity to Hamlet and is perhaps even pregnant, becoming "a breeder of sinners," which Hamlet warns her against (III.i). The "plucked" rose Hamlet holds in his hand, symbolizing his taking of her maidenhood, and the cherubs, looking down at her with childlike faces, reinforce this interpretation. Her death, therefore, also results in the death of her unborn child. Ultimately, Abeyta not only reads Ophelia through the lens of the La Llorona folklore, but he also writes the Greater Mexican legendary figure into European literature and history via Shakespeare's play, the effect of which suggests that before Shakespeare, there was La Llorona. The implication of Abeyta's painting is that we should actively seek out the intersections between Native and European storytelling traditions to lend new insights to both.[20]

The above represent only a few possibilities generated through the lens of *one* Greater Mexican artifact. I am not advocating the exclusive use of any one story as a critical lens, nor am I suggesting that every story found in Greater Mexican folklore will be a useful critical tool, but I do believe that there are untapped resources in Chican@ literature, history, philosophy, and lore that can serve as the foundation for new critical and theoretical strategies. The privileging of these new critical perspectives need not be at the expense of Eurowestern thought lest we be labeled "barrio-izers." Yet there is a need for us to explore and understand our relationship to our own cultural principles and how they shape our worldviews. Doing so can undermine usurping Euro-inflected ideologies used by those who attempt to define our cultural productions while ignoring us in the process. As La Llorona teaches us, we are not helpless victims without recourse for responding to these efforts. A wealth of Chican@ critical possibilities awaits those with the diligence, integrity, and imagination to find them.

In "La Llorona y El Grito/The Ghost and the Scream: Noisy Women in the Borderlands and Beyond," Rosemarie L. Coste warns: "Openly looking for a ghost is the surest way not to find her." Despite La Llorona's elusive nature, Mexican Americans and Chican@s continue to search for and turn to La Llorona to reflect critically on questions of gender, religion, sexuality, and class. La Llorona is a figure tied to cultural, social, and political movements, and my hope is that my work also demonstrates the need for transnational comparative analyses in, and throughout, Latin America to determine, for instance, how the stories operate in different national contexts or how the lore is expressed across genres. Whether cultural producers represent or revise the legend, position La Llorona as a champion for her people, or turn her toward new narrative possibilities, what matters is that for approximately five centuries she has held a powerful place in the cultural and political imaginations of her people.

Preface

1. My initial efforts to categorize Llorona narratives are useful for understanding the evolution of this project. See "Caminando con La Llorona."

2. For an analysis of Anaya's use of La Llorona as a motif, see Jane Rogers, "The Function of the *La Llorona* Motif."

3. In Bess Lomax Hawes' compelling compilation and analysis of recurring themes in folktales collected from a variety of female sources, she includes stories about La Llorona from Anglos and African Americans in addition to those gathered from Greater Mexican women. See Hawes, "La Llorona in Juvenile Hall."

4. My mother's mother, Eugenia Ortiz, died of pneumonia when my mother was only three, so she and her two younger siblings were raised by their maternal grandparents, whom they called Amá and Apá. Their father, Eduardo, raised my mother's four older brothers because they were old enough for him to take with him to labor in the fields. My mother remained separated from her father and brothers until she was a teenager. Family gatherings, like the one that was the setting for the Llorona stories I heard, were especially joyous and emotional for my mother, who spent so many years apart from the rest of her family.

5. The following is a list, in the order I found them, of my initial critical sources on La Llorona generated by Chicanas and Chicanos: Gloria Anzaldúa, *Border-*

lands/La Frontera: The New Mestiza (1987); José E. Limón, "La Llorona, The Third
Legend of Greater Mexico" (1990), Tey Diana Rebolledo, *Women Singing in the
Snow* (1995); and Cordelia Candelaria, "Letting La Llorona Go" (1993).

6. I am not the first to use this symbol (@) to designate Mexican American women
and men simultaneously. The "a" ending, which indicates the feminine in Spanish, is at the center of a stylized "o." The circle used to form the "o," which in
Spanish designates the masculine, is an extension of the "a" but not separate
from it, which is why I prefer to use this instead of the standard "a/o" ending
when talking about Chicanas and Chicanos. Rather than promote heterosexism
or gender separation, it symbolizes for many of us the complex relationship between Chicanas and Chicanos while placing women at the center, if at times only
symbolically. I use the term *dominative* instead of *dominant* to both acknowledge
and account for the power within subgroups that is not defined, exclusively, in
relation to the Anglo, Protestant, middle-class, heterosexual, male ideology that
shapes life in the United States.

Introduction

The epigraph is from Deanda, "Three Boys Found Dead in Vermont River." I have
replicated the entry as it appears on the blog.

1. The bumper stickers are available through Cinco Puntos Press and are free with
a purchase and available for purchase separately. When placing an online book
order, a person must be sure to request the item specifically.

2. Robert A. Barakat ("Aztec Motifs," 293) offers the following additional information about traditional narratives: "Significantly, the weeping woman does not
always return as a malevolent ghost [. . .]. Sometimes she returns simply to find
the bodies of her children whom she has not killed, but who have died [. . .]. She
is being punished by God for not taking care of her children, and must roam the
river banks, or streets, looking for their bodies. Granted that she is portrayed as a
malign ghost in numerous variants, but importantly she also is portrayed simply
as a woman who must search for her children's bodies."

3. Juana Léija attempted to murder her seven children by throwing them into Buf-
falo Bayou in Houston, Texas. The site has been the scene of other infanticides,
such as the one committed by Evonne Michelle Valdez, who beat her infant son,
Ramiro Isabel, to death and threw his plastic-wrapped body into the water of the
bayou. Léija was attempting to end her suffering and that of her seven children
caused by her violent and abusive husband. Two of the children died. During an
interview with José Limón, who was called upon by the defense to provide expert
testimony in regard to the cultural and social context that may have contributed
to Juana's suffering, the defendant made the declaration that she was La Llorona.
For details concerning the Valdez case, see Bardwell and Teachey, "Bayou Is
Searched for Baby." For a full accounting of Juana Léija's case and its situation

within a broader context of "maternal infanticide," see Heinzelman "'Going Somewhere.'"

4. Coffee Shop of Horrors, formerly in Gainesville, Georgia, but currently in search of a new home, offers on its Web site a La Llorona brand coffee. The La Llorona underwear is from a line of products once advertised on Cafepress.com to promote David Gwin's film *Cry for Me;* the connection between the legend and thong panties is unclear except that the discomfort, which some will undoubtedly experience as a result of wearing the garment, may cause them to weep like lloronas.

   Bernadine Santistevan created her Web site The Spirit of La Llorona (now The Cry: La Llorona [http://www.lallorona.com]) on 12 Feb. 1999 in an attempt to promote the development of her film project, then titled "The Crying Ghost" and since completed as *The Cry.* The film had its world premiere 12 May 2006, in Santa Fe, New Mexico. Promotional materials for Women's History Month in October 2004 at the University of Texas at San Antonio, which included a conference sponsored by the Women's Studies Institute, featured Monica Alaniz's etching *La Llorona* (http://www.utsa.edu/today/2004/02/26.cfm).

5. An article on La Llorona by Ariff Riza appeared on the Web site Singapore's First Online Ghost Stories. In it, Riza included illustrations from the Web sites The Cry and Legends of America, citing both as sources along with Jack Kutz's *Mysteries and Miracles of New Mexico* (1988). Kutz's book, subtitled *Guide Book to the Genuinely Bizarre in the Land of Enchantment,* is more of a travelogue offering directions to locales than an academic study. For Kutz's three-paragraph description of La Llorona, he cites Ray John de Aragón's *The Legend of La Llorona* (1980) as his only source. Anna Jarrett, a featured storyteller from New South Wales, told a Llorona story at Australia's National Storytelling Festival (29 Sept.–2 Oct. 2005) in Bicton, Western Australia.

6. Lhasa de Sela, *La Llorona* (1998); Chavela Vargas, *La Llorona* (2004); La Llorona featured in *The Death of Speedy* (1989), by Jaime Hernandez; La Llorona Park in Las Cruces, New Mexico; and La Llorona Art Gallery, Chicago.

7. Anaya, *Maya's Children;* Anzaldúa, *Prietita and the Ghost Woman;* Santa Barraza, for example, *La Llorona (1)* (1995); Isaura de la Rosa, *La Llorona* (n.d.); Lizz Lopez, *La Llorona;* (2004); Stevon Lucero, *La Llorona* (n.d.); and Kathleen Anderson Culebro, *La Llorona* (2002).

8. "Hell Hath No Fury" (16 Oct. 1997), *Cracker;* and "La Llorona, Part 1" (6 Feb. 2002) and "La Llorona, Part 2" (13 Feb. 2002), *American Family.*

9. *Mulholland Drive* (2001), directed by David Lynch. La Llorona is also the subject of at least three US films, including the feature-length films *The Cry* (2006) by Bernadine Santistevan; *The Wailer* (2006) by Andres Navía; and *Haunted from Within* [*Spirit Hunter: La Llorona*] (2004) by José L. Cruz.

10. See Chapter 2 for an analysis of Stephanie Saint Sanchez's film *The Legend of La Llorona* (2002).

11. I use both terms—*Mexican American* and *Chican@*—in an attempt to be inclu-

sive and to honor the ways that people self-identify. At times, I also use the term *Hispanic;* however, this designation is reserved for cultural informants or producers who identify as such, and when referring to how Latin@s and Chican@s are categorized en masse by the dominative Anglo culture and its bureaucratic institutions.

12. Though marketed under the name *Haunted from Within,* the title, as it appears at the beginning of the film, is *Spirit Hunter: La Llorona.*

13. I hasten to add that knowledge of La Llorona's story is in no way a measure of one's Chicanidad or Mexican-ness. The notion calls to mind the scene in Denise Chávez's *Face of an Angel* (1994), where the protagonist Soveida Dosamantes is asked to complete a "Chicano Culture Quiz" that, in one section, asks students to relate La Llorona's story (286). Apropos to this point is the fact that Cherríe Moraga and Inés Hernández-Ávila, both notable authors and leading figures in Chicana studies, have reflected on the fact that they did not grow up hearing stories about La Llorona, but once they did, the tale resonated immediately for them, particularly in the way that it reflected many of their own cultural and social concerns. See Moraga, *Loving in the War Years,* 142; and Keating, *Interviews,* 180.

14. This does not include instances when her name is identified as "Maria," which positions La Llorona as a failed Virgin Mary who, in the form of La Virgen de Guadalupe, is offered as a cultural ideal for Mexicanas and Chicanas in spite of the fact that her position is unattainable. La Llorona's failure to live up to an ideal kind of motherhood is implicit in traditional versions of the legend. Therefore, assigning her the name "Maria" conflates La Llorona's identity with that of Virgin Mary's and suggests that La Llorona's "crime," at least in part, is the result of her failure to perform chaste motherhood.

15. For example, Alma Lopez's "La Llorona Desperately Seeking Coyolxauhqui" series (2003) deserves more attention than I can give it in a single chapter. Works in the series include "La Llorona Desperately Seeking Coyolxauhqui in Juárez" (2003), which appears as cover art for Gaspar de Alba's book of poetry *La Llorona on the Longfellow Bridge; La Llorona Desperately Seeking Coyolxauhqui* (2003, serigraph, 22″ × 16″); and *La Llorona Desperately Seeking Coyolxauhqui* (2003; mixed-media installation). Numerous self-published books on La Llorona also warrant consideration, such as *Bruja: Legend of La Llorona* (2004) by Lucinda Leyba, and *La Llorona* (2003) by Juan Trigos. The quality of these works varies greatly, yet one cannot dispute the cultural work done in these productions, namely the dissemination of the lore to wider audiences. Both are available through online booksellers.

16. Though numerous sources point to the eminent folklorist Américo Paredes and his work on La Llorona, he had relatively little to say about her, limiting his commentary to placing her in wider discussions about other "Mexican legendry." Paredes cites and often criticizes the work done on La Llorona by Mexican and Euroamerican scholars, observing: "Most studies on La Llorona [. . .] make

sweeping historical generalizations for all Mexico on the basis of one or two variants. In spite of all that has been written about this legend, we know relatively little about its history and distribution, much less about the conditions under which it is told" ("Mexican Legendry," 106).

17. Though my work is informed by these studies, not all are cited directly.

18. There are indeed corresponding La Llorona figures in many cultures: Toad or Weeping Woman (Haida, American Indian), Lamia (Greek), Lilith (Jewish), the Woman in White (Filipino), or El Loron (particular to Durango, Mexico). Author Maxine Hong Kingston, in "No Name Woman," describes her Chinese aunt who had an adulterous affair and later murdered herself and the child she bore. Spirits like the aunt's weeping ghost lay in wait outside of wells, seeking to pull down people to take their places.

19. Mexican artist Victor Zubeldía painted a forty-piece treatise on La Llorona, one for each of the lyrics included in the Oaxacan folksong about her. The artist's portfolio, of this and other projects, is available on his Web site, http://www .victorzubeldia.com/.

20. Jean Franco ("The Return of Coatlicue") cites Gloria Anzaldúa as a key figure in a larger Chicana feminist project to reconsider Mexican icons such as the goddess Coatlicue.

21. I first offered these definitions of *myth* and *legend* in "Mitos y Leyendas," *The Oxford Encyclopedia of Latinos and Latinas in the United States* (2005).

22. Shirley L. Arora ("La Llorona") maintains that "Although one normally speaks and hears of 'the Llorona' as a singular entity, it is in fact misleading to refer to 'the Llorona legend.' It is, rather, a complex of legends, some closely related and others having nothing in common but the central figure of the female phantom who usually—though not always—weeps" (24). While I do not disagree with Arora's point about variations of the legend, I see these as emerging from the original event involving the woman heard crying in Tenochtitlan. As such, all represent versions of La Llorona's legend.

23. The term *Native* with a capital "N" is reserved exclusively for Indigenous people of the Americas.

24. This approach is akin to "Red Readings," a phrase coined by Jill Carter (Anishinabe) at the University of Toronto and one put into use by James H. Cox (*Muting White Noise*) in his readings of Native American novels.

Chapter One

1. Scene 1 is a contemporary encounter narrative told by two women and featuring two drunken men who pursue a beautiful woman who reveals herself to be La Llorona. Scene 2 establishes La Llorona as part of a dynamic Mexican storytelling tradition that is being passed on to the next generation, many of whom have taken up residence in the United States, carrying the stories with them. Scene 3, set in the United States, reflects the ways in which La Llorona stories can ac-

commodate a geographic change and incorporate social issues such as poverty or the persecution of Mexicans by the Texas Rangers. Scene 4 directly addresses the storytellers in the audience and implicates all present in La Llorona's "shame" (13).

2. See Lockhart, *We People Here*, 54–55.

3. The eight portents included (1) a comet; (2) the destruction by fire of Huitzilopochtli's temple; (3) lightning striking the temple of Xiuhtecuhtli, the god of fire; (4) fire raining down from the sky; (5) the waters of Lake Tetzcoco boiling and causing a flood; (6) a woman heard crying in the streets; (7) the appearance of strange fish and birds; (8) the appearance of two-headed beings that mysteriously disappeared. For a more detailed accounting see León-Portilla, *The Broken Spears*.

4. Motecuçoma (Nahuatl spelling) read these omens as heralding the return of the god/king Quetzalcoatl, "as the codices and traditions promised they would" (León-Portilla, 14). Popular interpretations cite Motecuçoma's belief as one reason the emperor allowed Cortés to march into Tenochtitlan unchallenged. In initial reports about the stranger, Cortés was described with features matching those of the exiled god.

5. According to the account included in León-Portilla's *The Broken Spears*, the priests escaped from prison by flying away and making "themselves invisible, which they do every night," so that they "can fly to the ends of the earth" (15). Motecuçoma's decision to kill their wives and children and the imagery of the priests flying through the night create a composite of a Llorona tale with protagonists. As such, the emperor's decree to murder the families of the priests emasculates the men and turns them into lloronas. Seen in this way, the woman howling in the streets, "Oh my children, we are about to go forever," was prophesizing the fate of the priests and their families as well as Motecuçoma's. The priests become ensnared in a narrative they helped to set in motion by translating Cihuacoatl's war cry into an expression of grief.

6. Lockhart briefly summarizes the debate over the publication date of the *Historia general de las cosas de la Nueva España* (General History of the Things of New Spain) or Florentine Codex, stating, "The process started about 1547, not until 1569 had most of the Nahuatl taken on a form close to that which we see in the Florentine Codex, and not until about 1577 was a Spanish version complete. The Florentine Codex itself was probably put on paper about 1578–1579. Book Twelve is thought to have been first drafted about 1555" (27).

7. Although other codices exist, the Florentine Codex is considered the most comprehensive accounting of Indigenous Mexican lifeways and worldviews before the arrival of the Spaniards.

8. English translations of both the Nahuatl and Spanish accounts of the same event reveal different characterizations of the woman's actions. Whereas an English translation of the Nahuatl reveals that the woman was heard "weeping and shouting," a translation of the Spanish has the woman merely "saying" that

she and her children are about to become lost. The language that reflects the
Nahuas' view indicates that the woman's mournful, even desperate cries require
some type of response. In Spanish, however, the woman is indifferent in her
pronouncement. This contrast mirrors, perhaps, the opposing views of conquest.
For the Nahua, it was something to bemoan and resist. As in the case with most
colonizers, for the Spanish the conquest was "inevitable." For the English translations of the account of the sixth omen in Nahuatl, see Lockhart, 54–55.

9. See León-Portilla's documenting of the sixth sign and its interpretation as Cihuacoatl's roar in *The Broken Spears* (6, 9–10).

10. According to the story a widow wishes to marry and misinterprets the causes
for her new paramour's resistance. She murders her children to clear a path
between her and her lover. The man, when he discovers her deed, is outraged
and of course does not marry the woman. See Kirtley, "'La Llorona' and Related
Themes," 157–158.

11. For a rendering of the painting, see the "Artwork" section of the artist's Web site
(http://www.carmenlomasgarza.com/gallery/lallorona.html) or her children's
book *In My Family/En Mi Familia*, 19.

12. The show is a part of regular programming on Radio Ranchito, KQUE (1230 AM).
La Llorona appeared under her English moniker, the Weeping Woman, in the
pilot episode of the WB's *Supernatural* (2005). She is also referred to in the episode as a "woman in white."

13. Additional works on La Llorona and the cultural history of Mexico relevant to
this analysis include José de Acosta, *Historia natural y moral de las Indias* (1590);
J. Frank Dobie, *The Mexico I Like* (1942); Fernando de Alva Ixtlilxóchitl, *Obras
históricas* (1952); León-Portilla, *Visión de los vencidos* (1959); Fernando Horcasitas and D. Butterworth, "La Llorona," (1963); Robert A. Barakat, "Aztec Motifs
in 'La Llorona'" (1965); Elaine K. Miller, comp., "La Xtabay" *Mexican Folk Narrative from the Los Angeles Area* (1973); César Pineda del Valle, *Cuentos y leyendas
de la costa de Chiapas* (1976); Elton Miles, *Tales Of The Big Bend* (1976) and *More
Tales from the Big Bend* (1988); Richard M. Dorson, "Leyendas," *Buying the Wind*
(1964); Stanley L. Robe, comp., *Mexican Tales and Legends from Veracruz* (1971)
and *Hispanic Legends from New Mexico: Narratives from the R. D. Jameson Collection* (1980); Keith Cunningham, "La Llorona in Yuma" (1981); John O. West, "The
Weeping Woman" (1981) and *Mexican-American Folklore* (1988); Mark Glazer,
"'La Llorona' in South Texas" (1984); Rosan A. Jordon, "The Vaginal Serpent"
(1985); Pamela Jones, "'There Was a Woman'" (1988); Ed Walraven, "Evidence for
a Developing Variant of 'La Llorona'" (1991); and Arturo Ramírez, "La Llorona:
Structure and Archetype" (1992).

14. In her second article on La Llorona, Leddy again mentions Neve's play but does
not consider it closely. See "La Llorona Again," 364.

15. See note 19, on Victor Zubeldia, in the introduction. The State of Oaxaca funded
a book cataloging Zubeldia's project, but the book is currently available only
in Mexico. Countless other folksongs about La Llorona exist. "La Llorona," by

Concha Michel from Tehuantepec, is included in a collection of songs and dance music. See Toor, *A Treasury of Mexican Folkways*. For additional examples, see Pablo Castañejo's performance of "La Llorona," *Mexico South: Traditional Songs and Dances from the Isthmus of Tehuantepec* (Folkways Records, 1976), as well as Oscar Chávez's, Carlos Jasso's, Rubén López's, and Mario Quiroz's performances of "Llorona, la Surianita, Zandunga," *Traditional Songs of Mexico* (Folkways Records, 1968). Also, John Donald Robb includes two additional versions in *Hispanic Folklore Music of New Mexico and the Southwest: A Portrait of a People* (Norman: University of Oklahoma Press, 1980). As indicated by Henrietta Yurchencho in the liner notes for *Mexico South,* songs about a "llorona" often have "no direct reference to the legend," but the name itself evokes a sense of tragedy. Because the singer, usually male, positions himself in the role of the lover in the song, singing about his separation from a particular woman, these performers are casting themselves within the folklore. While they may not directly reference the legend, they are personalizing the experience and drawing upon central features of the legend: separation, loss of love, tragedy. For additional information about the folksong, see Leach and Fried, eds., "Lilith" and "llorona." On the other hand, in naming her album *La Llorona,* Lhasa evokes La Llorona's qualities as a sirena and writes herself, playfully and respectfully, into this role.

16. Recent studies from both inside and outside the field of folklore, like *Media Sense: The Folklore-Popular Culture Continuum* (1986), edited by Peter Narváez and Martin Laba, and *Inventing Popular Culture: From Folklore to Globalization* (2003) by John Storey, have considered closely the relationship between folklore and popular cultural forms.

17. Figures 1 and 2 are from Encinas' unpublished children's book on La Llorona. Encinas' artwork appears on the cover of Craig Chalquist's *The Tears of Llorona: A Californian Odyssey on El Camino Real* (Lincoln, NE: iUniverse, 2004).

18. Although Santistevan includes "virgin" as a category into which some versions of La Llorona fall, this is a minority view, one not often seen or transmitted.

19. Some of the material included in this article appears in Candelaria, "La Llorona." An additional version, including photographs and artwork, is included in "Letting La Llorona Go, Or Re/reading History's 'Tender Mercies,'" *Heresies: A Feminist Publication on Art and Politics* 7 (27) (1993): 111–115.

20. According to Janvier ("Legend of La Llorona"), in the "Hispanicized" version of the tale, La Llorona murdered the children she had out of wedlock when her lover married another woman of his own higher position in society.

21. The following studies locate their analyses of La Llorona in a single discipline: Cynthia Ann Sanchez, "'Blessed is the Fruit of Thy Womb . . .': The Politics of the Representation and Reproduction of the Mythical Mother in New Mexico Cultural Traditions" (diss., New York University, 1998); and Linda Kinsey Spetter, "The Interrelationship of Myth and Legend in a Mexican-American Community in Chicago: The 'La Llorona' Legend as an Inversion of the Adam and Eve Sacred Narrative" (diss., Indiana University, 1998).

22. We see this particular kind of conflation in Trina Lopez's short film *La Llorona,*

where La Malinche is offered as an alternate positing of and name for La Llorona, and Abelardo Delgado's poem "La Llorona," in which he surmises that "la llorona" is a symbol "of all mothers / who have lost a child" (9.37–38). In Anaya's epic poem *The Adventures of Juan Chicaspatas,* the poet/narrator dedicates his narrative to the Malinche/Virgen/Llorona triad and to Juan's unnamed mother, addressing them as separate entities. The titular hero sees "la Llorona" as the "wailing woman at the water's edge" in whom he found his "manhood," a statement that goes unexplained, but one the reader assumes involves fear and sexuality (5). Later he identifies La Malinche as the "Llorona of our legends," thus conflating the two by offering her as the source of La Llorona's story (13). Whereas Anaya seemingly vacillates in this early work between conflating the two figures and treating them separately, he takes a different approach for La Llorona and her Mexica antecedent, Coatlicue. The epic heroes at the center of the poem view La Llorona and Coatlicue as separate entities. Al Penco, barrio vato loco, tells Juan: "'I saw la Llorona once / when I was on the la peda. / Pero esta Coatli has her beat'" (37).

23. The conflation of these two figures also appears in oral narratives collected for folkloric studies done on La Llorona. For example, consider the following account of La Llorona by "B.C.," a female informant from Houston who chose to be identified only by her initials:

> La Malence [*sic*] was a beautiful Aztec Indian princess who fell in love with the great conquistador Hernando Cortez. He had a beautiful castle built for her. She became his mistress. They soon had two sons whom they loved dearly. Hernando Cortez had the need for adventure and left La Malence and his two children. Shortly after his departure their sons were kidnapped. La Malence was frantic; she searched and searched for them but never found them. She cried and wailed for them. She mourned for her children and soon after she died. Shortly after her death the village people would hear her crying and wailing down the village streets in search of her children. La Malence became known as La Llorona (the cryer). (76)

B.C. here presents a melodramatic version of La Malinche's relationship with Cortés in which La Malinche becomes La Llorona. See Cunningham, "La Llorona in Yuma" 70–77.

24. Anaya's novella *The Legend of La Llorona* (1984) and his adaptation of the work in his unpublished one-act play "The Season of La Llorona" (2003) serve as a corrective to this damaging view. In Anaya's novella about La Malinche, a Spanish princess emerges as the "real" antagonist of the story; the captain is depicted as a sympathetic but conflicted figure who actually loves Malinche; and Malinche sacrifices her sons according to a directive given to her by Huitzilopochtli, the god of war. In "The Season of La Llorona," excluding the narrative frame set in the present, the primary differences between the novella and the portion of the play

set in the past are the Spanish princess' plot to drown Malinche's children on the passage back to Europe; Motecuçoma, rather than Huitzilopochtli, sending forth the vision for Malinche to sacrifice her children; and Motecuçoma's appearance before Malinche holding fire, which is symbolic of his desire for vengeance. Although Anaya has Abuelo in the framing narrative of the play blend La Malinche and La Llorona, upon concluding the historical portion of his story, he tells his grandchildren: "Some say that poor woman became la Llorona" (32.36). The statement seemingly undermines his previous narrative, in which he identifies Malinche as La Llorona. Furthering this complication is the fact that Abuelo later adds: "Long before Malinche the Aztecs already had a / goddess who cried in the streets for her children" (35.1–2). The inclusion of this information then points to an earlier "version" of La Llorona's story, one Indigenous in origin. A possible explanation for this trajectory of Anaya's Llorona story is offered in the mother's concluding query: "Is it possible? Every woman can be a Llorona?" (36.2). A character in the novel *Alburquerque* (1992) makes a similar observation. However, in the play the mother, whose son inexplicably disappeared years earlier, realizes that the fear induced by the legend is derived as much from La Llorona's actions as from the potential of every woman to become like her. In other words, inside every woman is a Llorona in waiting.

25. Bruce-Novoa explains that "*llorona* is slang for the police car siren, so the image transmutes through an interlingual metonomy" (42).

26. Virgil reads Dante's emotional vulnerability to the damned that are unworthy of any sympathy as an affront to God's ultimate authority. Later, when Dante wants to increase the torment of his old enemy, Filippo Argenti, whom he and the ancient poet encounter while crossing the Styx, the request pleases Virgil, for it serves as evidence of Dante's hardened heart. Before Dante and Virgil reach the other shore, the soul of Argenti is torn apart and dragged beneath the surface of the river. See *Inferno,* Canto VIII. I make this point to illustrate the depth of emotion and moral judgment that La Llorona and her legend inspire.

Chapter Two

1. Toscano's play was also adapted into the Mexican film *La Llorona* (1960) directed by René Cardona.

2. La Llorona was featured as the cover art of one of the installments in the series, which later appeared in *The Death of Speedy,* vol. 7 of *Love and Rockets.*

3. In the second panel of "Jerusalem Crickets," the story focusing on La Llorona, the band's name appears on a flyer on the wall of a dive. An image of an Indian warrior, smiling and holding the severed head of a European, appears below the band's name. The image clearly speaks to colonial conflict and represents Natives resisting European encroachment. The position of this image beneath La Llorona's name serves as a visual representation of the themes found within the legend from which the band takes its name. Although Hernandez does not

explicitly continue this conversation in the installment, it is certainly one he addresses through other Llorona-like characters found in the series, such as Luba and Tonantzin. The latter's name serves as evidence of the level of engagement with Greater Mexican cultural figures found in the series.

4. The image also lends itself to the reading strategy of recovery. Tonantzin's moons dangle from Monica's ears. The band's name, La Llorona, is written across Monica's Virgen posed body. In this image, Hopey replaces the role of the cherub traditionally seen at the Virgen's feet. Together these represent a fusing or re-working of several female cultural icons from Greater Mexico.

5. Cordelia Candelaria, in "The Literary Context of Chicano Poetry," provides readers with a history of the various influences affecting Chicano poets. Among these, she cites folklore and the corrido form in greater detail.

6. Consider the following lines from Gonzales' *I am Joaquín:* "I am / the black-shawled / faithful women / who die with me / or live / depending on the time and place" (42).

7. The use of La Virgen in the Chicano Civil Rights Movement recalls Father Hidalgo, who evoked the Virgen in his famous grito de dolores. See Gonzales, 21.

8. In the introduction to section one entitled "Chicana Feminism And the Politics of the Chicano Movement," Alma M. García outlines the grievances Chicana feminists had with the men of the "el movimiento" (*Chicana Feminist Thought*).

9. Angie Chabram-Dernersesian talks about the exclusionary Chican(o) in her article on Chicana absence from the male dominated literature of the Chicano Civil Rights Movement period ("I Throw Punches for My Race").

10. The poetry of the writers listed is included in García, *Chicana Feminist Thought.* Their inclusion here reveals the relationship between the development of Chicana feminist thought and poetry, for these poets voice their marginalized positions within Chicano culture and their struggle to draw attention to issues specific to Chicanas.

11. The version of the poem discussed in this section is from *Sueño de colibrí/Hummingbird Dream,* 8–9. In the "Notes on the Poems" at the back of the book, Quiñonez provides the following definition of La Llorona: "Legendary woman, goddess or witch who eternally laments her lost children" (76). Quiñonez offers two cultural interpretations of the figure, but complicates these further within the poem by posing additional possibilities.

12. "Madre perdida" means "lost mother" and "desgraciados" translates as "the wretched ones."

13. The blessed mother / the strong woman / the whore mother / the soldier girl / the loving Indian woman / the suffering woman.

14. The poem appears in Mora, *Agua Santa/Holy Water,* 115.

15. Victoria Moreno is the pen name of Chicana poet Carmen Tafolla, a heretofore unknown or little known fact. Tafolla describes her decision to write under Moreno's name: "When I first used it in the mid-70's, I was younger as a published poet, and the pen name was very freeing to break from the identity and persona that others ascribed to me" (pers. comm., 6 Feb. 2007).

16. La Llorona's age, as figured in the poem, indicates that she predates the conquest or emerges immediately before.

17. Chicana scholar Maria E. Cotera shared a similar story with me about "calling" La Llorona on the phone when she was younger, though she could not recall how they obtained La Llorona's phone number. She speculated that it was probably a fax number, but immediately countered that as a child she was certain it was La Llorona.

18. Chicana photographer, printmaker, and multimedia artist Delilah Montoya also includes this reversal in her Hotel Santa Fe bathroom installation, *For a Good Time Call 1-900-Llorona,* which is a part of her *La Lloronas* series with collaborator Asta Kuusinen. Her objective was to connect La Llorona with the "contemporary new story of young women that deny their pregnancy." According to Montoya, "Like the story of Llorona, these women are ostracized for killing their offspring." See the artist's Web site for photos of the installations in the series (http://www.delilahmontoya.com/ArtistsStatement.html).

19. Brule/Lakota activist Mary Crow Dog, in *Lakota Woman,* her autobiography coauthored with Richard Erdoes, discusses the issue of the forced sterilization of Indian women, such as her sister Barbara, at Bureau of Indian Affairs (BIA) hospitals on or near reservations: "For a number of years BIA doctors performed thousands of forced sterilizations on Indian and Chicana women without their knowledge or consent" (79). Through a coercive program in place until 1980, California regularly sterilized poor and/or undocumented women. While in some cases the state had obtained women's signatures consenting to the procedure, it did not provide translators to explain specifically the operation to which women were consenting. As a result of *Madrigal v. Quilligan,* filed by Mexican American women plaintiffs, the state agreed to provide bilingual consent forms and enforce an already-in-place seventy-two-hour waiting period prior to performing the operation. In Puerto Rico, a similar governmental policy/program instituted in the 1930s known as "la operacíon" resulted in the sterilization of approximately one-third of Puerto Rican women of childbearing age. For a book-length study of the program and its effects, see Gibson-Rosado, *The Sterilization of Women in Puerto Rico.*

20. Gish grounds his argument concerning La Llorona in Chicano literature in "magic realism," a term I distrust due to the tendency of some critics to invoke the label as a means of othering or primitivizing communities and/or the people associated with what outsiders see as "fantastical events."

21. Prior to the film, Mendoza had an established background directing episodes of comedies such as *The Chris Rock Show* and *The Bernie Mac Show.* Mendoza's film stylization harkens to "old fashioned screwball comedy from the '60s where everyone is beautiful" (DVD, "Director's Commentary"). Simón, a former teacher, gained national attention after directing the television documentary *Fear and Learning at Hoover Elementary* (1997), focusing on the caliber of education received by the immigrant students at the school where she taught.

22. On the cast commentary audio track of the DVD, Vergara states: "Everybody

in the Latin world knows who La Llorona is." Verástegui adds that when he was six years old in Mexico, his mother told him "if he went outside the house, La Llorona was going to get him." Sanchez points out that in Puerto Rico, La Llorona is one of many "cucus."

23. The rest of the film involves a counterfeiting scheme, a beauty pageant, and car chases, all of which take place while the women wait for Tomás to wake up and make his choice. In the course of these adventures, the women forge bonds of friendship and realize they do not need Tomás or any other Papi to be happy. When he finally awakens and is ready to announce his decision, each of the women, in turn, breaks up with him before he can state his choice. Tomás, in spite of his philandering, comes across as a nice-guy hero in the end, for he is the one responsible for bringing these women together, liberating them from their unsatisfying lives, and helping them realize their dreams: Cici becomes a dancer on a cruise ship; Pati, now independent from her parents and their money, gets a job at a gallery; and Lorena takes tango lessons and wears more revealing clothes.

24. See Clark, "Dull Chasing Papi," and Kehr, "Three Wronged Women."

25. *Realidades,* a short documentary series that followed Nava's *American Family,* featured the ad as the subject of one of its installments, which aired after the "La Llorona, Part 2" episode.

26. Language also presented itself as an obstacle to translating the ads from an English- to a Spanish-language market. In the past, advertisers attempting to reach Spanish speakers have run into this obstacle. The most famous, oft-repeated case is the American car manufacturer Chevrolet trying to sell "Nova" cars to Chican@s and Mexican@s in the late sixties and seventies, completely unaware that the name of the vehicle translates to "it doesn't go." Needless to say, Spanish speakers, while they may have appreciated the carmaker's honesty, were not anxious to buy cars that did not work. The "Got Milk?" campaign faced a linguistic problem of a more delicate nature because the catch phrase of the ad when translated literally into Spanish means, "Are you lactating?" Therefore, milk ads that eventually ran in Spanish-language markets had a slightly different focus and tag line. See Wartzman, "Read Their Lips."

27. "La Llorona Commercial Takes Hispanic Creative Honors."

28. "Milk Industry Turns to Ghostly Hispanic Legend."

29. See Chabria, "Spanish-language Milk Campaign Goes Mainstream."

30. See National Public Radio, "Got Milk? Ad."

31. The statement appeared at one time on the Art Center's Web site.

32. National Public Radio, "Got Milk? Ad."

33. Ibid.

34. Ibid.

35. From the back cover of the DVD.

36. Gene Hackman does not act in the film, but an image of him appears on screen

37. Saint Sanchez, pers. comm., letter to the author.

38. In their argument to the House Subcommittee on Communications and Power, the National Mexican-American Anti-Defamation Committee (NMAADC) used

the Frito Bandito as evidence of negative stereotypes of Mexican Americans in the media. One of the results of the hearings, as observed by Francisco Lewels, was that Chicano organizations shifted their attention from representation *in* to access *within* media, including for example, employment, production, and training (Noriega, *Shot in America,* 48). As a Chicana filmmaker and producer, Saint Sanchez engages the legacy of the Bandito in both the choice of product, Fritos, and the outcome, access. By wedding La Llorona to a consumer product that was once the focus of activists' groups protests concerning negative stereotypes of Chican@s, Saint Sanchez shifts the site of criticism from the mainstream media to Chican@s, thus illustrating how the latter, too, are not immune to corporate greed through the figure of Maria Tortilla.

Chapter Three

1. The latter poems in the series are discussed in Chapter 4. All references to "Go 'Way" are from *Arroyos to the Heart,* 74. An earlier version of the poem appears in Candelaria's *Ojo de la cueva* (Colorado Springs: Maize Press, 1984), 45.
2. In William Shakespeare's *King Lear,* Goneril rejects her violent and oppressive father (*The Riverside Shakespeare* [Boston: Houghton Mifflin, 1974]: 1249–1305).
3. Lopez's recounting emphasizes La Llorona's desire to secure her husband's affection by bearing his children. In the tale, La Llorona is in direct competition for her husband's affection with their children, so she murders them:

> La Llorona is an urban legend dating back to the 1500s in Aztec culture. Over time, various stories have developed and I think every young Texas girl hears the story from their mother differently. My mother and grandmother believed that La Llorona was a woman who wanted terribly to seduce a beautiful Mexican man who traveled by horse through her small town on business. She eventually was able to secure a relationship with him but for fear of losing him, she tried desperately to have his children. After some time, two children were born but instead of her husband falling more deeply in love with his wife, he paid more attention to the children. While the husband was away on business one day, the woman took the children to a river and drowned them. When her husband returned and found what she had done, he left her. She's said to have lived the rest of her life crying by that river for her children and legend has it that you can still hear her cries at night. (Gonzales et al.)

4. "Coatlicue Rules," "Malinche's Tips," "Consejos de Nuestra Señora de Guadalupe," and "Llantos de La Llorona," which comprise the "Cuarteto Mexicano," are found in Mora, *Agua Santa/Holy Water.*
5. "Llantos," 74–77.
6. In "Mayan Warning: The Legend of *Ixtabai* [*sic*]" (1985), Mora offers her inter-

pretation of the legend (*Chants*, (Houston: Arte Público) 25. The X-tabay (an alternate spelling) is said also to wander in white at night in the forested regions of the Yucatan. Her principal characteristic, however, is her desire to seduce men to their deaths. See Miller, "La Xtabay"; and Novelo, *Leyendas mayas*.

7. The last sentence of this stanza is the opening line of Mora's poem "Desert Women" (*Borders*, 80).

8. Other characters in Cisneros' short story collection resemble La Llorona. For example, in "One Holy Night," a young woman, Ixchel, bears the same name as a Mayan earth goddess, and her lover identifies himself as Chaq, a name that calls to mind the rain god Chaac. Ixchel becomes pregnant, and Chaq abandons her. Their relationship represents a different kind of "holy" union, one between a god and goddess. The story of Ixchel's impregnation, when severed from the realm of the gods and translated on an earthly plane, resembles a Llorona story full of tragedy. Also Clemencia, in "Never Marry a Mexican," bears a likeness to the vengeful Llorona. The protagonist is capable of any harmful act and seeks married white men with whom to have affairs. La Llorona is not named directly in either story, but we can read the stories through the lens of the lore to see the ways in which the women become entrenched further or liberate themselves from the Llorona-like narratives into which they have been inscribed, a technique I discuss fully in Chapter 6.

9. Alarcón comments directly on the limitations of Limón's feminist positioning of La Llorona, stating that "La Llorona fails to meet some of the modern and secularizing factors that Chicanas have felt they have needed in order to speak for themselves" (132 n51). See "Traddutora, Traditora."

10. A translation of the line reads: "Well, from the Indians way back, who knows." Ana María Carbonell ("From Llorona to Gritona") interprets this line as a key piece of evidence in her argument concerning "Woman Hollering Creek" as a narrative of resistance. By reading both Cisneros' and Viramontes' stories through the lens of Anzaldúa's the "Coatlicue State," found in *Borderlands*, Carbonell convincingly argues that both female protagonists represent resistant maternal figures whose antecedents include the Mexica goddesses Cihuacoatl and Coatilcue, a point made in spite of the fact that neither author, as Carbonell acknowledges, "explicitly invoke[s] La Llorona's pre-conquest antecedents in their writings" (54). While overt references to figures in the pantheon are certainly not necessary to produce such a cultural reading, her argument emphasizes a "returning" of La Llorona to her Mexica antecedents (see Chapter 4). Both stories, however, represent narratives of resistance independent of Anzaldúa's principle. Jacqueline Doyle ("Haunting the Borderlands") also makes connections between Cisneros' narrative and Anzaldúa's interpretation of La Llorona as Cihuacoatl.

11. Graciela tells Felice that Cleófilas only needs a ride to the bus station because she has her own money.

12. Saldívar-Hull provides an analysis of this particular kind of "popular feminism" practiced in Mexico. See *Feminism on the Border*, 105.

13. According to Saldívar-Hull, Popi's references to Tijuana, Mexico, and Sonya's recognition of the Mexican performer Vincente Fernández provide "cultural clues" that substantiate their national identity as Mexican (147).

14. The publication date is listed as 1985, but Saldívar-Hull (143) notes that the piece was written in 1984.

15. In the second part of *Borderlands,* Anzaldúa continues her theorization in poetry. Section 1, "Más antes en los ranchos," begins with an epigraph from the Mexican folksong "La Llorona." The lines from the song, emphasizing sorrow, death, and grief, not only set the tone, but also serve as a lens through which to view the poems included in the section. Gaspar de Alba uses a portion of these same lines as one epigraph for her novel *Desert Blood,* which I discuss in the conclusion.

    Critics—Rebolledo, Doyle, and myself included—have argued elsewhere that Anzaldúa's poem "My Black *Angelos*" represents a re-turning or more specifically a merging of La Llorona and Coatlicue and/or Cihuacoatl. My decision to omit the poem is based on the fact that La Llorona is not directly named in this piece, though she is readily identifiable through her wail in the same way that Coatlicue is by her "taloned hand" and "snake tongue" (18, 22). See Rebolledo, 77–78; Doyle, 53–70; and Perez, "'Words, Worlds in Our Heads.'"

16. The children's book was published under the title *Prietita and the Ghost Woman* (1995), which I analyze in Chapter 6. At this time, the fate of *Prieta* and *Lloronas* is unknown, though the literary estate has plans to publish Anzaldúa's work posthumously.

17. Moraga generously shared with me page proofs of the version of the play published in 2000. See Caridad Svich and María Teresa Marrero, eds., *Out of the Fringe: Contemporary Latina/Latino Theatre and Performance* (New York: Theatre Communications Group, 2000). For this study, however, I am using the version published in 2001 by West End.

18. In *The Last Generation,* Moraga states:

    > What was right about Chicano Nationalism was its commitment to preserving the integrity of the Chicano people. A generation ago, there were cultural, economic, and political programs to develop Chicano consciousness, autonomy, and self-determination. What was wrong about Chicano Nationalism was its institutionalized heterosexism, its inbred machismo, and its lack of a cohesive national political strategy. (149)

    The association between male power in the mythical Aztlán and male power in the creation of the Espiritual Plan de Aztlán is a less than subtle one. In el movimiento, women and queer folk were, with few exceptions, virtually invisible, a point underscored by Moraga who states that Chicano Nationalism "never accepted openly gay men and lesbians among its ranks" (147). The physical expulsion of queer folk from the nation represents an enactment of this rejection of difference within the Mechicano Nation.

19. Cihuacoatl is also known to wander the crossroads for Mixcoatl (Cloud Serpent), the child she abandoned there.
20. For Anzaldúa, the mother goddess is the one who initiated her rebirth into the "Coatlicue State" and a new mestiza consciousness, as discussed in *Borderlands*.
21. Located at the heart of Tenochtitlan was the Templo Mayor, with its twin shrines dedicated to Tlaloc, the rain god, and Huitzilopochtli. Coyolxauhqui's stone was positioned at the base of the temple. Sacrificial victims literally had to walk across the body of a female figure, whose image represented the ritual dismemberment many were about to face, before ascending. In other words, the vision of the stone prepared them for their fate. At the top of the temple on the platform outside of Tlaloc's and Huitzilopochtli's shrines was a Chacmol, where the victim's blood was or body parts were placed as an offering to the gods. The layout of the temple symbolizes male authority and the place of women in the empire and in the Mechicano Nation of Aztlán.
22. Moraga cites Bierhorst, ed., *The Hungry Woman*, as the source of this myth.

Chapter Four

1. The narrative included here is an abbreviated version of "Another Version of La Llorona's Story" that appears in Garza's collection *Creepy Creatures and Other Cucuys* (2004), which is discussed in Chapter 6. Readers will note that the spelling of the young woman's name is achieved by transposing the last two letters in "Christian," which represents further Garza's manipulation of religious icons and themes.
2. "La Llorona, Fact or Fiction?" under the title "La Llorona" is also included in *Creepy Creatures and Other Cucuys* and discussed in Chapter 6.
3. All future references to "La Llorona at Sixteen" and "La Llorona: Portrait by the River" are from *Arroyos to the Heart*, 75–76, 77. Earlier versions of both poems appear in Candelaria's *Ojo de la cueva*. "Portrait by the River" appears under the title "Herself Portrait." An alternate version of "La Llorona at Sixteen" appears in *Infinite Divisions: An Anthology of Chicana Literature*, edited by Tey Diana Rebolledo and Eliana S. Rivero (Tucson: Univ. of Arizona Press, 1993), 216–217.
4. A later version of the poem, which appears in Rebolledo and Rivero's anthology of Chicana literature, *Infinite Divisions*, omits the directive to sing, and includes changes in line breaks, words, and formatting, which alter the poem slightly, particularly its tone. My decision to focus on the earlier version of the poem is at Candelaria's request.
5. Additional lyrics of the song include lines such as "I'm dreaming dreams. I'm scheming schemes," the latter of which conveys a cunning not characteristic of the girl featured in the poem. For the complete lyrics, see Lyrics Drive, "I'm Forever Blowing Bubbles."
6. The phrase "¡ay, qué sorpresa!" translates as "Oh, what surprise!"; "grito a todas madres" translates as "she screamed to all mothers."
7. "Washing   crying   /   walking." Tehuantepec, located in Oaxaca, Mexico, is

known for the strength and beauty of its Native women. Located in the Mexican state of Sinaloa, Culiacán, is the site where two rivers merge to form a river named for the town. The place names evoke Native identity, female beauty, and water, ideas that comprise, in part, separate extra-textual Llorona narratives that allude to, in a very specific way, the vastness of her suffering. Yet the histories of and/or historical figures associated with each place, when taken together, represent elements of a national Llorona story, particularly when we consider that in the early colonial era in Mexico, Chief Chapalac of Chapala was baptized by Franciscans and given power by the new colonial Christian invaders. In exchange, Chapala publicly renounced Native religion, thus betraying la madre tierra and enslaving her people.

8. The eternal hunger.

9. The comparison between La Llorona and Medea unites them in their suffering while distinguishing their responses to their husbands' infidelity. Whereas Medea eliminates Jason's betrothed, La Llorona decides to focus her full attention on their sons and leave her husband's new lover alone.

10. Most often, she takes the shape of a mongoose, best known for its snake-killing abilities, which is facilitated by its capacity to tolerate the venom of multiple snakebites without dying. The symbolism is best understood if we liken the husband's neglect and infidelity as "bites" that slowly poison La Llorona without killing her.

11. Mexica midwives bathed newborns in a ritual that involved water and included a prayer to Chalchiuhtlicue asking, in part, to "Receive him, cleanse him, wash him, for he is especially entrusted to thee, for he is delivered into thy hands" (Sahagún, VI:175).

12. In this discussion, I distinguish between La Llorona and La Llorona/Chalchiuhtlicue, using the latter to reflect Luna's changing view of the legendary figure as a result of her grandmother's cuento.

13. Both Barakat (292) and Anzaldúa (*Borderlands,* 33) cite Chalchiuhtlicue as a precursor to La Llorona, but as a cultural symbol she has only recently come to the fore with great prominence. There are other non-Mexica Indigenous antecedents for La Llorona: the Mayan figures *ixtabai,* who live in the ceiba tree and to whom the poet Mora turns; and *xtaj* and *xpuch',* "two young women sent to the place called Tohil's Bath in order to seduce the gods," whom Dennis Tedlock cites as additional antecedents (*Popul Vuh,* 346). Tedlock also provides a detailed story about the young women (*Breath on the Mirror,* 45–58). Rather than scour the whole of Mesoamerica searching for those goddesses that either through their association or physical attributes resemble La Llorona, I have chosen to focus on those figures that are cited most often, in scholarly and creative works, as La Llorona's antecedents.

14. Though I have argued elsewhere that Anzaldúa's poem "My Black *Angelos*" represents a re-turning or more specifically a merging of La Llorona and Coatlicue and/or Cihuacoatl, I do not include an analysis of the poem in this chapter. Other critics, including Rebolledo and Doyle, make similar points, but my deci-

sion to omit the poem is based on the fact that La Llorona is not directly named in this piece, though she is readily identifiable through her wail in the same way that Coatlicue is by her "taloned hand" and "snake tongue." See Rebolledo, *Women Singing*, 77–78; Doyle, "Haunting"; and Perez, "'Words, Worlds in Our Heads.'"

15. In keeping with the way in which Montoya self-identifies, I refer to her throughout this section as Juana Alicia. For an image of the mural in detail see the artist's Web site (http://www.juanaalicia.com).

16. Amnesty International estimates the figure to be around 470. The Juárez murders have been the subject of a true-crime book, *Crossing to Kill: The True Story of the Serial-Killer Playground* (2000) by Simon Whitechapel; feature articles in *Ms. Magazine*, *The New Yorker*, *People* magazine, and *Glamour* (March 2007); newspaper articles in the *New York Times* and *Washington Post*; Gaspar de Alba's novel *Desert Blood* (2005), discussed in the conclusion; and Gregory Nava's feature film *Bordertown* (2006), starring Antonio Banderas and Jennifer Lopez.

17. See Sahagún, I:22.

18. For a full accounting of the conflict see Harris, "Bechtel, Bolivia Resolve Dispute."

19. Anzaldúa makes a similar observation about La Llorona's global appeal, stating "Potentially as a symbol, metaphor, and cultural figure la Llorona can be very empowering to the Chicana and the Indian because she was not only found in the Mexican tradition, but also in the Mayan and other cultures such as the Nigerian. There's a Native American figure dressed in white who cries and wails. She's transcultural" (Keating, 192).

20. The painting emphasizes characteristics that Cihuacoatl and Chalchiuhtlicue shared, but in the Codices, they are identified as separate entities.

21. León, like others before him, identifies Cihuacoatl as a precursor to La Llorona, but he does not mention Chalchiuhtlicue.

22. The demands of the goddesses in relationship to the male gods, with the exception of Cihuacoatl, seem paltry in relation to the alleged twenty thousand citizens and slaves said to have been sacrificed at the four-day dedication of the Templo Mayor, twin temples in the capital city devoted to Tlaloc (Rain God) and Huitzilopochtli. The actual number of people sacrificed during this nonstop ritualistic killing is highly disputed. Some people feel that the number was greatly exaggerated by the Spanish in the post-conquest era to emphasize the brutality and perceived savagery of the Mexica. The Discovery Channel devoted an episode of its series *Unsolved History*, "Aztec Temple of Blood" (2004), to testing the supposition and found that it was, in fact, feasible.

23. Specifically, a young woman was taken to the temple of the Tlalocs, where her chest was then cut open (Sahagún, I:22).

24. Dori Lemeh, in the chapter entitled "Myth, Reality, Legend: *El Poder de la Mujer*," includes a brief discussion of La Llorona's history and the renderings of her featured in Barraza's work.

25. Like her sister goddess Chalchiuhtlicue, the corn goddess required an annual

sacrifice. Her demands, as interpreted by the priests, were particularly gruesome. Victims were first decapitated and then flayed by a Chicomecoatl priest who later donned the skin of the victim in a ceremony dedicated to the goddess.

26. For an excellent study on the codex format in Chicano art, some of which include images of La Llorona, though none exclusively, see Ann Marie Leimer, "Performing the Sacred: The Concept of Journey in 'Codex Delilah,'" Ph.D. diss., University of Texas at Austin, 2005. Also see Patricia Draher, ed., *The Chicano Codices: Encountering Art of the Americas* (San Francisco: Mexican Museum, 1992).

27. The tattoos of the death mask covering her eyes and the hand over her mouth are included in later renderings of her and also addressed by Lemeh (76–87).

28. Their designation as a group before leaving Aztlán remains unknown.

29. León-Portilla (*The Broken Spears*, 4–12) cites different versions of the omens collected by Sahagún's informants and documented in the Florentine Codex. For a translation that identifies the woman's actions as "shouting" and "saying," see Lockhart, 54–55.

30. Delgadillo sees the novel as an articulation of a resistance narrative through the construction of "hybrid spirituality" ("Forms of Chicana Feminist Resistance"). Extant scholarship on *So Far From God* includes such works as "The Sardonic Powers of the Erotic in the Work of Ana Castillo" by Norma Alarcón; the chapter on Ana Castillo in *Postethnic Narrative Criticism* (2003) by Frederick Luis Aldama; and "Chicana/o Fiction from Resistance to Contestation: The Role of Creation in Ana Castillo's *So Far From God*" by Ralph E. Rodriquez, to name a few. But my exclusive focus on La Llorona has limited by critical engagement with these and other works on the novel.

31. I want to acknowledge Alicia Gaspar de Alba's terminology, "alter-Native," which she uses in *Chicano Art* to describe Chicana/o culture as being "both alien and indigenous to the landbase known as the 'West'" (xvi). While clearly inspired by her model, I mean, literally, other Native sources.

32. An earlier version of my argument, including some portions of this section, appears in "Crossing Mythological Borders."

33. For additional information on "Matlachiuatl" see Leddy, "La Llorona Again," 365. The poet Abelardo Delgado also cites a goddess from the Mexica pantheon as an antecedent to La Llorona that I have not been able to locate through other sources. Abelardo includes as an epigraph to his poem "La Llorona, Part III" a quotation from *Aztec* (1980), Gary Jennings' fictionalized account of the empire before and during the conquest. In it is a reference to "Chocacíuatl, the Weeping Woman, the first of all mothers to die in childbirth, forever wandering, forever bewailing her lost baby and her own lost life" (17). Whether this goddess is an actual figure from the pantheon is irrelevant. By imagining her before the advent of Spanish colonization, Abelardo re-turns La Llorona to a time before "the Europeans arrived" (11).

Chapter Five

1. I identified the cultural heritages of the producers included in this chapter through interviews and available biographical information.

2. One of the women featured in the print is partially nude. This aspect of the work raises troubling issues about the exoticization and objectification of Mexican@s and Chican@s. When I asked Jefferson about the nudity, I questioned whether or not the partial nudity was suggestive of literal or metaphoric rape. Jefferson responded:

> She is partially nude for a couple of reasons; it cements the relationship to the children—she has literally torn them from her own breast in the ultimate act of betrayal and it also alludes to the sexual nature of her madness. Has the infidelity of the man she can no longer possess become a reflection of her unattractiveness and self-loathing? Are the children a product of her being raped and a reminder of what she must escape? It may be that the appeal of this story is that clarity and reason meander into dark corners. As you may be able to tell, I too was drawn to the inexplicable elements of it. (pers. comm. 2005)

3. Alston, who identifies as African American, says that her decision to make a film on La Llorona was inspired by a conversation she had with a Tejano she met at a cocktail party her first week in Austin. La Llorona came up in that conversation, and Alston became fascinated with the legend. Even after making the film, she still wonders "how do the stories about [La Llorona] reflect how we think about powerful women?" (pers. comm. 2005).

4. See Alston's Web site, The Weeping Woman.

5. Vicki Trego Hill drew the original illustrations for the book, and seventeen years later, her daughter Mona Pennypacker added color to the illustrations for the hardback version. The book was the first children's book published by Cinco Puntos, which has since published more than 70,000 copies of the work. The press has a special affinity for Hayes and his work. As the press explains in the "About Us" section of their Web site, "The Weeping Woman (as she's known in English) has been such a steady seller that we can truly say Cinco Puntos Press is the (publishing) house that La Llorona built."

6. The quote is from the front flap of the hardcover book jacket.

7. Ibid.

8. Whereas Hayes' tale is conventional, Trego Hill's illustrations tell a slightly different, more interesting story, making visible the Native history and identity not directly cited in the story. Facing the title page in the softcover version (1987) is the head of a Mesoamerican Indian sculpture. Directly beneath the image are the words "La Llorona," implying that the sculpture is an image of La Llorona, the legend is Indigenous in origin, or simply that her history is ancient. Readers are therefore directed from the outset, via the illustration, to conceive of María's

identity as Indigenous, an idea supported in the text by her social class and physical features. In the 2004 hardcover color edition, the image stands alone, and "La Llorona" appears above the English translation of her name.

9. He identifies Malinche, without complication, as "the Native mistress of Hernán Cortés" (2004, 32).

10. In Roberta Zybach Yarbrough's pre-teen mystery *The Ghost Chasers: A Story of La Llorona* (2001), two characters go to the library to do research on La Llorona and come across Hayes' book, which is mentioned by name. The narrator states that Hayes describes "the legend" of La Llorona in his book, clearly an objectionable term from Hayes' point of view. Yarbrough cleverly presents and complicates La Llorona's story. The "use" of La Llorona by an opportunistic thief in Yarbrough's book parallels the action of Paula G. Paul's *The Wail of La Llorona,* but the difference is that in spite of the criminal's dismissive attitude about La Llorona, Yarbrough confirms in the end both the beliefs of the people and that La Llorona is an elusive presence. Yarbrough's respect for and attitude toward La Llorona is best illustrated in the front matter disclaimer: "Any similarity to any person, living or dead, except Joe Hayes and La Llorona, is purely coincidental." Yarbrough leaves the reader to decide who is living and who is dead. Her work is one of a host of self-published books about La Llorona written for a pre-teen or teen audience. These stories often emphasize the gory or horrific aspects of the legend, but a few are actually rooted in a historical and cultural, even Mexican Indian, context. Yarbrough's is one of the best.

11. Although Spain is unquestionably a part of Europe, Spanish is considered a Third World language in the United States. In the American cultural mainstream, Spaniards are often excluded from popular or critical conceptions of Europe. My use of the term *Eurowestern* reflects this exclusion. Also, because Anglos represent an ideological majority within Eurowestern culture, I often identify them separately.

12. My analysis in this chapter focuses exclusively on the artifacts these non-native cultural producers have generated that represent La Llorona. Their treatment of other subject matters in different works may represent a less enlightened view.

13. According to Enger, he is most likely of Scandinavian descent.

14. At one time this information appeared on the artist's Web page hosted by Arco Iris.

15. *Cry for Me,* a film about La Llorona scheduled for production in 2006, but since cancelled, promoted her as a horrific figure. David Gwin wrote the screenplay for the film, and Tiffany Sinclair was to direct. Though billed as horror, the screenplay focuses on Maria, an abusive mother, and the consequences of her actions. To promote and presumably fund the film, an effort that failed, a line of products attached to the movie was available from David Gwin productions on www .cafepress.com/davidgwinfilms. These products included throw pillows, sweatshirts, hoodies, T-shirts, and thong underwear. Featured on each item is an image of the sky, a forest, and what appears to be a desert bathed in red light or a river of blood. These scenes are stacked, in cross sections, inside a water drop-

let or a tear. While all of the products include the title of the film, not all feature references to La Llorona.

16. All of the quotes from Diana Bryer are from an e-mail she sent to me in March 2005.

17. The storyteller's conventional version of the tale includes a detail particular to La Llorona stories in and around Santa Fe, New Mexico: the chains, a feature associated with ghosts that haunt houses, and one that Bryer leaves out of her own rendition. An early study of New Mexican folklore done in English by Aurelio M. Espinosa includes a brief section on La Llorona, but neither infanticide nor adultery is noted as being attached to the "myth." Espinosa cites La Llorona as "peculiar" to Santa Fe and describes her as a "soul from purgatory" (401). Although Espinosa puts forth that La Llorona has committed some sin, he does not identify the specific transgression. An additional detail included in the account is that La Llorona's spirit is said to enter the houses of "those who are to be visited by great misfortunes," death in particular (401).

18. As Adam's first wife, Lilith refused to submit to his will and, as a result, was cast as demonic. For additional information on Lilith, see Maria Leach and Jerome Fried, eds., "Lilith," *Funk and Wagnalls Standard Dictionary of Folklore, Mythology and Legend,* 2 vols. (New York: Funk and Wagnalls, 1950), 622–623; and Marta Weigle, "Lilith—Adam's First Wife—and Her Legendary Kinswomen," *Spiders and Spinsters: Women and Mythology* (Albuquerque: Univ. of New Mexico Press, 1982), 252–260.

19. One such source is de Aragón's *The Legend of La Llorona.* In the introduction to his fictional account of La Llorona, de Aragon offers a fascinating history that directly connects La Llorona to Medea. His failure to cite a single source makes confirmation of this genealogy difficult if not impossible.

20. An earlier version of my analysis of Lynch's film appears in "Lost in the Cinematic Landscape."

21. La Llorona appears as the subject of major Mexican films such as *La Llorona* (1933) by Ramón Peón; *La Herencia de La Llorona* (1947) by Mauricio Magdaleno; *El Grito de la Muerte* (1958) by Fernando Mendez; *La Llorona* (1960) by René Cardona; *La Maldición de La Llorona* (1961)—a remake/adaptation of Peón's film—by Rafael Baledon; *La Venganza de La Llorona* (1974) by Miguel Delgado; and *Las Lloronas* (2004) by Lorena Villarreal. However, the only other films about La Llorona made by Chican@s are short films—for example, *La Llorona* (1998) by Trina Lopez and *The Legend of La Llorona* by Stephanie Saint Sanchez. In 2003, New Moon Films began production on a feature-length film about La Llorona starring Danny Trejo and Eva Longoria, but according to director Rudy Luna, they were only able to shoot one scene before they lost funding. New Moon is in the process of attempting to secure additional resources to complete the film. Longoria's celebrity status as a television star on the hit series *Desperate Housewives* may prevent the production, as originally cast, from moving forward. Notably, the producers have selected the image from La Llorona brand coffee to place on the Web site advertising the film.

22. Although Rebekah Del Rio, La Llorona de Los Angeles, is a character in the film, the singer Rebekah Del Rio, who calls herself La Llorona de Los Angeles, plays her. See her Web site (http://www.rebekahdelrio.com).

    Lynch drew upon knowledge from a cultural informant to name the singer. Relying upon a cultural reading of the chanteuse in Club Silencio, Geno Silva, who plays Cookie, devised his introduction for Rebekah: "You know that intro I do for Rebekah? I made that up: 'La Llorona de Los Angeles.' La Llorona in Southwestern legend, is a mythic, spooky character of your childhood. It is a wailing woman you hear at night. She's crying because she lost her two children in the Rio Grande. It is a story you hear all over the Southwest. When she was singing 'Crying' I said, 'David, how about we call her La Llorona—the crying woman—of Los Angeles, because that's what she's doing.' Some people will get it and some people won't" (Lost on Mulholland Drive, http://www.mulholland-drive. net/cast/rebekah.htm, accessed on 17 July 2007).

23. In an e-mail interview (June 2005), owner Brice Vorderbrug states that he tries to find representative figures from the countries where the coffee originates.

24. Vorderbrug sent Pullin "websites with a few variations of the myth," and the artist used these to create his own interpretation (pers. comm. 2005).

25. The concept is a key feature of Carlos Castañeda's spiritual practice as shared by Don Juan, but neither Daglow nor I rely on Castañeda's interpretation of the spiritual and metaphysical practice. Most of the existing material on the *nahualli* written in English was generated some time ago from white anthropologists and archeologists who do little with the idea except explain it. See Brundage, *The Fifth Sun*. Mexican theorist León-Portilla does discuss the nahualli as they appear in the flor y canto of the Mexicans but does not elaborate on their individual significance.

26. I would like to thank Don Daglow for generously agreeing to speak with me about a story he wrote more than twenty years ago. He is currently president and CEO of Stormfront Studios, which notably produced an interactive game for *The Lord of the Rings: The Two Towers*. In an e-mail interview (March 2005), Daglow offers the following insight into his decision to feature a young anthropologist at the center of his narrative:

> My Dad was trained as an anthropologist in the 1920s and studied with Lowie (his mentor) and Kroeber (who didn't care for him) at Berkeley at the time of the Scopes trial. The depression robbed him of his true calling, but even as he supported the family as an accountant he would beam and go to his books any time the topic of anthropology came up. So I was raised around a classically trained anthropologist and some of the attitude must have gotten through my thick skull. The fact that he never got the chance to live through the academic politics probably also left him with an untarnished love of his area of study that my college professors didn't always have . . . that's in the Sorteaux character as well.

When I commented on his decision to problematize the position of a field researcher, which for many current cultural anthropologists is now a standard practice, but one that was dismissed at the time, Daglow admitted: "I was (and am) also heavily influenced by the bilingual-multicultural educational movement of the 1970s, which taught me so much about how we fit in the world (and how hard it is to really understand what others see about how we fit), and that dovetails with the foundations of the story" (pers. comm. 2005).

27. The Spanish phrases translate as "Do you have a soul for me, sir?"; "It's time you should go back to your own people"; and "You can see me, but never understand me."

28. Daglow at first could not recall the exact source of his information about the nahualli, but later remembered the following:

> Around 1976 I had found this very cool coloring book (in those days we often bought them as ditto masters) with Aztec gods and legends depicted. Perfect stuff for the diverse mix of a multi-cultural classroom. I'd rotate one or two of its images through art time about once a month so the kids periodically were coloring the images, discussing the stories, re-telling the stories etc. When I woke up this morning, clear as a bell, I remembered the pages for Mictlantecuhtli and Quetzalcoatl and how much fun we all had discussing the stories in class. So that's where I was exposed to the legend. (pers. comm. 2005)

Concerning his decision to assign La Llorona an Indigenous identity, he states: The idea that "'the reality behind the story of La Llorona' would be indigenous to the Americas . . . I guess I never considered any alternative to that" (pers. comm. 2005).

29. Daglow's discussion of the nahualli has fueled my own research on the subject. As a native concept of doubling, the principle, along with In Lak'ech, allows for multiple subjectivities and positionalities that counter Western notions of the self and other. For scholarly discussions of the concept, see Yolanda Broyles-Gonzalez, *El Teatro Campesino: Theater in the Chicano Movement* (Austin: Univ. of Texas Press, 1994); Rosa Linda Fregoso, *The Bronze Screen: Chicana and Chicano Film Culture* (Minneapolis: Univ. of Minnesota Press, 1993).

30. In her essay "Stop Stealing Native Stories," Lenore Keeshig-Tobias (Canadian Ojibway) reminds us: "Stories, you see, are not just entertainment. Stories are power. They reflect the deepest, the most intimate perceptions, relationships and attitudes of a people. Stories show how a people, a culture, thinks. Such wonderful offerings are seldom reproduced by outsiders" (71). Her views on the importance of stories and storytelling mirror those of Leslie Marmon Silko (*Ceremony*) and Thomas King (*The Truth About Stories*).

Chapter Six

1. Successive productions were staged in 1997, directed by Ed Muth; 2000, directed by Edith Pross; and in 2003, directed by Trish Rigdon (Silver, pers. comm. 2005).
2. From a flyer from the 2002–2003 season.
3. Tafoya first learned about La Llorona after moving from Kentucky to New Mexico. Tafoya admits to restricting herself from doing extensive research on the legend or looking for images, choosing instead to "draw only on [her] memories, experiences, and what the neighbors had told [her]" (pers. comm. 2005).
4. This is the same image found in his multimedia piece discussed in Chapter 4.
5. The choice of ruda as the ingredient Prietita must find is an interesting one for it is native to Europe and Asia—not the Americas. Also, the long and at times violent relationship between Mexicans and the owners of the King Ranch is well documented. See Don Graham, *Kings of Texas: The 150-Year Saga of an American Ranching Empire* (Hoboken: Wiley, 2003); and Jane Clements Monday and Betty Bailey Colley, *Voices from the Wild Horse Desert: The Vaquero Families of the King and Kenedy Ranches* (Austin: Univ. of Texas Press, 1997).
6. The book features a foreword by Anaya. According to Vigil, the play was commissioned by the Denver Center Theater Company and produced as a part of its school touring program.

Conclusion

1. Like La Llorona, the runaway slave Margaret Garner also murdered her children, but did so to protect them from a slave catcher. Her story, as recounted in the article "A Tale of Horror" served as inspiration, in part, for Morrison's *Beloved*. See the *Cincinnati Daily Enquirer*, 29 Jan. 1856. Candelaria, in "Letting La Llorona Go," and Catrióna Rueda Esquibel, in *With Her Machete in Her Hand: Reading Chicana Lesbians* (2006), also make this comparison between La Llorona's story and Morrison's *Beloved*.
2. Lara, Pablito's heroin-addicted mother, loses custody of her son when she leaves him in a locked car while she goes inside a hotel room to get high; Elena's child, who is an American citizen, is taken from her when she is deported after searching for her husband, who was detained in an INS roundup.
3. "There are those dead who make no sound, Llorona / And their suffering is far greater" (translation mine). One possible interpretation of these lines is that while La Llorona can at least wail, some have no outlet for their suffering.
4. David Lynch's *Mulholland Drive* (2001) is also included in this analysis. For my reading of Chicana characters in films that do not include La Llorona by name, see "Lost in the Cinematic Landscape."
5. This is an interesting use of the term "Others," for at present, the Others literally refers to those individuals whose identities are unknown. The Others are also the initial "residents" [read: Natives] on the island before the arrival of Oceanic flight 815 survivors.

6. The vitriol that Ana's character has inspired on blogs and other Web sites is impressive. She is most often referred to as "homicidal" and a "bitch." Also, people who stated that they wished she would "fucking die" seem to, for now, have gotten their wish. At the time of her death, she was not the only character, or person of color, who was murdered on the island. She was, however, the only character of color in a leadership role. Ana Lucia was directly responsible for the survival of the "tailies," the people at the back of the plane. Although some attributed their loathing of Ana Lucia to Rodriguez's "bad acting" skills, comments also reveal that they resented her "taking up so much screen time." I would argue that what they really objected to was a woman using power and violence in the same way as a man and the fact that as a brown woman, she did not know her "place." According to these views, her role should have been supportive rather than a lead like Jack's character. See "List of Reasons We Hate Ana Lucia," 24 Nov. 2005, (http://lost-forum.com/archive/index.php/t-22288.html) or "Ana's Got a Gun, Comments," 28 Nov. 2005 (http://www.tvgasm.com/archives/lost/001465.php) for a sample of this outrage.

7. Another important detail of the scene is that Ana Lucia is comforted in the river by Mr. Eko, who has been silent for forty days following his killing of three Others in self-defense. Mr. Eko assures Ana Lucia that she is "going to be okay." In later episodes, Mr. Eko is a staunch defender of Ana Lucia's actions, but later he too is killed.

8. Reading Ana Lucia as a Llorona clarifies and contextualizes her rage. Her last name, Cortéz, directs Chican@ cultural readers, and those familiar with Mexican history, to the long-standing source of her fury. Seen in this way, killing the white man who murdered her unborn child becomes a revolutionary act. Careful viewers will also note that in this scene Ana Lucia is wearing a shirt with a snake pattern, which looks like a second skin, while the man is wearing a shirt with a cross in the center. Rather than pit good versus evil, the scene harkens to an Old and New World conflict between religions: Ana Lucia as Coatlicue (creator and destroyer) versus the dead guy as Christ (redeemer).

9. ABC has found critical and commercial success with the dramedy *Ugly Betty* (2006).

10. Other examples include a corporate logo on a shark's fin and other characters appearing in the background of flashback scenes that provide characters' histories.

11. Ironically, Michael kills Ana Lucia as a part of a complicated plot to get his son, Walt, back from the Others, who have kidnapped him. Michael succeeds but kills two women in the process. Ana Lucia's murder represents part of a disturbing trend on the show: the killing off, criminalizing, or implied mental instability of its ethnic characters.

12. The review of the installation that appeared in the *San Francisco Chronicle* incorrectly identifies Michael Findley as the creator. See Tyche Hendricks, "Dia de los Muertos: Artists from Around the Globe Share in Rites, Traditions of the Otherworldly," *San Francisco Chronicle,* 31 Oct. 2003, A21.

13. At one point, Aguilar included on his Web site the quotation from www
    .lallorona.com about Smith as a "modern-day Llorona" that accompanies the
    Tillery Brothers' image of Susan Smith. This association may have served as an
    additional inspiration for his reading of Smith as a Llorona. Inquiries made to
    the artist were not answered, and the information no longer appears on the site.
    Numerous other sources identify *Time*'s "reference" to Susan Smith as a Llorona.
    After an extensive search, I have been unable to locate the primary source that
    includes this direct comparison, which leads me to believe that the "fact" is now
    a story unto itself. The originating point of the "fact" seems to be the wording
    that accompanies an illustration included in the art gallery of the "Tribute"
    section of the pull-down menu on The Cry Web site. The 1994 illustration com-
    missioned by *Time* from Hungry Dog Studios features Susan Smith weeping with
    her hands clasped in prayer. Underneath the image reads: "*Time Magazine,* 1994,
    'Susan Smith, A Modern Day Llorona.'" See Janice C. Horowitz and Lina Lofaro,
    Hungry Dog Studios, Tillery Brothers, illus. "The Year in Caricature," *Time* (25
    Dec. 1995–1 Jan. 1996), 45. Hungry Dog Studios did not assign the title attributed
    to the piece. The way in which the information is presented on the site, in terms
    of punctuation, leads the reader to believe that *Time* is the one who identifies
    Smith as a modern-day Llorona, which is not the case. The "fact" is repeated
    online by sites such as Wikipedia and *USA Today.*

14. Smith's allegations were meant to throw the already skeptical police off track by
    sending them in search of a black man fitting Smith's vague description. In hind-
    sight, close inspection of the police composite reveals the image of a caricature
    or a black minstrel. The lead investigator in the case had begun to suspect Smith
    and did not, much to the relief of many in the black community, vigorously pur-
    sue the lead. See Lacayo, "Stranger in the Shadows."

    Smith's position and "innocence" were further thrown into question by the
    arrival of Polly Klaas' father, Marc, a well-known advocate for children, whose
    own daughter had been kidnapped and murdered. Marc arrived on the scene
    to help with the investigation, bringing with him a psychologist to help create a
    more useful and detailed sketch of the alleged suspect. Smith's refusal to meet
    with Mr. Klaas, along with the actual details of the case, aroused further suspi-
    cion of her involvement in their disappearance.

15. The same is true of comparisons made between Smith and Medea. In fact, one
    article that appeared in *Time* begins with the following epigraph from *Medea:*
    "Forget that you once loved them, that of your body they were born. For one
    short day, forget your children; afterwards, weep. Though you kill them, they
    were your beloved sons" (Gibbs and Booth, "Death and Deceit," 43). The writers
    misinterpret key lines Medea utters about killing her children, although they
    appear in the same passage as Medea's statement: "with all / haste I shall kill
    my children and leave this country. I shall / not delay and so surrender them to
    other, crueler hands to / kill" (Euripides, *Medea,* 1236–1240). In Medea's own
    words, she kills her children to prevent their becoming slaves or being murdered.

16. Jeremiah 31:17 reads: "That *your* children shall come back to their own border."
17. For a reading of *Moby Dick* that relies on a Native Nationalist perspective, one that includes a consideration of the marginalization of Tashtego, even within Native studies, see Cox, *Muting White Noise,* 224–236.
18. I distinguish between "Ophelia" in the play and "Ofelia" in the painting through the different spellings of her name.
19. For an analysis of absent mothers in Shakespeare's plays, see Mary Beth Rose, "Where Are the Mothers in Shakespeare? Options for Gender Representation in the English Renaissance," *Shakespeare Quarterly* 42 (3) (1991): 291–314.
20. Though the play is believed to have been written in 1601, *Hamlet* is set during the Medieval period, well before the Spanish conquest of Mexico (1519–1521). Therefore, we may determine that La Llorona's identity, at the time in which the scene occurs, is exclusively Native. However, the images and various artistic styles present in the painting represent a wide range of influences from many different periods, including the English Renaissance and the architecture of American movie houses during Hollywood's Golden Age. Together, these convey the timelessness of the play's and painting's central themes.

Acosta, José de. *Historia natural y moral de las Indias.* 1590. Ed. Jane E. Mangan, trans. Frances M. López-Morillas. Durham, NC: Duke Univ. Press, 2002.

Alarcón, Norma. "Chicana's Feminist Literature: A Re-Vision Through Malintzin/ or Malintzin: Putting Flesh Back on the Object." In *This Bridge Called My Back: Writings By Radical Women of Color,* ed. Cherríe Moraga and Gloria Anzaldúa, 182–190. 1981. New York: Kitchen Table Women of Color Press, 1983.

———. "Traddutora, Traditora: A Paradigmatic Figure of Chicana Feminism." In *Scattered Hegemonies: Postmodernity and Transnational Feminist Practices,* ed. Inderpal Grewal and Caren Kaplan, 110–133. Minneapolis: Univ. of Minnesota Press, 1994.

Alcalá, Rita Cano. "From Chingada to Chingona: La Malinche Redefined Or, A Long Line of Hermanas." *Aztlán: A Journal of Chicano Studies* 26 (2) (2001): 33–61.

Alston, Angela. Personal communication "Re: La Llorona." E-mail to the author, 14 June 2005.

———. The Weeping Woman: Tales of La Llorona. 2001. http://www.sparklehouse .com/angela/Weeping.html. Accessed 24 Oct. 2004.

Alurista. "must be the season of the witch." In *Floricanto en Aztlán,* 26. Los Angeles: Univ. of California, Chicano Studies Center, 1976.

Alva Ixtlilxóchitl, Fernando de. *Obras históricas de Don Fernando de Alva Ixtlilxóchitl*

publicadas y anotadas por Alfredo Chavero. 2 vols. 1891–1892. México: Editora
Nacional, 1952.

Anaya, Rudolfo A. *The Adventures of Juan Chicaspatas.* Houston: Arte Público,
1985.

———. *Bless Me, Ultima.* Berkeley, CA: Tonatiuh-Quinto Sol, 1972.

———. "'I'm The King': The Macho Image." In *Muy Macho: Latino Men Confront
Their Manhood,* ed. Ray González, 57–73. New York: Anchor, 1996.

———. *The Legend of La Llorona.* Berkeley, CA: Tonatiuh-Quinto Sol, 1984.

———. "La Llorona, El Kookoóee, and Sexuality." *Bilingual Review* 17 (1) (1992):
50–55.

———. *Maya's Children: The Story of La Llorona.* Illus. Maria Baca. New York:
Hyperion, 1997.

———. *My Land Sings: Stories from the Rio Grande.* Illus. Amy Córdova. New York:
Morrow Junior Books, 1999.

———. *Rio Grande Fall.* New York: Warner Books, 1996.

———. "The Season of La Llorona." Unpublished play. 2003.

Anzaldúa, Gloria. *Borderlands/La Frontera: The New Mestiza.* San Francisco: Aunt
Lute, 1987.

———. *Prietita and the Ghost Woman/Prietita y la Llorona.* Illus. Christina
Gonzalez. San Francisco: Children's Book Press, 1995.

Aragón, Ray John de. *The Legend of La Llorona.* Las Vegas, NM: Pan American
Publishing, 1980.

Arora, Shirley L. "Ethnic Identity and Narrative Strategies in a Mexican-American
Memorate." *Plenary Papers: The 8th Congress for the International Society for Folk
Narrative Research, Bergen, June 12th–17th, 1984,* ed. Reimund Kvideland and
Torunn Selberg, 11–20. Bergen, Norway: International Society for Folk Narrative
Research, 1984.

———. "Hear and Tell: Children and the Llorona." *Contemporary Legend: The
Journal of the International Society for Contemporary Legend Research* 3 (2000):
27–44.

———. "La Llorona: The Naturalization of a Legend." *Southwest Folklore* 5 (1) (1981):
23–40.

Arteaga, Alfred. *Chicano Poetics: Heterotexts and Hybridities.* Berkeley and New York:
Cambridge Univ. Press, 1997.

Avila, Alfred. *Mexican Ghost Tales of the Southwest.* Comp. Kat Avila. Houston:
Piñata Books, 1994.

Barakat, Robert A. "Aztec Motifs in 'La Llorona.'" *Southern Folklore Quarterly* 29 (4)
(1965): 288–296.

Bardwell, S. K., and Lisa Teachey. "Bayou Is Searched for Baby After Mother Admits
Slaying." *Houston Chronicle on the Web,* 29 Jan. 1997. http://www.chron.com/
content/chronicle/page1/97/01/30/baby.html. Accessed 31 Jan. 1997.

Barnes, Kim. "A Leslie Marmon Silko Interview." *Journal of Ethnic Studies* 13 (4)
(Winter 1986): 83–105.

Barraza, Santa C. "Santa C. Barraza, An Autobiography." In *Santa Barraza: Artist of the Borderlands,* ed. María Herrera-Sobek, 3–49. College Station: Texas A&M Univ. Press, 2001.

Baudrillard, Jean. *Seduction.* Trans. Brian Singer. New York: St. Martin's, 1990.

Bierhorst, John, ed. *The Hungry Woman: Myths and Legends of the Aztecs.* New York: Morrow, 1984.

Blea, Irene I. *La Chicana and the Intersection of Race, Class, and Gender.* New York: Praeger, 1992.

Bobo, Jacqueline. *Black Women as Cultural Readers.* New York: Columbia Univ. Press, 1995.

Bruce-Novoa, Juan. *Chicano Poetry: A Response to Chaos.* Austin: Univ. of Texas Press, 1982.

Brundage, Burr Cartwright. *The Fifth Sun: Aztec Gods, Aztec World.* Austin: Univ. of Texas Press, 1979.

Bryer, Diana. Personal communication "Re: La Llorona." E-mail to the author, 15 March 2005.

California Milk Processor Board (CMPB). "Got Milk? Commercial Takes Hispanic Creative Honors." Got Milk? News, 3 Oct. 2002. http://www.gotmilk.com/news/news_009.html. Accessed 6 Feb. 2006.

Camacho, Alicia Schmidt. "Body Counts on the Mexico-U.S. Border: Feminicidio, Reification, and the Theft of Mexicana Subjectivity." *Chicana/Latina Studies: The Journal of Mujeres Activas en Letras y Cambio Social* 4 (1) (2004): 22–60.

Candelaria, Cordelia. *Arroyos to the Heart.* Ed. Ernesto Padilla. Santa Monica, CA: Lalo Literature Division, Santa Monica College Press, 1993.

———. "La Llorona." In *The Oxford Companion to Women's Writing in the United States,* ed. Cathy N. Davidson et al., 468. New York: Oxford Univ. Press, 1995.

———. "Letting La Llorona Go, Or, Re/reading History's 'Tender Mercies.'" In *Arroyos to the Heart,* 125–131. Santa Monica, CA: Lalo Literature Division, Santa Monica College Press, 1993.

———. *Chicano Poetry: A Critical Introduction.* Westport, CT: Greenwood, 1986.

Carbonell, Ana María. "From Llorona to Gritona: Coatlicue In Feminist Tales by Viramontes and Cisneros." *Melus* 24 (2) (1999): 53–74.

Castañeda Shular, Antonia, Tomás Ybarra-Frausto, and Joseph Sommers, eds. "la llorona." In *Literatura Chicana: Texto y Contexto/Chicano Literature: Text and Context,* 97–108. Englewood Cliffs, NJ: Prentice-Hall, 1972.

Castillo, Ana. *Massacre of the Dreamers: Essays on Xicanisma.* 1994. New York: Plume, 1995.

———. *So Far From God.* New York: W. W. Norton, 1993.

Catacalos, Rosemary. *Again for the First Time.* Santa Fe, NM: Tooth of Time, 1984.

Chabon, Michael. *Summerland.* New York: Miramax/Hyperion, 2002.

Chabram-Dernersesian, Angie. "I Throw Punches for My Race, but I Don't Want to Be a Man: Writing Us—Chica-nos (Girl, Us)/Chicanas—into the Movement

Script." In *Cultural Studies,* ed. Lawrence Grossberg et al., 81–95. New York: Routledge, 1992.

Chabria, Anita. "Spanish-language Milk Campaign Goes Mainstream." *PR Week US,* 28 Jan. 2002: 2. *Factiva.* Dow Jones Reuters Business Interactive. UT at Austin Libraries. http://global.factiva.com. Accessed 17 Jan. 2006.

Chasing Papi. Story by Laura Angélica Simón and Steven Antin. Dir. Linda Mendoza. Perf. Roselyn Sanchez, Sofia Vergara, Jaci Velasquez, Eduardo Verástegui, Laurie Carrasco. 20th Century Fox, 2003.

Chávez, Denise. *Face of an Angel.* New York: Warner, 1994.

————. *Last of the Menu Girls.* Houston: Arte Público, 1986.

ChUSMA. Biography. Teatro ChUSMA! 2004. http://www.chusma.com/biography .htm. Accessed 26 Oct. 2004.

Cinco Puntos Press. About Us. http://www.cincopuntos.com. Accessed 28 May 2005.

Cisneros, Sandra. "Woman Hollering Creek." In *Woman Hollering Creek and Other Stories,* 43–56. New York: Random House, 1991.

Clark, Mike. "Dull *Chasing Papi* Goes Nowhere Fast." *USA Today,* 16 Apr. 2003: 3D.

"Collision." *Lost.* ABC. KVUE, Austin, TX, 23 Nov. 2005.

Cook, Barbara J. "La Llorona and a Call for Environmental Justice in the Borderlands: Ana Castillo's *So Far From God.*" *Northwest Review* 39 (2) (2001): 124–133.

Cortez, Constance. "Aztlán in Tejas: Chicano/a Art From the Third Coast." In *Chicano Visions: American Painters on the Verge,* ed. Cheech Marin, 33–42. Boston: Bulfinch Press, 2002.

Coste, Rosemarie. "La Llorona y El Grito/The Ghost and The Scream: Noisy Women in Borderlands and Beyond." 15 Dec. 2000. http://www.womenwriters.net/ editorials/lallorona.htm. Accessed 31 May 2005.

Cox, James H. *Muting White Noise: Native American and European American Novel Traditions.* Norman: Univ. of Oklahoma Press, 2006.

Crow Dog, Mary, with Richard Erdoes. *Lakota Woman.* New York: HarperCollins, 1990.

Cuádraz, Gloria Holguín. "Diary of *La Llorona* With a Ph.D." In *Telling to Live: Latina Feminist Testimonios,* ed. the Latina Feminist Group, 212–217. Durham, NC: Duke Univ. Press, 2001.

Cuellar, Israel, and Robert E. Roberts. "Psychological Disorders Among Chicanos." In *Chicano Psychology,* ed. Joe L. Martinez Jr. and Richard H. Mendoza, 133–161. 2nd ed. Orlando: Academic Press, 1984.

Cunningham, Keith. "La Llorona in Yuma." *Southwest Folklore* 5 (1) (1981): 70–77.

The Cry. Dir. Bernadine Santistevan. Perf. Miriam Colon and Carlos Leon. No distributor, 2006.

Cypess, Sandra Messinger. *La Malinche in Mexican Literature: From History to Myth.* Austin: Univ. of Texas Press, 1991.

Daglow, Don L. "The Blessing of La Llorona." *The Magazine of Fantasy and Science Fiction* 62 (4) (1982): 33–67.

———. Personal communication "Re: The Blessing of La Llorona." E-mail to the author, 15 Mar. 2005.

———. Personal communication "Re: La Llorona and Thanks." E-mail to the author, 23 Mar. 2005.

Dávila, Arlene. *Latinos, Inc.: The Marketing and Making of a People.* Berkeley: Univ. of California Press, 2001.

Dawes, Kwame. "Re-appropriating Cultural Appropriation." In *Borrowed Power: Essays on Cultural Appropriation,* ed. Bruce Ziff and Pratima V. Rao, 109–121. New Brunswick, NJ: Rutgers Univ. Press, 1997.

Deanda, Mayra. "Three Boys Found Dead in Vermont River, Comments." La Llorona . . . The Cry. Blog. 21 June 2005. http://thecry.typepad.com/thecry/2005/05/three_boys_foun.htm#comments. Accessed 7 July 2005.

Del Rio, Rebekah. http://www.rebekahdelrio.com. Accessed 15 Jan. 2005.

del Valle, César Pineda. *Cuentos y leyendas de la costa de Chiapas.* México, D.F.: B. Cost-Amic, 1976.

Delgadillo, Theresa. "Forms of Chicana Feminist Resistance: Hybrid Spirituality in Ana Castillo's *So Far From God.*" *Modern Fiction Studies* 44 (4) (1998): 888–916.

Delgado, Abelardo B. *La Llorona: 43 Lloronas de Abelardo.* Arvada, CO: Barrio Publications, 1997.

Deloria, Vine, Jr. *Custer Died For Your Sins: An Indian Manifesto.* New York: Macmillan, 1969.

Dobie, J. Frank. *The Mexico I Like.* Dallas: University Press in Dallas, Southern Methodist University, 1942.

Dorson, Richard M. "Leyendas." In *Buying the Wind: Regional Folklore in the United States,* 436–441. Chicago: Univ. of Chicago Press, 1964.

Doyle, Jacqueline. "Haunting the Borderlands: La Llorona in Sandra Cisneros's 'Woman Hollering Creek.'" *Frontiers* 16 (1) (1996): 53–70.

Endrezze, Anita. "La Llorona, the Crying Woman." In *Throwing Fire at the Sun, Water at the Moon,* 156–158. Tucson: Univ. of Arizona Press, 2000.

Enger, Dan K. Arco Iris Web Designs. http://www.arco-iris.com/enger/images/llorona.jpg. Accessed 24 May 2005.

———. Personal communication "Re: La Llorona." E-mail to the author, 16 June 2005.

Espinosa, Aurelio M. "New-Mexican Spanish Folk-lore." *Journal of American Folklore* 23 (90) (Oct.–Dec. 1910): 395–418.

Estés, Clarissa Pinkola. *Women Who Run With the Wolves: Myths and Stories of the Wild Woman Archetype.* New York: Ballantine, 1995.

Euripides. *Medea and Other Plays.* Trans. James Morwood. New York: Oxford Univ. Press, 1998.

Fernández, Roberta. "Esmeralda." In *Intaglio: A Novel in Six Stories,* 109–132. Houston: Arte Público, 1990.

Figueredo, Maria L. "The Legend of *La Llorona:* Excavating and (Re)Interpreting the Archetype of the Creative/Fertile Feminine Force." In *Latin American Narratives and Cultural Identity: Selected Readings,* ed. Irene Maria Blayer and Mark Cronlund Anderson, 232–243. New York: Peter Lang, 2004.

Fish, Stanley. *There's No Such Thing As Free Speech: And It's a Good Thing, Too.* New York: Oxford Univ. Press, 1994.

Franco, Jean. "The Return of Coatlicue: Mexican Nationalism and the Aztec Past." *Journal of Latin American Cultural Studies* 13 (2) (Aug. 2004): 205–219.

Frida. Screenplay by Clancy Sigal, Diane Lake, Gregory Nava, and Anna Thomas. Dir. Julie Taymor. Perf. Salma Hayek, Alfred Molina, Geoffrey Rush, Ashely Judd. Miramax, 2002.

Fuentes, Víctor. "Chicano Cinema: A Dialectic Between Voices and Images of the Autonomous Discourses Versus Those of the Dominant." In *Chicanos and Film: Representation and Resistance,* ed. Chon A. Noriega, 207–217. Minneapolis: Univ. of Minnesota Press, 1992.

Fusco, Coco. *English is Broken Here: Notes on Cultural Fusion in the Americas.* New York: New Press, 1995.

García, Alma M., ed. *Chicana Feminist Thought: The Basic Historical Writings.* New York: Routledge, 1997.

Garcia, Mario S. "Holding *La Llorona*'s Feet to the Fire." Mr. Garcia's English Class. Los Angeles Unified School District, John F. Kennedy High School staff Web site, 1–2. 1998. http://www.lausd.k12.ca.us/Kennedy_HS/staff/garcia/. Accessed 8 Feb. 2005.

Garza, Carmen Lomas. *In My Family/En Mi Familia.* San Francisco: Children's Book Press, 1996.

Garza, Xavier. *Creepy Creatures and Other Cucuys.* Houston: Piñata Books, 2004.

———. Personal communication "Re: La Llorona." E-mail to the author, 7 Feb. 2005.

Gaspar de Alba, Alicia. *Chicano Art Inside/Outside the Master's House: Cultural Politics and the CARA Exhibition.* Austin: Univ. of Texas Press, 1998.

———. *Desert Blood: The Juárez Murders.* Houston: Arte Público, 2005.

———. *La Llorona on the Longfellow Bridge: Poetry y otras movidas, 1985–2001.* Houston: Arte Público, 2003.

———. "Malinche's Rights." In *Currents From the Dancing River: Contemporary Latino Fiction, Nonfiction, and Poetry,* ed. Ray González, 261–266. New York: Harcourt Brace, 1994.

———. Personal communication. Letter to the author, 1 Oct. 2006.

Gaspar de Alba, Alicia, María Herrera-Sobek, and Demetria Martínez. *Three Times a Woman: Chicana Poetry.* Tempe, AZ: Bilingual Press/Editorial Bilingüe, 1989.

The Ghost of La Llorona. By Rodney Rincon. Dir. Trish Rigdon. Express Children's Theatre, Houston, 2003.

The Ghost of La Llorona. By Rodney Rincon. Dir. Ed Muth. Express Children's Theatre, Houston, 1997.

Gibbs, Nancy, and Kathy Booth. "Death and Deceit." *Time,* 14 Nov. 1994, 42–48.

Gibson-Rosado, Erica M. *The Sterilization of Women in Puerto Rico Under the Cloak of Colonial Policy: A Case Study on the Role of Perception in U.S. Foreign Policy and Population Control.* Washington, D.C.: Johns Hopkins Univ. Press, 1993.

Gish, Robert Franklin. "La Llorona, Magic Realism, and the Frontier." In *Beyond Bounds: Cross-Cultural Essays on Anglo, American Indian, and Chicano Literature,* 110–127. Albuquerque: Univ. of New Mexico Press, 1996.

Glazer, Mark. "'La Llorona' in South Texas: Tradition and Modernity in a Mexican American Legend." In *Plenary Papers: The 8th Congress for the International Study of Folk Narrative Research, Bergen, June 12th–17th, 1984,* 205–212. Bergen, Norway: International Society for Folk Narrative Research, 1984.

Gleick, Elizabeth, and Lisa H. Towle. "It Did Happen Here." *Time,* 19 Dec. 1994, 60–61.

Gómez-Peña, Guillermo. *Warrior for Gringostroika: Essays, Performance Texts, and Poetry.* St. Paul, MN: Graywolf, 1993.

Gonzales, Robert, Karim Chatila, and Ronnie Pontiac. "Los Angelina." *Newtopia Magazine: A Journal of the New Counterculture.* http://www.newtopiamagazine .net/archives/content/issue14/newart/losangelina.php. Accessed 14 Mar. 2006.

Gonzales, Rudolfo. *I am Joaquín.* 1967. New York: Bantam, 1972.

González Obregón, Luis. "La Llorona." In *Las Calles de México: Leyendas y sucedidos, vida y costumbres de otros tiempos,* 9–10. 1922. Reprint, México, D.F.: Editorial Porrúa, 1988.

Gonzalez S., Silvia. *La Llorona Llora: A Play in One Act.* Woodstock, IL: Dramatic Publishing, 1996.

Hall, Douglas Kent. Personal communication "Re: La Llorona." E-mail to the author, 16 June 2005.

Hanson, Eric. "Infanticide Cases Still Evoke Shock, Horror in Jaded Public." *Houston Chronicle on the Web,* 29 Jan. 1997. http://www.chron.com/content/chronicle/ page1/ 97/01/30/infanticide.html. Accessed 31 Jan. 1997.

Harlow, Barbara. *Resistance Literature.* New York: Methuen, 1987.

Harris, Paul. "Bechtel, Bolivia Resolve Dispute: Company Drops Demand Over Water Contract Canceling." *San Francisco Chronicle,* 19 Jan. 2006, A3.

Haunted From Within [Spirit Hunter: La Llorona]. Dir. José L. Cruz. Perf. Rina Fernandez, David Green, Kurt Sinclair, and Tamra Marez. DVD. York, 2004.

Hawes, Bess Lomax. "La Llorona in Juvenile Hall." *Western Folklore* 27 (1968): 153–170.

Hayes, Joe. *Here Comes the Storyteller.* El Paso: Cinco Puntos, 1996.

———. *La Llorona, The Weeping Woman: An Hispanic Legend Told in Spanish and English.* Illus. Vicki Trego Hill. El Paso: Cinco Puntos, 1987.

———. *La Llorona, The Weeping Woman: An Hispanic Legend Told in Spanish and English.* Hardcover with color illustrations. Illus. Vicki Trego Hill and Mona Pennypacker. El Paso: Cinco Puntos, 2004.

Heinzelman, Susan Sage. "'Going Somewhere': Maternal Infanticide and the Ethics of Judgment." In *Literature and Legal Problem Solving: Law and Literature as Ethical Discourse,* ed. Paul J. Heald, 73–97. Durham, NC: Carolina Academic Press, 1998.

"Hell Hath No Fury." *Cracker.* ABC. KLKN, Lincoln, NE, 16 Oct. 1997.

Hernandez, Gilbert. "La Llorona: The Legend of the Crying Woman." In *Fear of Comics,* vol. 17 of *Love and Rockets,* 69–72. Seattle: Fantagraphics Books, 2000.

Hernández, Guillermo E. *Chicano Satire: A Study in Literary Culture.* Austin: Univ. of Texas Press, 1991.

Hernandez, Jaime. *The Death of Speedy,* vol. 7 of *Love and Rockets.* Seattle: Fantagraphics Books, 1989.

Hernandez, Leticia. "Juana Alicia: A Muralist Takes a Global Look at the Spirit of Women." http://www.juanaalicia.com/sections/recently-completed/. Accessed 26 Oct. 2004.

Herrera-Sobek, María. "Introduction." In *Santa Barraza, Artist of the Borderlands,* ed. María Herrera-Sobek, xv–xx. College Station: Texas A&M Univ. Press, 2001.

———. *The Mexican Corrido: A Feminist Analysis.* Bloomington: Indiana Univ. Press, 1990.

———, ed. *Santa Barraza, Artist of the Borderlands.* College Station: Texas A&M Univ. Press, 2001.

Hillerman, Tony. *The Wailing Wind.* New York: HarperCollins, 2002.

Holy Bible: The New King James Version. Carmel, NY: Guideposts, 1982.

Horcasitas, Fernando, and Douglas Butterworth. "La Llorona." In *Tlalocan: Revista de Fuentes para el Conocimiento de las Culturas Indígenas de México* 4 (1963): 204–224.

Hong Kingston, Maxine. "No Name Woman." In *Woman Warrior: Memoirs of a Girlhood Among Ghosts,* 1–16. New York: Vintage, 1975.

Huerta, Jorge A. "La Llorona." Unpublished play. 1978.

"I'm Forever Blowing Bubbles." Lyrics Drive. http://www.lyricsdrive.com/lyrics/jaan-kenbrovin/356952/im-forever-blowing-bubbles/. Accessed 15 Mar. 2007.

Janvier, Thomas A. "Legend of La Llorona." In *Legends of the City of Mexico,* 134–138, 162–165. New York: Harper and Brothers, 1910.

Jefferson, Rob. Personal communication "Re: La Llorona." E-mail to the author, 20 June 2005.

Jennings, Gary. *Aztec.* New York: Atheneum, 1980.

Jones, Pamela. "'There Was a Woman': *La Llorona* in Oregon." *Western Folklore* 47 (3) (1988): 195–211.

Jordon, Rosan A. "The Vaginal Serpent and Other Themes From Mexican-American Women's Lore." In *Women's Folklore, Women's Culture,* ed. Rosan A. Jordon and Susan J. Kalcik, 26–44. Philadelphia: Univ. of Pennsylvania Press, 1985.

Kearney, Michael. "La Llorona as a Social Symbol." *Western Folklore* 28 (3) (1969): 199–206.

Keating, AnaLouise, ed. *Interviews/Entrevistas/Gloria E. Anzaldúa.* New York: Routledge, 2000.

Keeshig-Tobias, Lenore. "Stop Stealing Native Stories." In *Borrowed Power: Essays on Cultural Appropriation,* ed. Bruce Ziff and Pratima V. Rao, 71–73. New Brunswick, NJ: Rutgers Univ. Press, 1997.

Kehr, Dave. "3 Wronged Women Scratch Out Insight, Not One Another's Eyes." *New York Times,* 16 Apr. 2003, E5.

Keller, Gary D., Mary Erickson, and Pat Villeneuve. *Chicano Art For Our Millennium: Collected Works From the Arizona State University Community.* Tempe, AZ: Bilingual Press/Editorial Bilingüe, 2004.

Kennedy, Desiree. "More Deaths in Iraq, Comments." La Llorona . . . The Cry. Blog. 20 June 2005. http://thecry.typepad.com/thecry/2005/05/more_deaths_in_ .html#comments. Accessed 7 July 2005.

King, Thomas. *The Truth About Stories: A Native Narrative.* Toronto: House of Anansi, 2003.

Kirtley, Bacil F. "'La Llorona' and Related Themes." *Western Folklore* 19 (3) (1960): 155–168.

Klor de Alva, J. Jorge. "Foreword." In *The Broken Spears: The Aztec Account of the Conquest of Mexico,* trans. Lysander Kemp, ed. Miguel León-Portilla, xi–xxiv. 1959. Expanded and updated, Boston: Beacon Press, 1992.

Kraul, Edward Garcia, and Judith Beatty, comps. and eds. *The Weeping Woman: Encounters With La Llorona.* Illus. Tony Sanchez. Santa Fe, NM: Word Process, 1988.

Kutz, Jack. *Mysteries and Miracles of New Mexico: Guide Book to the Genuinely Bizarre in the Land of Enchantment.* Corrales, NM: Rhombus, 1988.

La Llorona. Short film. Dir. and prod. Trina Lopez. No distributor, 1998.

"La Llorona" coffee. Coffee Shop of Horrors. http://www.coffeeshopofhorrors.com/ isell/product.php?id=79. Accessed 24 Oct. 2004.

"La Llorona, Part 1." *American Family.* PBS. KERA, Dallas, 6 Feb. 2002.

"La Llorona, Part 2." *American Family.* PBS. KERA, Dallas, 13 Feb. 2002.

"La Llorona, Parts 1 and 2." *American Family.* Dir. Gregory Nava. Perf. Edward James Olmos, Sonia Braga, Constance Marie, Esai Morales, Raquel Welch, A. J. Lamas, Rachel Ticotin, and Austin Marques. DVD. 20th Century Fox, 2003.

"La Llorona Commercial Takes Hispanic Creative Honors." *Hispania News,* 9 Oct. 2002. http://www.hispanianews.com/archive/2002/10/09/14.htm. Accessed 7 Nov. 2004.

"La Llorona Park Opens." *Las Cruces Sun-News,* 15 Oct. 1995, A4.

"La Llorona: Jaime Hernandez." In *Barrio Streets, Carnival Dreams: Three Generations of Latino Artistry,* ed. Lori Marie Carlson, 108–109. New York: Henry Holt, 1996.

Lacayo, Richard. "Stranger in the Shadows." *Time,* 14 Nov. 1994, 46–47.

Lane, Anthony. "Road Trips: David Lynch and John Dahl Look Back." *New Yorker,* 8 Oct. 2001, 88–89.

Leach, Maria, and Jerome Fried, eds. "llorona." In *Funk and Wagnalls Standard*

Dictionary of Folklore, Mythology and Legend, 639. 2 vols. New York: Funk and Wagnalls, 1950.

Leddy, Betty. "La Llorona Again." *Western Folklore* 9 (4) (1950): 363–365.

———. "La Llorona in Southern Arizona." *Western Folklore* 7 (3) (1948): 272–277.

The Legend of La Llorona. Dir. and prod. Stephanie Saint Sanchez. DVD. No distributor, 2002.

Lemeh, Dori. "Myth, Reality, Legend: *El Poder de la Mujer.*" In *Santa Barraza, Artist of the Borderlands,* ed. María Herrera-Sobek, 76–87. College Station: Texas A&M Univ. Press, 2001.

León, Luis D. *La Llorona's Children: Religion, Life, and Death in the U.S.-Mexican Borderlands.* Berkeley: Univ. of California Press, 2004.

León-Portilla, Miguel. *Visión de los vencidos: Relaciones indígenas de la conquista.* México, D.F.: Universidad Nacional Autónoma de México, 1959.

———, ed. *The Broken Spears: The Aztec Account of the Conquest of Mexico.* Trans. Lysander Kemp. 1959. Expanded and updated. Boston: Beacon Press, 1992.

Leyba, Lucinda. *Bruja: The Legend of La Llorona.* Otsego, MI: PageFree Publishing, 2004.

Limón, José E. "La Llorona, The Third Legend of Greater Mexico: Cultural Symbols, Women, and the Political Unconscious." In *Between Borders: Essays on Mexicana/Chicana History,* ed. Adelaida R. Del Castillo, 399–432. Encino, CA: Floricanto Press, 1990.

Lockhart, James, ed. and trans. *We People Here: Nahuatl Accounts of the Conquest of Mexico.* Vol. 1. Berkeley: Univ. of California Press, 1993.

Luna Lemus, Felicia. *Trace Elements of Random Tea Parties.* Emeryville, CA: Seal Press, 2003.

"The Making of La Llorona Got Milk." *Realidades.* PBS. KERA, Dallas, 13 Feb. 2002.

Magical Rain Theaterworks. About Us. http://www.magicalrain.com/about5.htm. Accessed 23 June 2006.

———. "La Llorona Dolorosa." http://www.magicalrain.com/lallorona5.htm. Accessed 23 June 2006.

Manríquez, B. J. "Ana Castillo's *So Far From God:* Imitations of the Absurd." *College Literature* 29 (2) (Spring 2002): 37–49.

Mesa-Bains, Amalia. "El Mundo Femenino: Chicana Artists of the Movement—A Commentary On Development and Production." In *Chicano Art: Resistance and Affirmation, 1965-1985,* ed. Richard Griswold Del Castillo, Teresa McKenna, and Yvonne Yarbro-Bejarano, 131–140. Los Angeles: Wight Art Gallery, UCLA, 1991.

Miles, Elton. *More Tales of the Big Bend.* College Station: Texas A&M Univ. Press, 1988.

———. *Tales of the Big Bend.* College Station: Texas A&M Univ. Press, 1976.

"Milk Industry Turns to Ghostly Hispanic Legend in Ad Campaign." *San Francisco Chronicle,* 13 Jan. 2002. http://sfgate.com/cgi-bin/article.cgi?file=/n/a/2002/01/13/state0948EST0013.DTL. Accessed 14 May 2004.

Miller, Elaine K., comp. "La Xtabay." *Mexican Folk Narrative from the Los Angeles Area, 99.* Austin: Univ. of Texas Press, 1973.

Minh-ha, Trinh T. *Woman, Native, Other: Writing Postcoloniality and Feminism.* Bloomington: Indiana Univ. Press, 1989.

Montoya, Delilah. "It's All About the Apple, Or Is It?" Delilah Montoya: Women Artists of the American West. http://www.cla.purdue.edu/WAAW/Ressler/artists/montoyastat.html. Accessed 17 Jan. 2006.

Mora, Pat. *Agua Santa/Holy Water.* Boston: Beacon, 1995.

———. *Borders.* Houston: Arte Público, 1986.

———. *Chants.* Houston: Arte Público, 1985.

Moraga, Cherríe L. *The Hungry Woman: A Mexican Medea.* Albuquerque: West End, 2001.

———. *The Last Generation: Prose and Poetry.* Boston: South End, 1993.

———. *Loving in the War Years: Lo que nunca pasó por sus labios.* Expanded 2nd ed. Cambridge, MA: South End, 2000.

Moreno, Victoria. "La Llorona, Crying Lady of the Creekbeds, 483 Years Old, and Aging." In *The Third Woman: Minority Women Writers of the United States,* ed. Dexter Fisher, 319–320. Boston: Houghton Mifflin, 1977.

Morrison, Toni. *Beloved.* New York: Knopf, 1987.

Morton, Carlos, and Angel Vigil. *Cuentos.* In *Una Linda Raza: Cultural and Artistic Traditions of the Hispanic Southwest,* ed. Angel Vigil, 153–172. Golden, CO: Fulcrum, 1998.

Mulholland Drive. Dir. David Lynch. Perf. Laura Elena Harring, Naomi Watts, and Justin Theroux. Universal Studios, 2001.

Murray, Yxta Maya. "La Llorona: A Story." *The North American Review* 281 (6) (1996): 24–27.

National Public Radio (NPR). "Got Milk? Ad Campaign Redirects Its Efforts Towards Teen-agers in California by Using an Old Mexican Legend." *All Things Considered,* host. Liane Hansen. 7 Feb. 2002. *Factiva.* Dow Jones Reuters Business Interactive. UT at Austin Libraries. http://global.factiva.com. Accessed 17 Jan. 2006.

Noriega, Chon A. *Shot in America: Television, the State, and the Rise of Chicano Cinema.* Minneapolis: Univ. of Minnesota Press, 2000.

Novelo, Narciso Souza. "La X-Tabay." *Leyendas mayas,* 107–113. Mérida, Yucatán, México: Distribuidora de Libros Yucatecos, 1970.

"The Other 48 Days." *Lost.* ABC. KVUE, Austin, TX, 16 Nov. 2005.

Odom, Mel. *Bruja.* New York: Pocket Pulse, 2001.

Onekama Consolidated Schools. "Fourth Graders Produce a Scarey [sic] Play." 2001. http://www.onekama.k12.mi.us/n2002/music/spooky4th.htm. Accessed 27 Nov. 2005.

The Others. Dir. Alejandro Almenábar. Perf. Nicole Kidman. Dimension Films, 2001.

Owen Moore, Deborah. "*La Llorona* Dines at the Cariboo Cafe: Structure and

Legend in the Work of Helena María Viramontes." *Studies in Short Fiction* 35 (3) (1998): 277–286.

Palacios, Monica. "La Llorona Loca: The Other Side." In *Chicana Lesbians: The Girls Our Mothers Warned Us About,* ed. Carla Trujillo, 49–51. Berkeley, CA: Third Woman, 1991.

Paredes, Américo. "Mexican Legendry and the Rise of the Mestizo: A Survey." In *American Folk Legend: A Symposium,* ed. Wayland D. Hand, 97–107. Berkeley: Univ. of California Press, 1971.

———, ed. and trans. *Folktales of Mexico.* Chicago: Univ. of Chicago Press, 1970.

Paul, Paula G. *The Wail of La Llorona.* New York: Airmont Publishing, 1977.

Paz, Octavio. *The Labyrinth of Solitude: Life and Thought in Mexico.* Trans. Lysander Kemp. New York: Grove, 1961.

Perez, Domino Renee. "Caminando con La Llorona: Traditional and Contemporary Narratives." In *Chicana Traditions: Continuity and Change,* ed. Norma E. Cantú and Olga Nájera-Ramírez, 100–113. Urbana: Univ. of Illinois Press, 2002.

———. "Crossing Mythological Borders: Revisioning La Llorona in Contemporary Fiction." *Proteus: A Journal of Ideas* 16 (1) (1999): 49–54.

———. "Lost in the Cinematic Landscape: Chicanas as Lloronas in Contemporary Film." In *Velvet Barrios: Popular Culture and Chicana/o Sexualities,* ed. Alicia Gaspar de Alba, 229–247. New York: Palgrave, 2003.

———. "Mitos y Leyendas." In *The Oxford Encyclopedia of Latinos and Latinas in the United States,* ed. Deena J. González, Suzanne Oboler et al., 165–166. New York: Oxford University Press, 2005.

———. "'Words, Worlds in Our Heads': Reclaiming La Llorona's Aztecan Antecedents in Gloria Anzaldúa's 'My Black *Angelos.*'" *Studies in American Indian Literatures, Special Edition: Indigenous Intersections* 15 (3–4) (Fall 2003/Winter 2004): 51–63.

Perez, Maria. Personal interview by author, 10 Mar. 1998.

Pérez, Soledad. "Mexican Folklore From Austin, Texas." In *The Healer of Los Olmos and Other Mexican Lore,* ed. Wilson M. Hudson, 71–76. Dallas: Southern Methodist Univ. Press, 1951.

Pérez-Torres, Rafael. *Movements in Chicano Poetry: Against Myths, Against Margins.* New York: Cambridge, 1995.

phulana2. "At least the illustrations are good." Review of *Prietita and the Ghost Woman/Prietita y la Llorona,* by Gloria Anzaldúa, illus. Christina Gonzalez. "Amazon.com Customer Reviews." 24 June 2001. http://www.amazon.com/ Prietita-Ghost-Woman-llorona/dp/0892391677/ref=pd_bbs_sr_1/105-1801557- 9197248?ie=UTF8&s=books&qid=1184776333&sr=8-1. Accessed 18 July 2007.

"Pilot." *Supernatural.* WB. KNVA, Austin, TX, 13 Sept. 2005.

Quiñonez, Naomi. *Sueño de colibrí/Hummingbird Dream: Poems.* Los Angeles: West End, 1985.

Ramírez, Arturo. "La Llorona: Structure and Archetype." In *Chicano Border Culture and Folklore*, ed. José Villarino and Arturo Ramírez, 19–26. San Diego: Marin Publications, 1992.

raúlrsalinas. *Un Trip Through the Mind Jail y Otras Excursions: Poems*. San Francisco: Editorial Pocho-Che, 1980.

Rebolledo, Tey Diana. "Myths and Archetypes." In *Infinite Divisions: An Anthology of Chicana Literature*, ed. Tey Diana Rebolledo and Eliana S. Rivero, 189–195. Tucson: Univ. of Arizona Press, 1993.

———. *Women Singing in the Snow: A Cultural Analysis of Chicana Literature*. Tucson: Univ. of Arizona Press, 1995.

River of Women/Río de Mujeres. By Hector Armienta. Dir. José Maria Condemi. Theater Artaud, San Francisco, 10 May 2001.

Robe, Stanley L. *Hispanic Legends from New Mexico: Narratives from the R. D. Jameson Collection*. Berkeley: Univ. of California Press, 1980.

———, comp. "Classification: G264 *La Belle Dame Sans Merci*." In *Mexican Tales and Legends from Veracruz*, 110–111. Berkeley: Univ. of California Press, 1971.

Rodriguez, Ralph E. "Chicana/o Fiction from Resistance to Contestation: The Role of Creation in Ana Castillo's *So Far From God*." *MELUS* 25 (2) (Summer 2000): 63–82.

Rogers, Jane. "The Function of the *La Llorona* Motif in Rudolfo Anaya's *Bless Me, Ultima*." In *Latin American Literary Review: Special Issue of Chicano Literature* 5 (10) (1977): 64–69.

Romero, Rolando, and Amanda Nolacea Harris, eds. *Feminism, Nation and Myth: La Malinche*. Houston: Arte Público, 2005.

Rosenthal, Phil. "ABC Gets Top Marks From Minority Groups." *Austin American-Statesman*, 5 Dec. 2005, E8.

Sahagún, Fray Bernardino de. *Historia general de las cosas de la Nueva España: Florentine Codex*. 1578. Trans. Arthur J. O. Anderson and Charles E. Dibble. 12 vols. Santa Fe, NM: School of American Research; Salt Lake City: Univ. of Utah Press, 1950–1982.

Saint Sanchez, Stephanie. Personal communication. Letter to the author, [2005].

Salas, David. "La Llorona." http://www.eyetooth7.com. Accessed 17 July 2007.

Saldívar, José David. *Border Matters: Remapping American Cultural Studies*. Berkeley: Univ. of California Press, 1997.

Saldívar-Hull, Sonia. *Feminism on the Border: Chicana Gender Politics and Literature*. Berkeley: Univ. of California Press, 2000.

San Miguel, Susan. "La Llorona of Leon Creek." In *Texas Short Stories*, ed. Billy Bob Hill, 482–497. Dallas: Browder Springs Publishing, 1997.

Sánchez, Ricardo. *Hechizospells: Poetry/stories/vignettes/articles/notes on the human condition of Chicanos and pícaros, words and hopes within soulmind. . . .* Los Angeles: University of California, Chicano Studies Center, 1976.

Santistevan, Bernadine. The Spirit of La Llorona. 2005. http://www.lallorona.com. Accessed 7 July 2005.

Sela, Lhasa de. *La Llorona.* Album. Atlantic, 1998.

Shakespeare, William. *Hamlet.* In *The Riverside Shakespeare,* 1141–1197. Boston: Houghton Mifflin, 1974.

Silko, Leslie Marmon. *Ceremony.* New York: Viking, 1977.

Silver, Patricia A. Personal communication "Re: La Llorona, Again." E-mail to the author, 5 June 2005.

Tafolla, Carmen. Personal communication "Re: Thank you." E-mail to the author, 6 Feb. 2007.

Tafoya, Mary J. Personal communication "Re: La Llorona." E-mail to the author, 14 Sept. 2005.

Tedlock, Dennis. *Breath on the Mirror: Mythic Voices and Visions of the Living Maya.* San Francisco: HarperSanFrancisco, 1993.

———. *Popol Vuh: The Definitive Edition of the Mayan Book of the Dawn of Life and the Glories of Gods and Kings.* New York: Simon and Schuster, 1996.

Tillery, Val and Bob. Personal communication "Re: *Time* Magazine." E-mail to the author, 8 Feb. 2005.

Toelken, Barre. *The Dynamics of Folklore.* Boston: Houghton Mifflin, 1979.

Toor, Frances A. *A Treasury of Mexican Folkways.* New York: Crown, 1947.

Toscano, Carmen. *La Llorona.* México, D.F.: Tezontle, 1959.

———. "La Llorona." Dramatic dialogue. In *Literatura Chicana: Texto y Contexto/ Chicano Literature: Text and Context,* ed. Antonia Castañeda Shular, Tomás Ybarra-Frausto, and Joseph Sommers, 103–104. Englewood Cliffs, NJ: Prentice-Hall, 1972.

Trigos, Juan. *La Llorona: Hemofiction Literature.* Bloomington, IN: First Books Library, 2003.

Vargas, Chavela. *La Llorona.* Album. Wea International, 2004.

Vigil, Angel. "La Llorona's Final Cry" and "The Weeping Woman (La Llorona)." In *The Corn Woman: Stories and Legends of the Hispanic Southwest/La mujer del maíz: Cuentos y leyendas del sudoeste hispano,* trans. Jennifer Audrey Lowell and Juan Francisco Marín, 184–189, 11–13. Englewood, CO: Libraries Unlimited, 1994.

Villanueva, Alma Luz. *Weeping Woman: La Llorona and Other Stories.* Tempe, AZ: Bilingual Press/Editorial Bilingüe, 1994.

Viramontes, Helena María. "The Cariboo Cafe." In *The Moths and Other Stories,* 65–79. 1985. Houston: Arte Público, 1995.

———. *Under the Feet of Jesus.* New York: Dutton, 1995.

Vorderbrug, Brice. Personal communication "Re: La Llorona Coffee." E-mail to the author, 27 June 2005.

Walraven, Ed. "Evidence for a Developing Variant of 'La Llorona.'" *Western Folklore* 50 (April 1991): 208–217.

Wartzman, Rick. "Read Their Lips: When You Translate 'Got Milk' for Latinos, What

Do You Get?—The Answer Was a Surprise For a Marketing Group Courting Hispanic Teens—The Meaning of Biculturalism." *Wall Street Journal*, 3 June 1999, A1. *Factiva*. Dow Jones Reuters Business Interactive. UT at Austin Libraries. http://global.factiva.com. Accessed 17 Jan. 2006.

The Weeping Woman: Tales of La Llorona. Dir. Angela Alston. Perf. Renée Nuñez. VHS. No distributor, 1993.

West, John O. *Mexican-American Folklore: Legends, Songs, Festivals, Proverbs, Crafts, Tales of Saints, of Revolutionaries, and More.* Little Rock: August House, 1988.

———. "The Weeping Woman: La Llorona." In *Legendary Ladies of Texas*, ed. Francis Edward Abernethy, 30–36. Dallas: E-Heart Press, 1981.

Wulf, Steve, and Lisa H. Towle. "Elegy for Lost Boys." *Time*, 31 July 1995, 36.

Yarbro-Bejarano, Yvonne. "The Lesbian Body in Latina Cultural Production." In *¿Entiendes?: Queer Readings, Hispanic Writings*, ed. Emilie L. Bergmann and Paul Julian Smith, 181–197. Durham, NC: Duke Univ. Press, 1995.

Yarbrough, Roberta Zybach. *The Ghost Chasers: A Story of La Llorona.* Philadelphia: Xlibris, 2001.

"Woman Hollering Creek," 83–87; La
Llorona story as tool of, 83–84, 95, 96;
Mexican patriarchal oppression, 95–
96; in Montoya's *La Llorona's Sacred
Waters*, 132, 134–135; Moraga on,
130–131; in Moraga's *Hungry Woman:
A Mexican Medea*, 97–107; in *Mulhol-
land Drive*, 164, 166; in Murray's "La
Llorona: A Story," 122–126; resistance
to, in Lopez's *La Llorona*, 76–79; in
Villanueva's *Weeping Woman*, 129; in
Viramontes' "Cariboo Cafe," 87–94
Paul, Paula G., 152, 230n10
Pecado de la Llorona (Lozoya), 24, 26
Pennypacker, Mona, 229n5
Peón, Ramón, 21, 231n21
Perez, Gina "Genie," 25
Pérez, Soledad, 7, 20
Pérez-Torres, Rafael, 19
Pineda del Valle, César, 215n13
plays. *See* theatre productions
Pocho (Villarreal), 44
poetry: by Chicana feminists, 45–53,
219n10; conventional productions in,
28, 31, 32, 33, 34, 217n22; examples of,
3; resistance narratives of La Llorona
in, 72, 74–76, 79–83; in re-turning and
recuperation narratives of La Llorona,
110, 118–122; revisions of La Llorona
lore in, 5–6, 38, 42, 45–53. *See also
specific poets and titles of poems*
pollution. *See* environmental issues
poverty, 29, 113, 115, 148, 155–156, 180–181
Prietita and the Ghost Woman
(Anzaldúa), 3, 10, 184–186, 191, 193,
211n7, 224n16, 234n5
Pross, Edith, 234n1
Puccini, Giacomo, 18
Puerto Rico, 220n19, 221n22
Pullin, Gary, 168, 170, 232n24

Quiñonez, Naomi, 8, 38, 42, 45–47,
219nn11–13
Quiroz, Mario, 216n15

Rachel, 204–205
radical recuperations of La Llorona

legend. *See* re-turning and recuperation narratives of La Llorona
radio, 19, 61, 215n12
Ramano, Joe, 182
Ramirez, Albert, 23
Ramírez, Arturo, 8, 215n13
Ramírez, José, 110, 135–137
rape. *See* sexual assault
raúlrsalinas, 34
Realidades, 221n25
Rebolledo, Tey Diana: on Anzaldúa's
"My Black *Angelos*," 224n15, 226n14;
on Chicanas' use of La Llorona, 41–
42, 73; on contemporary renderings
of La Llorona, 21; on endless wandering of La Llorona, 18; *Infinite Divisions* edited by, 225n4; on interweav-
ing of Indian and Spanish folklore
and legends in La Llorona, 19; on
La Llorona as darker aspect of the
self, 76; on La Llorona as negative
mother image, 29–30; on La Llorona
as representation of Chican@s' marginality, 200–201; on La Llorona
as sexual object, 28, 29–30; on La
Malinche and La Llorona, 30, 32; on
Mexica goddesses, 100; on Palacios'
"La Llorona Loca: The Other Side," 62;
scholarship on La Llorona by generally, xv, 7
recuperation of La Llorona. *See* re-
turning and recuperation narratives
of La Llorona
"Red Readings," 213n24
reinterpretation of La Llorona lore. *See*
revisions of La Llorona lore
Rennard, José, 60, 62
reproductive rights, 49–52, 220nn18–19
resistance narratives of La Llorona:
Anaya on, 97; in artwork, 72, 76–79;
by Chicanas generally, 73–74, 97; in
fiction, 72, 83–94; and imagining of
a new nation, 95–107; meanings of
resistance literature, 72–73; in *Mulholland Drive*, 160–166, overview of, 6;
in poetry, 72, 74–76, 79–83; and rejection of La Llorona, 74–76; in theater

PERMISSIONS ACKNOWLEDGMENTS

Material from "Llantos de La Llorona: Warnings from the Wailer" © 1995 by Pat Mora. First appeared in AGUA SANTA/HOLY WATER, published by Beacon Press. Now appears in AGUA SANTA/HOLY WATER. Reprinted by permission of Curtis Brown, Ltd.

Material from "Coatlicue's Rules: Advice from an Aztec Goddess" © 1994 by Pat Mora. First appeared in *Prairie Schooner*, Lincoln: University of Nebraska. Now appears in AGUA SANTA/HOLY WATER. Reprinted by permission of Curtis Brown, Ltd.

Material from "La Llorona" © 1985 by Naomi Quiñonez. First appeared in *Sueño de colibrí/Hummingbird Dream: Poems*, Los Angeles: West End Press. Reprinted by permission of the author.

Material from "Go 'Way From My Window, La Llorona," "La Llorona at Sixteen," and "Portrait by the River" © 1993 by Cordelia Candelaria. Reprinted from *Arroyos to the Heart*, Santa Monica: Lalo Literature Division, Santa Monica College Press. Reprinted by permission of the author.

Epigraph for Chapter 3 © 2000 by Cherríe L. Moraga. First appeared in *Loving in the War Years: Lo que nunca pasó por sus labios*, published by South End Press, 1983. Now appears in *Loving in the War Years: Lo que nunca pasó por sus labios* (expanded 2nd ed.), 2000. Reprinted by permission of South End Press.

Epigraph for Chapter 5 copyright © 1993 by Guillermo Gómez-Peña. Reprinted